An Atlas of the
WILD FLOWERS
of Britain and Northern
Europe

An Atlas of the
WILD FLOWERS
of Britain and Northern Europe

Alastair Fitter

Collins St. James's Place, London

William Collins & Co Ltd
London · Glasgow · Sydney · Auckland
Toronto · Johannesburg

First published 1978

© Alastair Fitter 1978

ISBN 0 00 219181 4

Filmset by Jolly & Barber Ltd, Rugby

Made and Printed in Great Britain by
William Collins Sons & Co Ltd, Glasgow

Contents

Acknowledgments

This book would never have taken shape without the constant support of my wife, who has helped with many aspects of its preparation, and the encouraging faith of Michael Walter. My father checked all the maps in manuscript and made many valuable comments. I owe, of course, an immense debt to the thousands of field botanists whose observations over many years have made mapping of these plants a possibility.

Introduction

This book has been designed as a companion volume to *The Wild Flowers of Britain and Northern Europe*, by Marjorie Blamey and Richard and Alastair Fitter. It shows the distribution of nearly 2000 wild plants in Europe between the Alps and Iceland, including all of those described in that book except for a few casuals and introduced species. It therefore represents an attempt at comprehensively mapping the flora of northern Europe, and as such its maps provide information which cannot be obtained from any other single source.

There are many problems associated with such a comprehensive mapping scheme. For some species the available information is very poor but I have produced preliminary maps even for these. Ideally in any mapping project such as this, the published information should be accepted as a basis for drawing a map, and the full distribution should then be constructed from further field recording. Clearly this is impossible for one person and can only be accomplished by a team, and over a very long period.

There is at present in progress a mapping scheme for the whole of Europe, known as the *Atlas Florae Europaeae*, which is an attempt to produce sophisticated dot-maps for all of the plants in the still unfinished *Flora Europaea*. Dot-maps are produced by dividing an area up into squares and then discovering by field work and from published records, whether the species grows in each square. If it does, a dot is put in the square, and eventually a complete map is built up. This project is being carried out by a team of workers in Helsinki, helped by representatives from all the European countries, and in time they will produce accurate maps for all the plants in this book (and many others besides), but as yet information is only available for seven (the Gymnosperms), and it is inevitable that it will be many years before the *Atlas* is complete.

The maps in this book are not always so detailed, but I believe they will still prove valuable to all interested in wild plants. For their compilation I have relied on existing published information, supplemented in some cases by my own field observations, and this inevitably means that the accuracy of the information varies greatly from one part of the range covered to another. For example there are published volumes giving accurate information on the British Isles (*The Atlas of the British Flora*), Scandinavia (*Hulten's 'Atlas över Växternas utbrednings i Norden'*), and Belgium (*Atlas de la Flore Belge et Luxembourgeoise*). All three books are practically comprehensive and give detailed distributional information; without them it would have been impossible to attempt the preparation of these maps and I therefore owe a great debt to them. Wherever possible I have additionally tried to update the information obtained from these sources by incorporating records of new localities published by individual botanists in such journals as *Watsonia* (for Britain), *Blyttia* (for Norway), *Svensk Botanisk Tidskrift* (for Sweden) and several others. If readers find unfamiliar records in the maps, therefore, they may have been recently published in these journals.

For the rest of the area covered here, in other words Central Europe, Northern France, and Iceland the information is much less conveniently located. I have used the

7

standard Floras of these countries listed in the Bibliography on p. 247 to give the general outline of the distribution of each species and have then attempted to fill in the detail with more accuracy from maps and records scattered throughout a very diffuse and often obscure literature. One major source of information was of great value, though the maps it contains are often on a much smaller scale even than those published here – the *Vergleichende Chorologie der Zentraleuropäischen Flora* by Meusel, Jäger, and Weinert, of which one volume has been published. Though the maps there illustrate the full range of each of a selection of Central European plants, again the quality of the information varies, being most accurate for Central Germany and least for France.

Information on plant distribution in northern France is very hard to come by, and although work is at present in progress on a mapping scheme for the French flora, I have had to rely on the distributional information given in standard Floras to a great extent, supplemented wherever possible by the reports of the excursions of the Société Botanique de France, published in their Bulletin. Nevertheless, generally it is for France that the information in these maps is likely to be least reliable overall. It is possible, therefore, that users of the book will occasionally find a plant growing outside its stated range.

Finally, the distributions given for the Alps are likely to be less reliable than for other areas, as this region is strictly outside the scope of the book but has been included for cartographic convenience. Because of the great habitat contrasts that occur over very small distances in the Alps, the distribution given represents a general average rather than a detailed guide.

How to use the maps

Colours

Different colours and hatchings have been used to distinguish areas of the distribution of each species of different status and abundance.

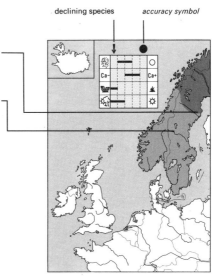

Solid green represents the core of each species' range, that part in which it is both native or well-established and more or less abundant.

Hatched green denotes the area over which the species occurs as a native or well-established introduction but much less frequently. Where information is poor this colour may represent a small number of scattered localities for which no precise information exists.

The distinction between solid and hatched green on the grounds of abundance is an arbitrary one, and varies from species to species. If a plant is very common in large areas (for example daisy, hawthorn) it may in fact be commoner in the areas shown as green hatching than another plant shown as solid green. Abundance cannot therefore be compared between maps.

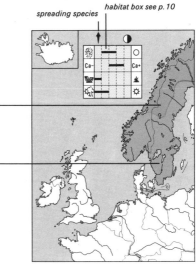

Red is used to delineate the introduced range of the species; in this part the plant usually occurs in obviously man-made habitats. For plants where the native and introduced ranges are not clearly separable, where the introduction was made a long time ago (as is the case with many weeds), or where the introduction is well-established, no distinction is made and the range is treated as native. No indication of abundance is given for the introduced range, as by its nature it tends to be very variable.

Blue is used to indicate the area over which the plant may occur as a casual, always associated with human activity and unlikely to be constant from year to year. Casuals are rarely found in native vegetation, such as woodlands and grasslands, but typically grow in disturbed ground. Clearly a casual may suddenly turn up in a new locality not marked on the map and some species are casual over such wide areas that it would be misleading to depict it on the map – such cases are indicated in the Notes (p. 243).

Habitats

As discussed in the next section, the ranges of plants are largely determined by climate, but within that area each species will be found only within certain habitats, such as deciduous woods or limestone cliffs, though some species, particularly wide-ranging ones, may occupy many different habitats. It is therefore inadequate to show merely the range of a species, for any field botanist will want to know in what parts of that range to look for the plant. I have therefore tried to give as much habitat information as possible by classifying them on a 5-point scale under four different headings (wetness, acidity, fertility, and shade) and providing a box diagram with each map providing this information. A key to the boxes is given below, with some examples.

wet	⬚	water	wet	damp	moist	dry	◯	dry
acid	Ca−	very acid	mild acid	neutral	mild calc	very calc	Ca+	calcareous
fertile	⬚	very fertile	fertile		poor	very poor	⬚	poor
shaded	⬚	dense woods	woods	open woods	scrub	open	☀	open

Wetness - Dryness: many habitats differ with respect to the amount of water in the soil and very different plants are found in these. At one extreme are water-plants growing actually in flowing or stagnant water (e.g. water crowfoot, *Ranunculus fluitans*) and at the other, plants which are found only on very dry soils (e.g. rockrose, *Helianthemum nummularium*). The five categories here represent:

1. Standing water above the soil surface for all or most of the year – lakes, rivers, wetter parts of marshes, fens and bogs.
2. Wet soils which are saturated with water for most of the year.
3. Damp soils which may be occasionally wet.
4. 'Normal' moist soils, such as a typical field soil.
5. Dry soils which crumble to the touch and are usually found on high ground or above very porous rock.

Acidity: this is a very important soil property which depends on the amount of basic minerals (mainly chalk and limestone providing calcium) in the soil and is crucial in controlling the habitats of most plants. A few plants can tolerate both acid and calcareous (base rich) soils but most grow either on acid soils (calcifuges) or basic (calcicoles), or on neutral soils if they can tolerate neither extreme. In this classification salty soils are treated as calcareous as they are similar in many respects and the categories are therefore:

1. Very acid soils with no chalk or limestone and usually found in sandy or peaty areas.

2. Slightly acid soils which are often again found on sands and peats but also on milder soils which have become acid because of the plants growing on them, such as pines, gorse and sometimes beech.

3. Neutral soils typical of lowland meadows and river-plains. These soils tend to be farmed.

4. Slightly calcareous soils formed over chalks and limestones but without bits of the rock in the soil.

5. Very calcareous soils which are usually very thin, formed on chalk and limestone and with pieces of the rock visible in the soil or lying on the surface. Limestone cliffs and pavements fit in here too, and saltmarsh soils are included for convenience.

Fertility: this is an obvious characteristic that can often be judged by the height of the vegetation; fertile soils tend to have tall, lush plants growing on them, and hence small, slow-growing plants are confined usually to poor soils. This factor is rather tied up with the last two, however, since the most fertile soils are often the moist (4), neutral (3) soils, but it can still be a useful pointer. The categories are simply graded from very fertile to very poor.

1. Very fertile soils often fertilised, with vigorous, tall vegetation or trees with dense undergrowth.

2. Fertile soils, usually in lowland sites or on alluvial deposits.

3. Intermediate fertility, typical of well-developed but unfertilised soils.

4. Poor soils, usually with a complete plant cover, but of short plants, or trees with little undergrowth.

5. Very poor soils, often with large patches of bare ground.

Shade: this is the only factor I have used which does not refer to the soil, but it is obviously important as nearly all plants require light to grow. The few which do not (e.g. bird's-nest orchid, *Neottia nidus-avis*) grow in the deepest shade. The categories are:

1. Very dense shade, as in some beechwoods and conifer plantations.

2. Most woodlands fall into this category with full shade cast particularly in summer.

3. Open woods with the trees well-spaced, so that the sun still reaches the ground at times, e.g. natural pinewoods.

4. Hedges, open scrub, and woodland edges, where the light is still bright but the full sun may be shielded off.

5. Open habitats with no trees or tall shrubs, e.g. grasslands, lakes, heaths.

As a guide to the use of these habitat boxes I have given three examples below which would represent plants occupying the following habitats:

a) a plant growing in fertile, slightly calcareous or neutral water, never shaded, for example many river plants.

b) a plant of very dry, very acid, very poor soils in the open or on woodland edges, such as many heath plants.

c) a plant of damp or moist, calcareous, moderately fertile soils in deep or very deep shade, such as you might find in a limestone wood.

Examples

a   b   c

Spreading and declining species

Many flowering plants are declining in northern Europe for a variety of reasons – collecting by botanists and others, destruction of habitat, particularly of wetlands, and subtler factors such as climatic changes. Such species are given the symbol↓ above the map. Conversely a few species, mainly recent introductions such as New Zealand willowherb, are spreading in the area and are given the opposite symbol ↑. Doubled arrows are occasionally used where the changes are occurring very rapidly. It must be expected that declining species will soon be extinct in some of the localities shown and that spreading species will occur outside the range shown.

Accuracy

As mentioned above accuracy varies between the different geographical regions on the maps and also between maps, and a general indication of the reliability of each map is therefore given, as a symbol on top of the box in the bottom right-hand corner. These represent:

- The map should be reliable and accurate, though probably more so in some parts (e.g. the British Isles and Scandinavia) than in others.
- ◑ Parts of the range shown are uncertain, but the general outline is likely to be correct.
- ○ The map as a whole is provisional and reliable data are not available. This is particularly true in groups whose taxonomy is complex and where two or more species are not properly distinguished in many of the records.

The symbol ○ also applies to the areas given as casual distribution on otherwise accurate maps, since casuals do not have clearly defined ranges.

Species omitted

A number of species which have only been recognised as separate very recently could not be mapped because no distributional information exists, and similarly the species of the so-called 'critical' groups (*Rubus, Sorbus, Hieracium, Taraxacum*) have been grouped into sections or other convenient groups and composite maps for these shown.

As a general rule plants have only been mapped if they occur as natives (or long-established introductions) over part of the area. Plants which only occur as casuals are not mapped, and those which are only found as introductions only if they are particularly common or well-established, or if they are typically in natural vegetation rather than as weeds.

Finally this book, like the *Wild Flowers of Britain and Northern Europe,* leaves out the grasses, sedges, and rushes. These will be covered in a later volume.

Plant distribution

Anyone who studies plants in the field soon comes to realise the importance of the distinction between *flora* and *vegetation.* The flora of an area is simply the list of species found growing there, but obviously they do not all grow together; rather they are found each in its own habitat, and since several species will all tend to favour one particular habitat they will then compose the vegetation of that habitat. Flora then is a geographical term whereas vegetation is an ecological one.

For a group of species to grow in one habitat, however, they must be adapted not only to its peculiar features that distinguish it from other habitats (for example acid rather than calcareous soil, sunny rather than shaded), but also, of course, to the climate of the whole area – they must in other words be part of the flora of the area. Clearly tropical plants do not grow out of doors in northern Europe for they would be killed by frost, but many Mediterranean plants which will grow in gardens cannot survive in the wild because the climate is not quite right; as a result they are not part of our flora even though suitable habitats, dry limestone rocks perhaps, can be found here.

It is possible therefore to have two sorts of maps of plant distribution: firstly, species maps which tell you in what areas a particular species grows and secondly, vegetation maps which tell you which groups of plants out of the flora of an area form the vegetation of particular parts. At the end of this section I have included some vegetation maps for northern Europe which show where you can expect to find various sorts of woodlands, heathlands, peatlands, and so on and which can, I hope, be used in conjunction with the habitat boxes for the individual species.

The range of a particular species, then, is controlled by three groups of factors:

a. *climatic* factors which govern the limits of the range of a species and determine whether or not it is a member of the flora of a particular area. Clearly a plant completely intolerant of frost or requiring a rainfall of 200 inches a year will not be found wild in northern Europe;

b. *habitat* factors, particularly of soil and shade which decide at which localities within the climatically determined range the plant will be able to grow, and produce the resultant mosaic; and

c. the *accessibility* of any particular locality. This means that islands and areas cut off by mountain barriers, for example, may not have in them all the plants that their flora could contain.

This last point is obviously of particular importance to the flora of the British Isles, since 10,000 years ago, as the ice retreated after the last glaciation, it left behind a very barren landscape and nearly all the plants growing in Britain today must have recolonised since then. As a result it is possible to recognise very clearly in the British Flora a number of *elements* or groups of species which have very different ranges outside the British Isles. These were first discussed in detail by Matthews and an excellent summary of the concept is given by Good in *The Geography of the Flowering Plants.*

13

In this context they are worth considering, for although they refer primarily to Britain they can be recognised in the whole north European flora, though the perspective given to them may be very different. For example, a plant that appears to have a southern distribution to a British botanist as it grows in southern Britain and France, may seem to have a western distribution to a German botanist.

The number of elements varies with different authors and three schemes are listed below:

Matthews (1955)		Good (1974)
Wide		Wide
Eurasian	Cosmopolitan	Eurasian
European		European
Mediterranean		Southern: mediterranean
Oceanic southern	Mediterranean	oceanic southern
Oceanic west European	Atlantic	oceanic west European
Continental southern		continental southern
Continental	Continental	Continental
Continental northern		Northern: continental northern
Northern-montane	Northern	northern montane
Oceanic northern		oceanic northern
North American	N. American	(inc. in oceanic northern)
Arctic-subarctic		Arctic-alpine: arctic
Arctic-alpine	Arctic-alpine	arctic-alpine
Alpine		alpine
Endemic	Endemic	Endemic

The central column represents a simplified scheme which is used here.

Cosmopolitan

Cosmopolitan species are those which have a more or less ubiquitous distribution, being found at least throughout Europe and in some cases throughout the world. They tend to be weeds or plants of man-made habitats, as these are the only habitats with a similarly cosmopolitan distribution, for example chickweed (*Stellaria media*) or groundsel (*Senecio vulgaris*).

Mediterranean

Mediterranean species tend to be very intolerant of frost and are therefore generally confined to the southern shores of the British Isles and the west coast of France where the winters are mild and the summer warm. Typical species are:

Wild Leek	*Allium ampeloprasum*	1855
Sea-Heath	*Frankenia laevis*	934
Gladiolus	*Gladiolus illyricus*	1902
Sea Holly	*Eryngium maritimum*	986

These species are largely coastal plants in the northern part of their range but many grow further inland in the Mediterranean countries and North Africa. In addition this group includes the *Lusitanian* element which differs in occurring primarily in Spain, Portugal, and south-west France (and therefore out of our area) but with outlying stations in south and west Ireland and (occasionally) Cornwall. These plants differ in not requiring high summer temperatures, but merely freedom from frost. Typical are:

Strawberry Tree	*Arbutus unedo*	1111
St Dabeoc's Heath	*Daboecia cantabrica*	1102
Dense-flowered Orchid	*Neotinea intacta*	1934

Atlantic

Atlantic species are a very large and important group and are defined very differently depending on which country's flora you are considering. For example the oblong-leaved sundew (*Drosera intermedia*) might seem to have an Atlantic distribution to a Central European botanist but from Britain appears to be a continental northern plant. Many Atlantic species are widespread in the British Isles and France but rare in central and eastern Europe, for they are typically sensitive to severe winters but tolerant of cool, wet summers. The Atlantic zone is usually defined as including all Ireland, most of Britain, and the coast of Europe from south Norway and Jutland to Lisbon, extending inland perhaps 100 miles in Germany, but including most of France and northern Spain. Some characteristic Atlantic plants are:

Wild Cabbage	*Brassica oleracea*	481
Heaths	*Erica* spp.	1095–1101
Foxglove	*Digitalis purpurea*	1371
Pale Butterwort	*Pinguicula lusitanica*	1475
Bluebell	*Endymion non-scriptus*	1868

Because of their climatic requirements most Atlantic species are endemic to western Europe and for some their whole range is given in the maps in this book. After the last glaciation they must have colonised northern Europe from France and Spain.

Continental

Continental species, by contrast, have as the centres of their distribution areas of central and south-eastern Europe. They are very frost-tolerant and require hot summers with rather little rainfall – conditions typical of continental climates, well away from the moderating influence of the sea. In the British Isles the nearest approach to such a climate occurs in East Anglia, and particularly in the Breckland, an area of dry, strongly leached, very infertile sandy soils with a heathy vegetation, where a number of continental plants otherwise very rare in Britain are congregated. Typical species of this group include:

Pasque Flower	*Pulsatilla vulgaris*	288
Field Wormwood	*Artemisia campestris*	1610
Hornbeam	*Carpinus betulus*	51
Field Eryngo	*Eryngium campestre*	987
Military Orchid	*Orchis militaris*	1917
Spring Speedwell	*Veronica verna*	1393
Maiden Pink	*Dianthus deltoides*	259

The continental species are often difficult to distinguish from those with a general

European distribution, but generally they are absent from the Atlantic fringe of Europe and from the more northern parts, which have a specialised, cold-tolerant flora of their own.

Northern

Northern species differ from those with a continental distribution in being tolerant of short, cold summers as well as cold winters. Some, known as continental northern species, are extremely hardy as they are adapted to a very rigorous climate, whereas oceanic northern species, which inhabit the coastal fringes of northern Europe are not normally exposed to such cold winters. On the whole the northern element is a very heterogeneous one, but they are typically found in northern England, and Ireland, Scotland, Scandinavia, and north-east Germany, for example:

Frog Orchid	*Coeloglossum viride*	1940
Twinflower	*Linnaea borealis*	1499
Mossy Saxifrage	*Saxifraga hypnoides*	539
Hairy Stonecrop	*Sedum villosum*	518
Globeflower	*Trollius europaeus*	273

Some northern plants, however, have more striking distributions, notably the so-called *North American* element in the European flora. Many species occur on both sides of the Atlantic ocean (and they are known as Amphi-Atlantic species) but rather few of them are primarily American species. There is, however, a small group of six or more such species, found mainly in Ireland and to a lesser extent in Wales and the Hebrides, which appear to have made the crossing of their own accord. These include:

Pipewort	*Eriocaulon septangulare*	1807
Welsh Mudwort	*Limosella australis*	1340
American Pondweed	*Potamogeton epihydrus*	1783
Blue-eyed Grass	*Sisyrinchium bermudianum*	1896
Irish Lady's Tresses	*Spiranthes romanzoffiana*	1965

There are other American plants in Europe which have clearly made the journey with man's assistance (such as several St John's worts) but those listed appear to have arrived naturally and it is an interesting botanical problem as to how they managed it. One intriguing theory is that some came across as seeds on the feet of migrating geese.

All the northern plants discussed so far have been species of the lower-lying habitats, and have not included the true mountain plants, though many of the northern plants do occur in the south of Europe on mountains. There is another group of predominantly montane or northern plants, however, the *arctic* and *alpine* elements, which are either true mountain plants or else occur mainly on mountains in our area. *Arctic* plants grow in the mountains of northern Europe and down to sea-level in the Arctic, but do not occur in the Alps and other Central European mountains. Typical species are:

Arctic Sandwort	*Arenaria norvegica*	156
Diapensia	*Diapensia lapponica*	1086
Woolly Willow	*Salix lanata*	17
Tufted Saxifrage	*Saxifraga caespitosa*	536

Alpine species are generally confined of course to the Alps and rather few of them are found in the mountains of northern Europe, and even then some appear to have been introduced, for gardeners have a fascination for the plants of Europe's highest mountains. Definite natives are:

Cyphel	*Cherleria sedoides*	173
Spring Gentian	*Gentiana verna*	1169
Mountain Milk vetch	*Oxytropis halleri*	702
Alpine Pennycress	*Thlaspi alpestre*	465

Although all these alpine species grow in upland areas, most are not found in high mountain habitats in northern Europe for mountain climates there are very much more severe than in the Alps at similar or even much greater heights. The bulk of the mountain plants of northern Europe have in fact an *arctic-alpine* distribution, being found both at lower levels in the Arctic and on the mountains of Central Europe. This group includes many of the showiest members of the mountain flora, such as:

Mountain Avens	*Dryas octopetala*	585
Alpine Gentian	*Gentiana nivalis*	1166
Mountain Azalea	*Loiseleuria procumbens*	1088
Alpine Cinquefoil	*Potentilla crantzii*	604
Rock Speedwell	*Veronica fruticans*	1377

This very brief and simplified survey of the major distributional groupings in the north European flora has, perhaps, served to underline the importance of climate in determining which plants are likely to be found in any one place, subject to habitat constraints of soil, water, and shade. The distribution of plants is not, however, a static affair, which can be delineated once and for all. Ranges are continually changing, whether because of simple discoveries of a plant outside its known range (though it may have been there all along), or because of extinctions, caused by human activities or climatic change. Equally these last two agents can cause a species to spread, as is certainly true of many weeds. Finally a species can itself evolve to increase its tolerance of climate or soil type, and so increase its range by pressure from within. In the last analysis, however, the range of any plant is determined by its climatic tolerances and its distribution within that range by ecological factors of the habitat.

The climate and other factors which delimit the ranges of plants are presented in the climate, soil, and vegetation maps on p.18–21. These show:

1. January mean temperature
2. July mean temperature
3. Annual precipitation
4. July precipitation
5. Annual precipitation – evaporation
6. Calcareous and acid soils
7. Main wetland vegetation types
8. Land use
9. Potential vegetation

17

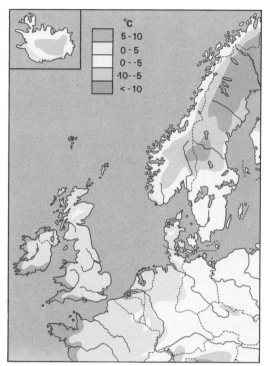

January mean temperature   **July mean temperature**

Temperature maps

The two *temperature maps* illustrate the important switch from a north-south difference in summer weather to an east-west difference in winter weather. This leads to a subdivision of the area into four quarters, as follows:

SW – warm summers, mild winters
NW – cool summers, mild winters
SE – warm summers, cold winters
NE – cool summers, cold winters

These correspond roughly to the Mediterranean, Atlantic, Continental, and Northern elements in the flora.

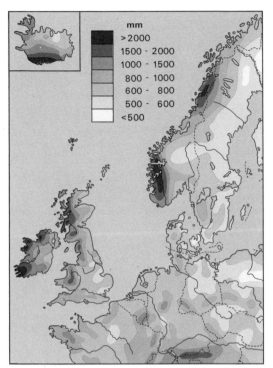

Annual precipitation

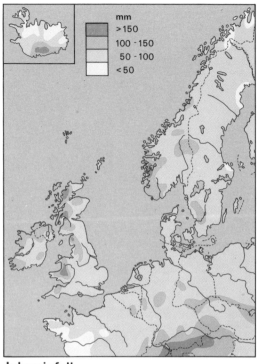

July rainfall

Rainfall maps

The *rainfall maps* show the annual precipitation, the precipitation in midsummer, which may be more important in producing drought and the annual difference between rainfall (precipitation) and evaporation. This last map gives the best idea of how dry an area is, as a small rainfall may, in a cold area with little evaporation, produce a moister climate than a much larger rainfall in a hotter place. Owing to the difficulty of calculating the difference, however, the map is very approximate.

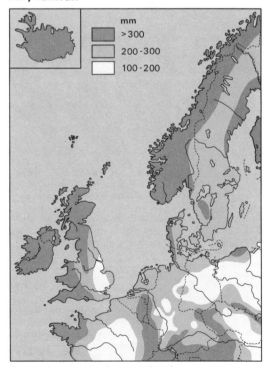

Annual excess of precipitation over evaporation

19

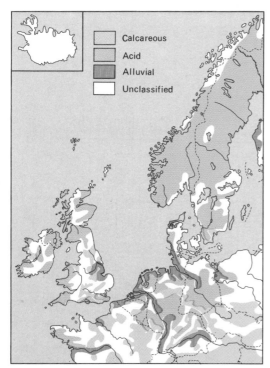

Soil types

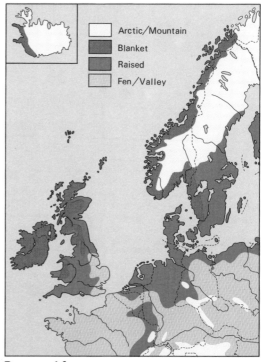

Bogs and fens

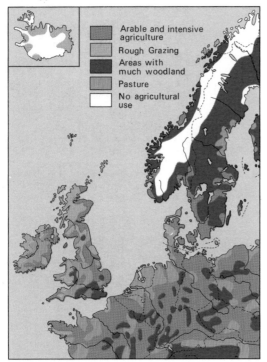

Major land use

Vegetation, Land use and Soil maps

These four maps can be used to provide a picture of the likely vegetation types to be found in an area. The map of potential vegetation shows what is to be expected on sites relatively free of human influence – in practice agricultural and other disturbance has meant that actual existing vegetation is too fragmented to map; the land use map can be used in conjunction with the potential vegetation map to indicate this pattern. The wetlands map (bogs and fens) is included since these habitats are not well demonstrated by the vegetation map. The map of acid and calcareous soils, which shows only the major areas and ignores small patches, can be used in conjunction with both the vegetation maps, to locate areas of calcareous grassland for example, and the habitat boxes on the individual plant maps.

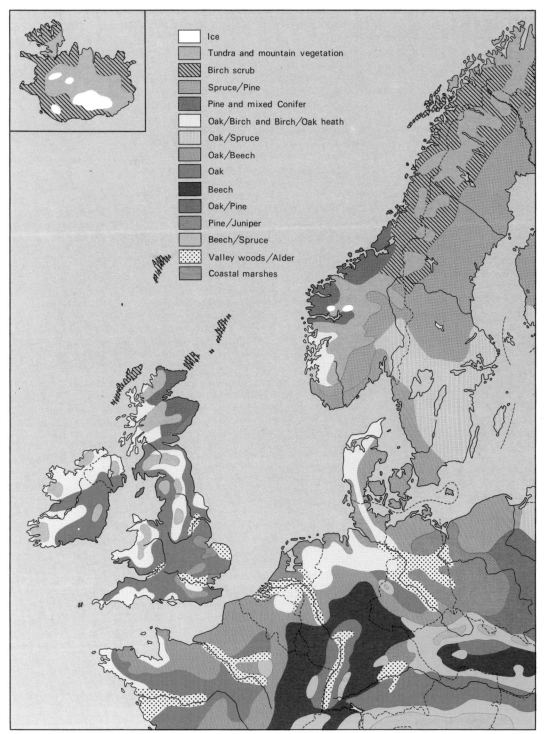

	Ice
	Tundra and mountain vegetation
	Birch scrub
	Spruce/Pine
	Pine and mixed Conifer
	Oak/Birch and Birch/Oak heath
	Oak/Spruce
	Oak/Beech
	Oak
	Beech
	Oak/Pine
	Pine/Juniper
	Beech/Spruce
	Valley woods/Alder
	Coastal marshes

Potential vegetation

The maps

The plants mapped on the following pages are arranged in systematic order. The numbers preceding each Latin name refer to the Checklist on pages 249–62, and are also used in the Indexes at the end of the book.

The letter 'n' after a plant's Latin name indicates that there is an entry on that species in the section 'Notes on the maps' on pages 243–6.

For an explanation of the colours and symbols used, see pages 9–11.

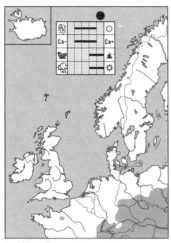

1 *Abies alba* N
Silver Fir

2 *Picea abies* N
Norway Spruce

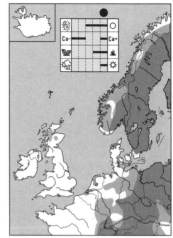

3 *Pinus sylvestris* N
Scots Pine

4 *Pinus mugo* N

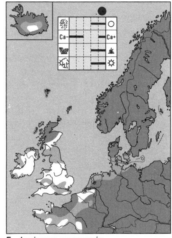

5 *Juniperus communis* N
Juniper

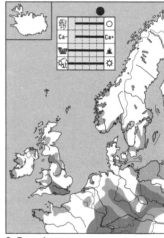

6 *Taxus baccata* N
Yew

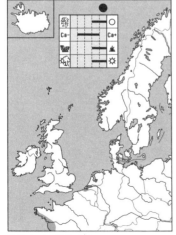

7 *Ephedra distachya* N
Joint Pine

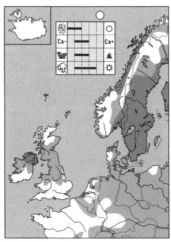

8 *Salix pentandra*
Bay Willow

9 *Salix alba* N
White Willow

Willow Family · Salicaceae

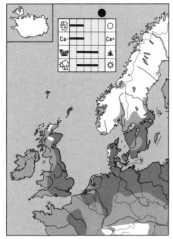

10 *Salix fragilis*   N
Crack Willow

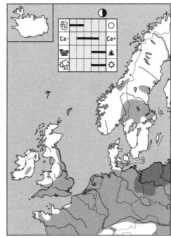

11 *Salix triandra*   N
Almond Willow

12 *Salix reticulata*
Net-leaved Willow

13 *Salix herbacea*
Dwarf Willow

14 *Salix polaris*

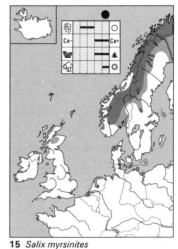

15 *Salix myrsinites*
Whortle-leaved Willow

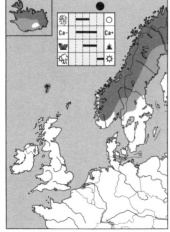

16 *Salix glauca*   N
Bluish Willow

17 *Salix lanata*
Woolly Willow

18 *Salix glandulifera*

24

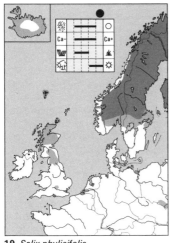

19 *Salix phylicifolia*
Tea-leaved Willow

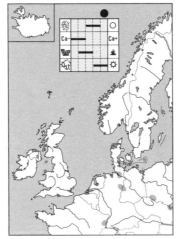

20 *Salix bicolor*

21 *Salix hibernica*
Irish Willow

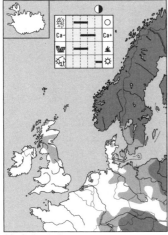

22 *Salix nigricans* N
Dark-leaved Willow

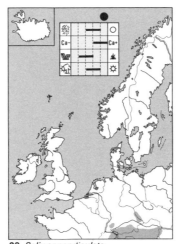

23 *Salix appendiculata*

24 *Salix cinerea* N
Grey Willow

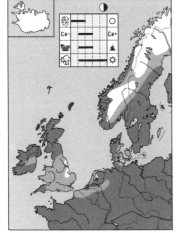

25 *Salix aurita*
Eared Willow

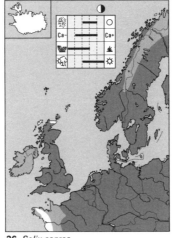

26 *Salix caprea*
Goat Willow

27 *Salix coaetanea* N

25

Willow Family · Salicaceae

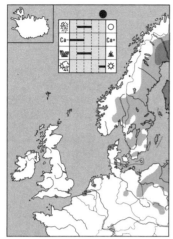

28 *Salix starkeana*

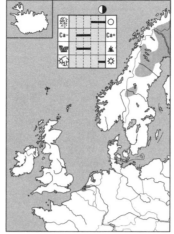

29 *Salix xerophila*

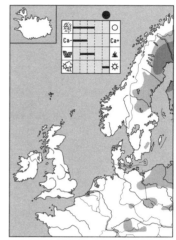

30 *Salix myrtilloides*

31 *Salix repens* N
Creeping Willow

32 *Salix arbuscula*
Mountain Willow

33 *Salix hastata*

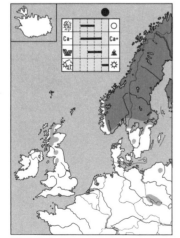

34 *Salix lapponum*
Downy Willow

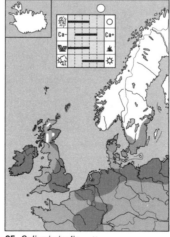

35 *Salix viminalis* N
Osier

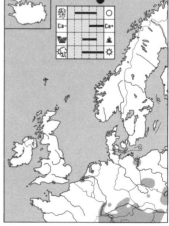

36 *Salix eleagnos*

26

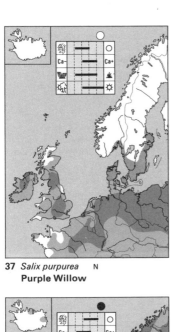

37 *Salix purpurea* N
Purple Willow

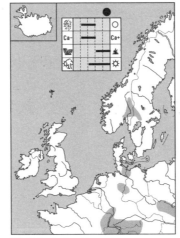

38 *Salix daphnoides* N
Violet Willow

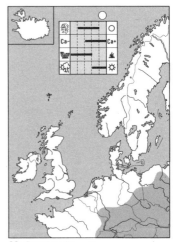

39 *Populus alba* N
White Poplar

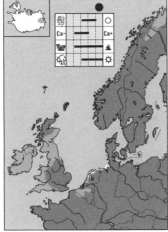

40 *Populus tremula*
Aspen

41 *Myrica gale*
Bog Myrtle

42 *Betula pendula*
Silver Birch

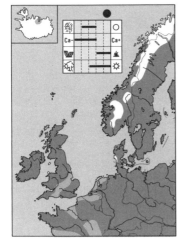

43 *Betula pubescens*
Downy Birch

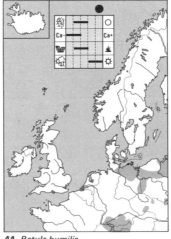

44 *Betula humilis*

45 *Betula nana*
Dwarf Birch

27

46 *Betula callosa*

47 *Betula tortuosa*

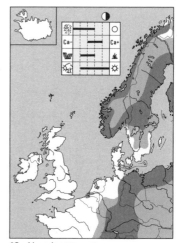

48 *Alnus incana* N
Grey Alder

49 *Alnus viridis*
Green Alder

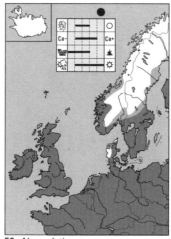

50 *Alnus glutinosa*
Alder

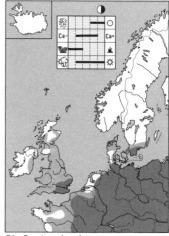

51 *Carpinus betulus* N
Hornbeam

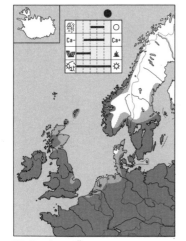

52 *Corylus avellana*
Hazel

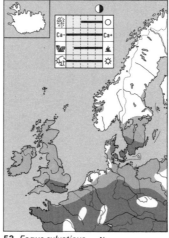

53 *Fagus sylvaticus* N
Beech

54 *Quercus ilex* N
Holm Oak

55 *Quercus petraea*
Sessile Oak

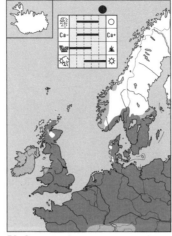

56 *Quercus robur*   N
Pedunculate Oak

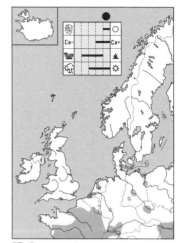

57 *Quercus pubescens*
White Oak

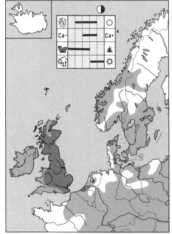

58 *Ulmus glabra*
Wych Elm

59 *Ulmus procera*   N
English Elm

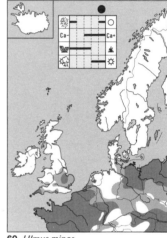

60 *Ulmus minor*
Small-leaved Elm

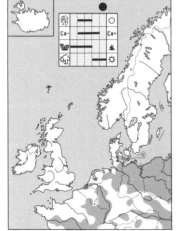

61 *Ulmus laevis*
Fluttering Elm

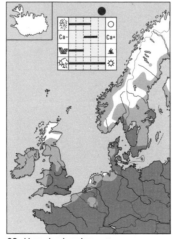

62 *Humulus lupulus*   N
Hop

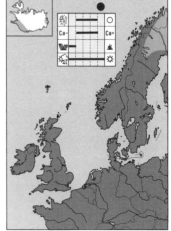

63 *Urtica dioica*
Nettle

64 *Urtica kioviensis*

65 *Urtica urens*
Annual Nettle

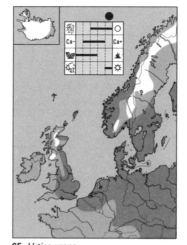

66 *Parietaria officinalis*

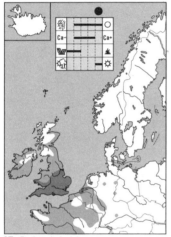

67 *Parietaria judaica*
Pellitory-of-the-Wall

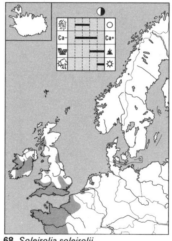

68 *Soleirolia soleirolii*
Mind Your Own Business

69 *Thesium alpinum*

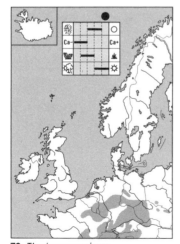

70 *Thesium pyrenaicum*

71 *Thesium ebracteatum*

72 *Thesium rostratum*

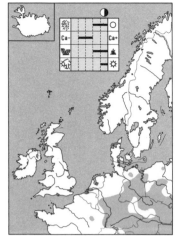

73 *Thesium bavarum*

74 *Thesium linophyllon*

75 *Thesium divaricatum*

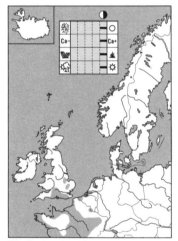

76 *Thesium humifusum*
Bastard Toadflax

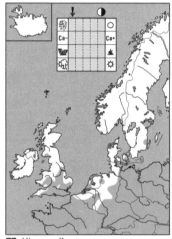

77 *Viscum album*
Mistletoe

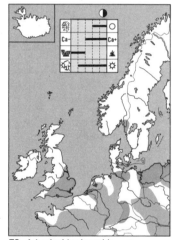

78 *Aristolochia clematitis* N
Birthwort

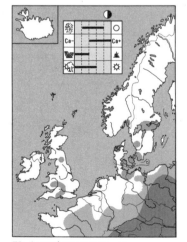

79 *Asarum europaeum* N
Asarabacca

80 *Koenigia islandica*
Iceland Purslane

81 *Polygonum maritimum*
Sea Knotgrass

82 *Polygonum oxyspermum*
Ray's Knotgrass

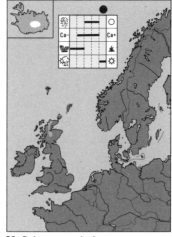

83 *Polygonum aviculare* N
Knotgrass

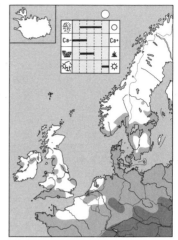

84 *Polygonum minus*
Small Water-pepper

85 *Polygonum foliosum*

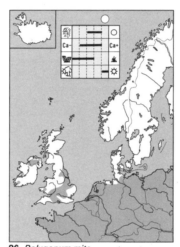

86 *Polygonum mite*
Tasteless Water-pepper

87 *Polygonum hydropiper*
Water-pepper

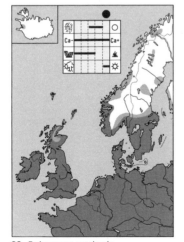

88 *Polygonum persicaria*
Redshank

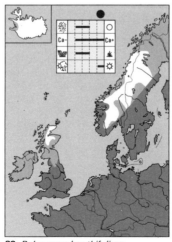

89 *Polygonum lapathifolium*
Pale Persicaria

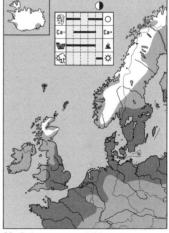

90 *Polygonum amphibium*
Amphibious Bistort

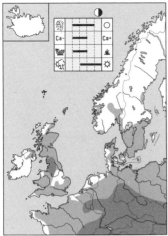

91 *Polygonum bistorta*
Bistort

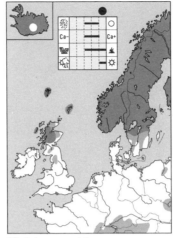

92 *Polygonum viviparum*
Alpine Bistort

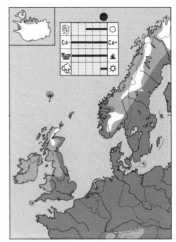

93 *Bilderdykia convolvulus*
Black Bindweed

94 *Bilderdykia dumetorum*
Copse Bindweed

95 *Oxyria digyna*
Mountain Sorrel

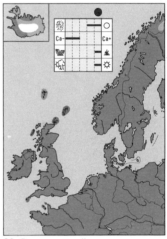

96 *Rumex acetosella*
Sheep's Sorrel

97 *Rumex scutatus*
French Sorrel

98 *Rumex arifolius*

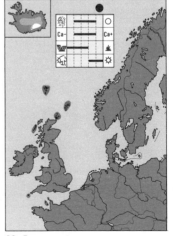

99 *Rumex acetosa*
Common Sorrel

33

Dock Family · Polygonaceae

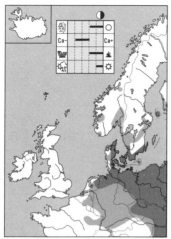

100 *Rumex thyrsiflorus*

101 *Rumex alpinus*
Monk's Rhubarb

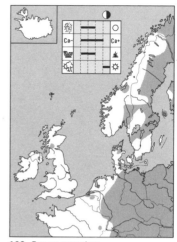

102 *Rumex aquaticus*
Scottish Dock

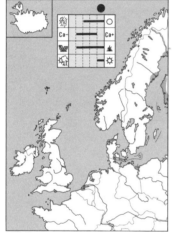

103 *Rumex pseudonatronatus*

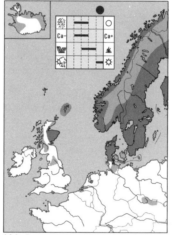

104 *Rumex longifolius*　N
Northern Dock

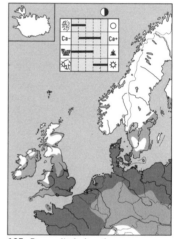

105 *Rumex hydrolapathum*
Water Dock

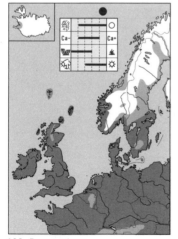

106 *Rumex crispus*
Curled Dock

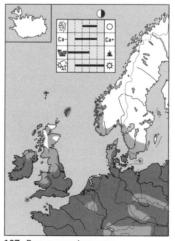

107 *Rumex conglomeratus*
Clustered Dock

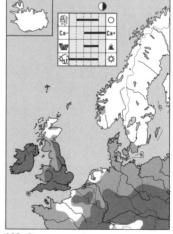

108 *Rumex sanguineus*
Wood Dock

109 *Rumex rupestris*
Shore Dock

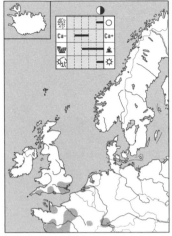

110 *Rumex pulcher*   N
Fiddle Dock

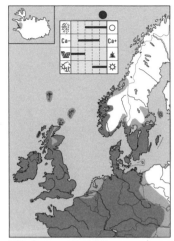

111 *Rumex obtusifolius*
Broad-leaved Dock

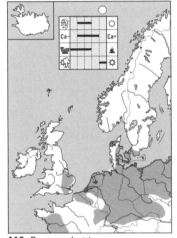

112 *Rumex palustris*
Marsh Dock

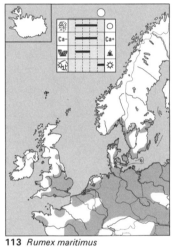

113 *Rumex maritimus*
Golden Dock

114 *Polycnemum majus*
Polycnemum

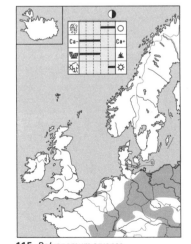

115 *Polycnemum arvense*

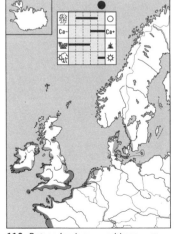

116 *Beta vulgaris ssp maritimus*   N
Sea Beet

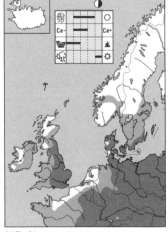

117 *Chenopodium bonus-henricus*   N
Good King Henry

Goosefoot Family · Chenopodiaceae

118 *Chenopodium glaucum* N
Oak-leaved Goosefoot

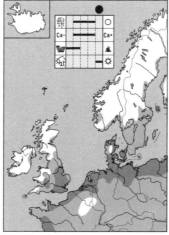

119 *Chenopodium rubrum* N
Red Goosefoot

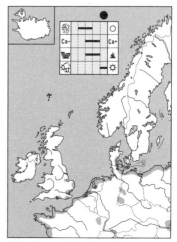

120 *Chenopodium botryodes* N
Small Red Goosefoot

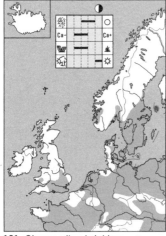

121 *Chenopodium hybridum* N
Maple-leaved Goosefoot

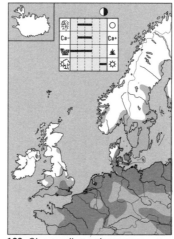

122 *Chenopodium polyspermum* N
Many-seeded Goosefoot

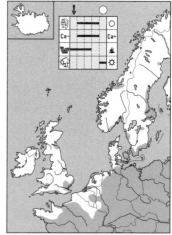

123 *Chenopodium vulvaria* N
Stinking Goosefoot

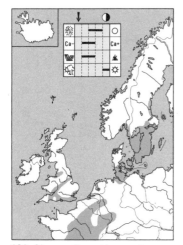

124 *Chenopodium urbicum* N
Upright Goosefoot

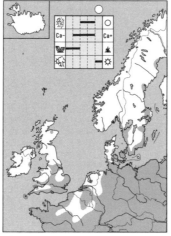

125 *Chenopodium murale* N
Nettle-leaved Goosefoot

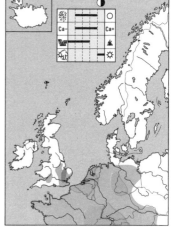

126 *Chenopodium ficifolium* N
Fig-leaved Goosefoot

36

127 *Chenopodium album* N
Fat Hen

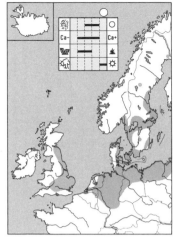

128 *Chenopodium suecicum* N
Green Goosefoot

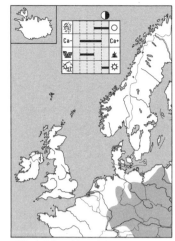

129 *Atriplex oblongifolia*

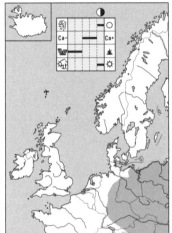

130 *Atriplex rosea*

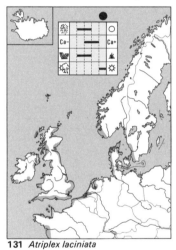

131 *Atriplex laciniata*
Frosted Orache

132 *Atriplex tatarica*

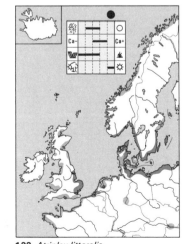

133 *Atriplex littoralis*
Grass-leaved Orache

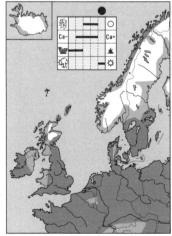

134 *Atriplex patula*
Common Orache

135 *Atriplex calotheca*

37

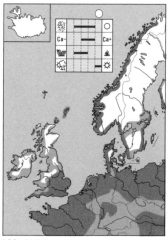

136 *Atriplex hastata*
Spear-leaved Orache

137 *Atriplex glabriuscula*

138 *Atriplex longipes*   N

139 *Halimione portulacoides*
Sea Purslane

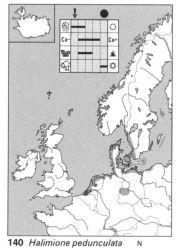

140 *Halimione pedunculata*   N
Stalked Orache

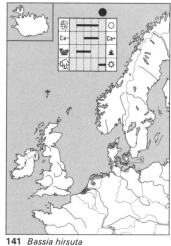

141 *Bassia hirsuta*
Hairy Seablite

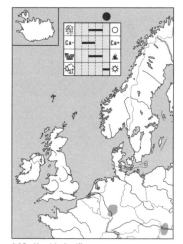

142 *Kochia laniflora*   N

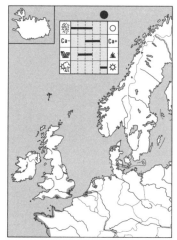

143 *Arthrocnemum perenne*
Perennial Glasswort

144 *Salicornia europaea*
Glasswort

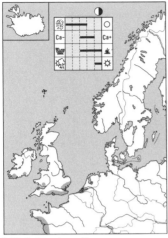

145 *Salicornia pusilla*

146 *Salicornia procumbens* N

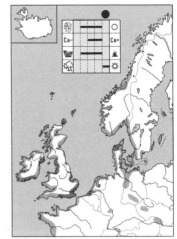

147 *Suaeda maritima*
Annual Seablite

148 *Suaeda vera*
Shrubby Seablite

149 *Salsola kali* N
Prickly Saltwort

150 *Carpobrotus edulis*
Hottentot Fig

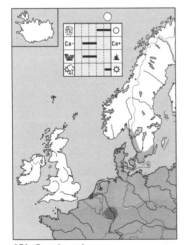

151 *Portulaca oleracea*

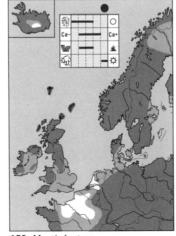

152 *Montia fontana*
Blinks

153 *Montia perfoliata*
Spring Beauty

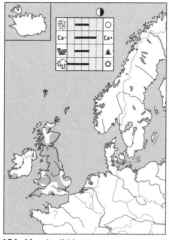

154 *Montia sibirica* N
Pink Purslane

155 *Arenaria humifusa*

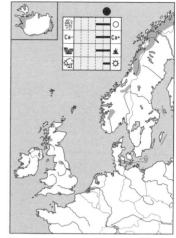

156 *Arenaria norvegica*
Arctic Sandwort

157 *Arenaria gothica*

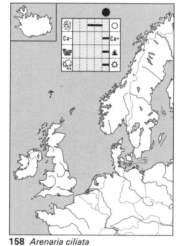

158 *Arenaria ciliata*
Fringed Sandwort

159 *Arenaria serpyllifolia* N
Thyme-leaved Sandwort

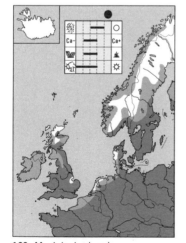

160 *Moehringia trinervia*
Three-veined Sandwort

161 *Moehringia lateriflora*

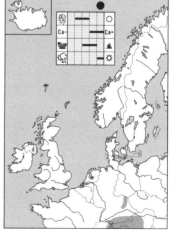

162 *Moehringia muscosa*

40

163 *Minuartia viscosa*

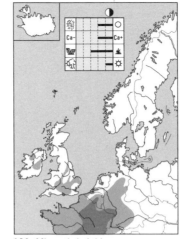

164 *Minuartia hybrida*
Fine-leaved Sandwort

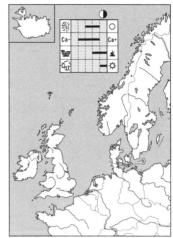

165 *Minuartia mediterranea*

166 *Minuartia rubra*

167 *Minuartia setacea*

168 *Minuartia recurva*
Curved Sandwort

169 *Minuartia verna*
Spring Sandwort

170 *Minuartia rubella*
Mountain Sandwort

171 *Minuartia stricta*
Teesdale Sandwort

172 *Minuartia biflora*

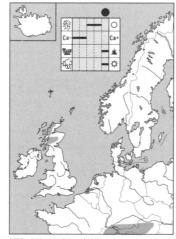

173 *Minuartia sedoides*
Cyphel

174 *Honkenya peploides*
Sea Sandwort

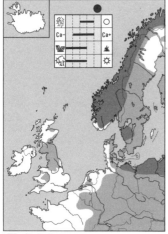

175 *Stellaria nemorum*
Wood Stitchwort

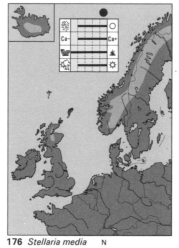

176 *Stellaria media* N
Common Chickweed

177 *Stellaria holostea*
Greater Stitchwort

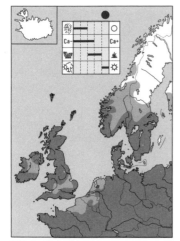

178 *Stellaria alsine*
Bog Stitchwort

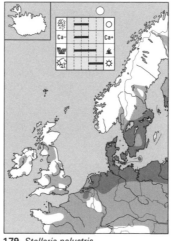

179 *Stellaria palustris*
Marsh Stitchwort

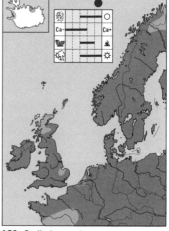

180 *Stellaria graminea*
Lesser Stitchwort

181 *Stellaria crassipes*

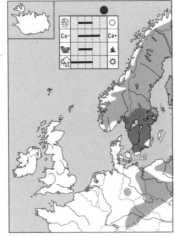

182 *Stellaria longifolia*

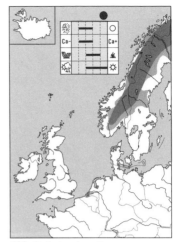

183 *Stellaria calycantha*

184 *Stellaria crassifolia*

185 *Stellaria humifusa*

186 *Holosteum umbellatum*
Umbellate Chickweed

187 *Cerastium cerastoides*
Starwort Mouse-ear

188 *Cerastium dubium*

189 *Cerastium arvense*
Field Mouse-ear

Pink Family · Caryophyllaceae

190 *Cerastium alpinum*
Alpine Mouse-ear

191 *Cerastium arcticum*
Arctic Mouse-ear

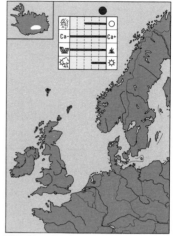

192 *Cerastium fontanum*
Common Mouse-ear

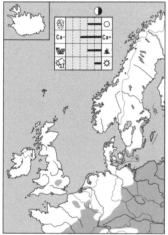

193 *Cerastium brachypetalum*
Grey Mouse-ear

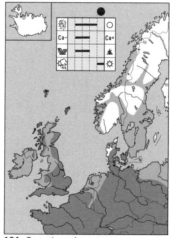

194 *Cerastium glomeratum*
Sticky Mouse-ear

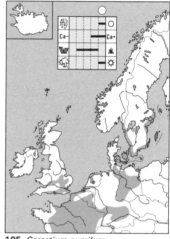

195 *Cerastium pumilum*
Dwarf Mouse-ear

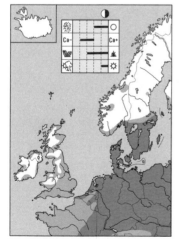

196 *Cerastium semidecandrum*
Little Mouse-ear

197 *Cerastium diffusum*
Sea Mouse-ear

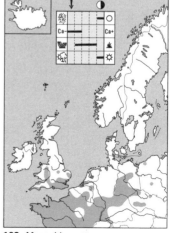

198 *Moenchia erecta*
Upright Chickweed

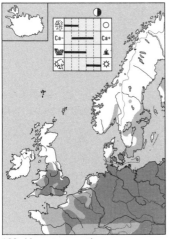

199 *Myosoton aquaticum*
Water Chickweed

200 *Sagina nodosa*
Knotted Pearlwort

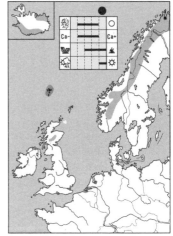

201 *Sagina intermedia*
Snow Pearlwort

202 *Sagina caespitosa*

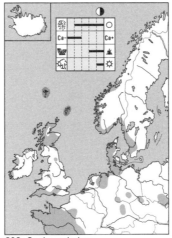

203 *Sagina subulata*
Heath Pearlwort

204 *Sagina saginoides*   N
Alpine Pearlwort

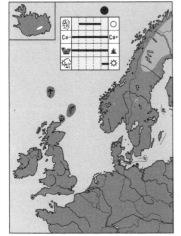

205 *Sagina procumbens*
Procumbent Pearlwort

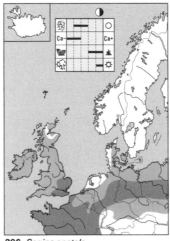

206 *Sagina apetala*
Annual Pearlwort

207 *Sagina maritima*
Sea Pearlwort

208 *Scleranthus perennis*
Perennial Knawel

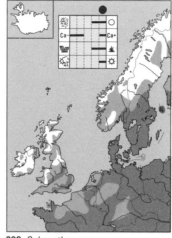

209 *Scleranthus annuus*
Annual Knawel

210 *Corrigiola litoralis*
Strapwort

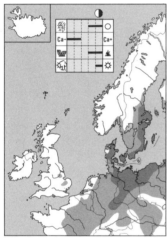

211 *Herniaria glabra*
Smooth Rupturewort

212 *Herniaria ciliolata*
Fringed Rupturewort

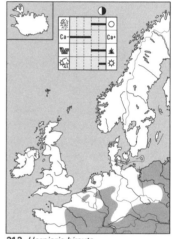

213 *Herniaria hirsuta*
Hairy Rupturewort

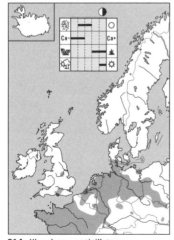

214 *Illecebrum verticillatum*
Coral Necklace

215 *Spergula arvensis*
Corn Spurrey

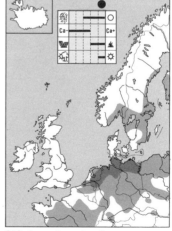

216 *Spergula morisonii*
Pearlwort Spurrey

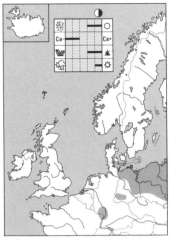

217 *Spergula pentandra*

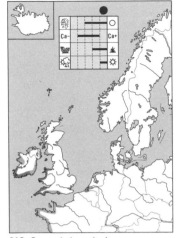

218 *Spergularia rupicola*
Rock Sea-spurrey

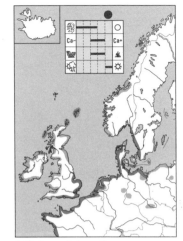

219 *Spergularia media*
Greater Sea-spurrey

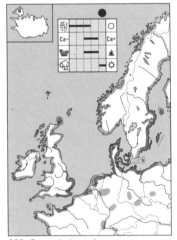

220 *Spergularia marina*
Lesser Sea-spurrey

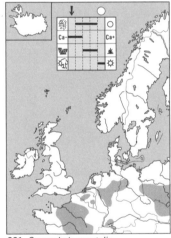

221 *Spergularia segetalis*

222 *Spergularia bocconii*
Greek Sea-spurrey

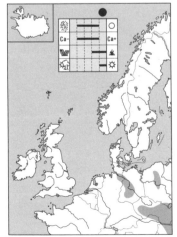

223 *Spergularia echinosperma*

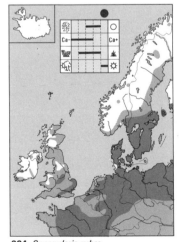

224 *Spergularia rubra*
Sand Spurrey

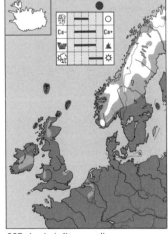

225 *Lychnis flos-cuculi*
Ragged Robin

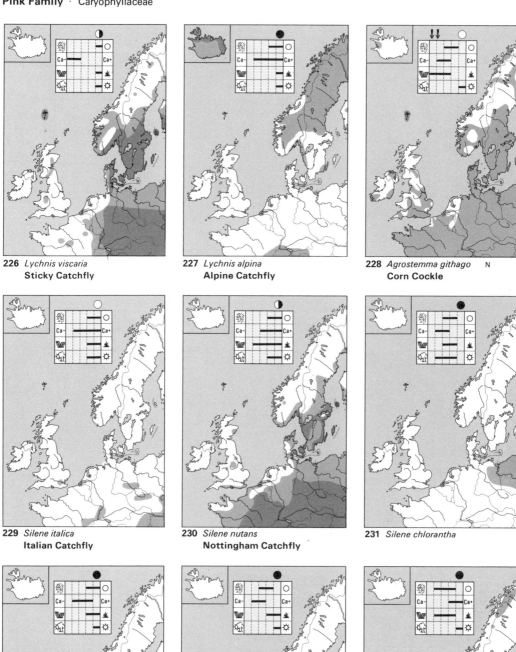

226 *Lychnis viscaria*
Sticky Catchfly

227 *Lychnis alpina*
Alpine Catchfly

228 *Agrostemma githago*   N
Corn Cockle

229 *Silene italica*
Italian Catchfly

230 *Silene nutans*
Nottingham Catchfly

231 *Silene chlorantha*

232 *Silene viscosa*
White Sticky Catchfly

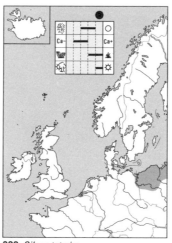

233 *Silene tatarica*

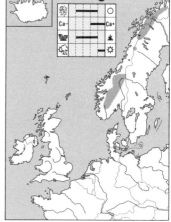

234 *Silene wahlbergella*
Northern Catchfly

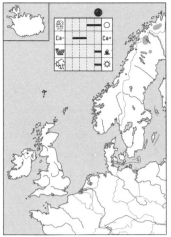

235 *Silene furcata*

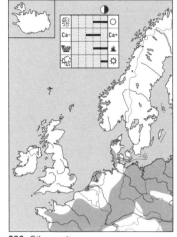

236 *Silene otites*
Spanish Catchfly

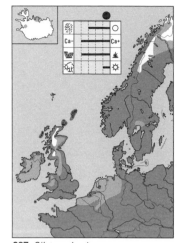

237 *Silene vulgaris*
Bladder Campion

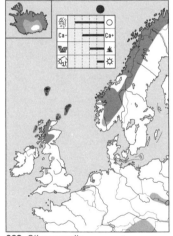

238 *Silene acaulis*
Moss Campion

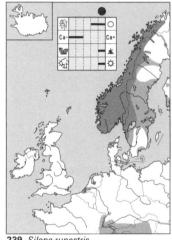

239 *Silene rupestris*
Rock Catchfly

240 *Silene armeria*

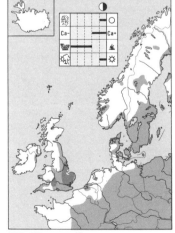

241 *Silene noctiflora* N
Night-flowering Catchfly

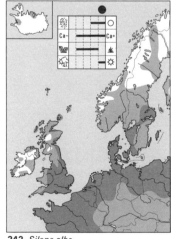

242 *Silene alba*
White Campion

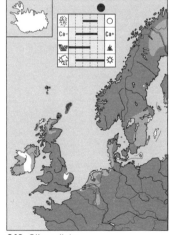

243 *Silene dioica*
Red Campion

244 *Silene linicola*
Flaxfield Catchfly

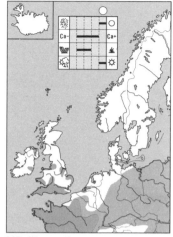

245 *Silene gallica*
Small-flowered Catchfly

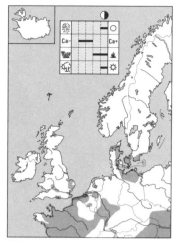

246 *Silene conica*
Sand Catchfly

247 *Cucubalus baccifer*
Berry Catchfly

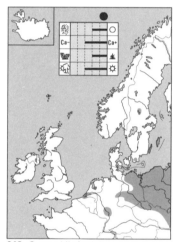

248 *Gypsophila fastigiata*
Fastigiate Gypsophila

249 *Gypsophila repens*

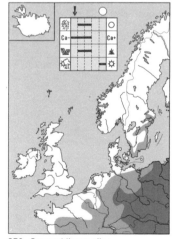

250 *Gypsophila muralis*
Annual Gypsophila

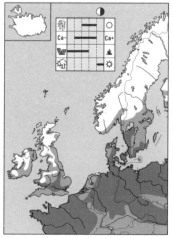

251 *Saponaria officinalis*
Soapwort

252 *Vaccaria pyramidata*
Cow Basil

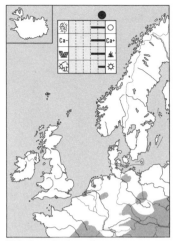

253 *Petrorhagia saxifraga*
Tunic Flower

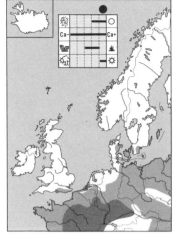

254 *Petrorhagia prolifera*   N
Proliferous Pink

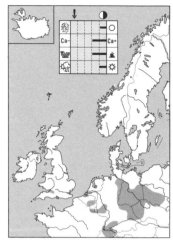

255 *Dianthus gratianopolitanus*   N
Cheddar Pink

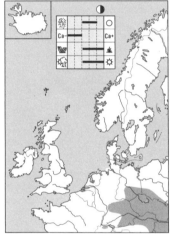

256 *Dianthus seguieri*

257 *Dianthus superbus*
Large Pink

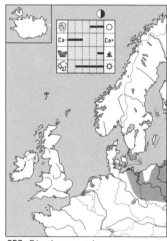

258 *Dianthus arenarius*

259 *Dianthus deltoides*
Maiden Pink

260 *Dianthus armeria*
Deptford Pink

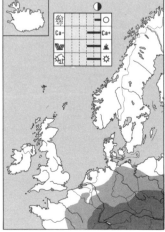

261 *Dianthus carthusianorum*
Carthusian Pink

262 *Dianthus gallicus*
Jersey Pink

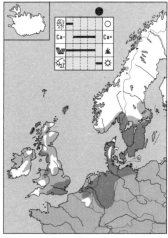

263 *Nymphaea alba*
White Water-lily

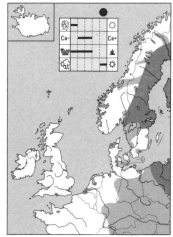

264 *Nymphaea candida*

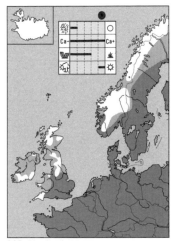

265 *Nuphar lutea*
Yellow Water-lily

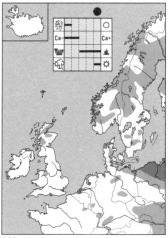

266 *Nuphar pumila*
Least Water-lily

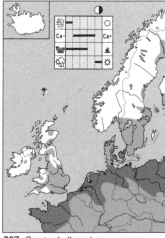

267 *Ceratophyllum demersum*
Rigid Hornwort

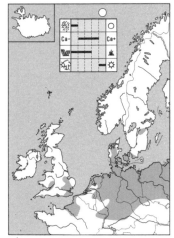

268 *Ceratophyllum submersum*
Soft Hornwort

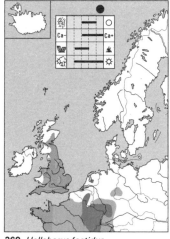

269 *Helleborus foetidus*
Stinking Hellebore

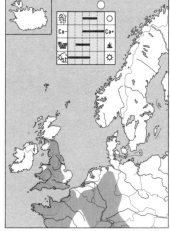

270 *Helleborus viridis*
Green Hellebore

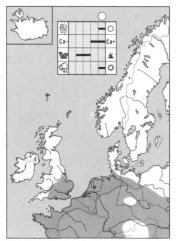

271 *Nigella arvensis*

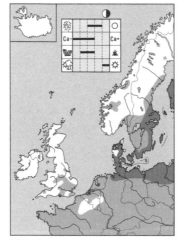

272 *Myosurus minimus*
Mousetail

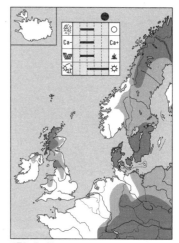

273 *Trollius europaeus*
Globeflower

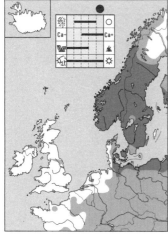

274 *Actaea spicata*
Baneberry

275 *Actaea erythrocarpa*

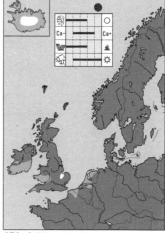

276 *Caltha palustris*
Marsh Marigold

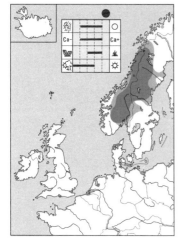

277 *Aconitum septentrionale*
Northern Wolfsbane

278 *Aconitum vulparia*
Wolfsbane

279 *Aconitum variegatum*

53

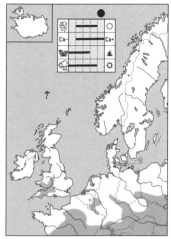

280 *Aconitum napellus*
Monkshood

281 *Consolida regalis*
Forking Larkspur

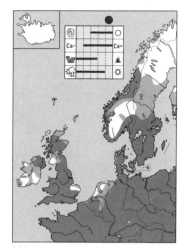

282 *Anemone nemorosa*
Wood Anemone

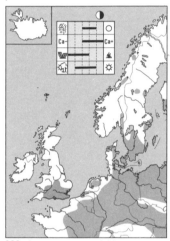

283 *Anemone ranunculoides*
Yellow Anemone

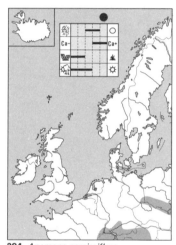

284 *Anemone narcissiflora*

285 *Anemone sylvestris*
Snowdrop Windflower

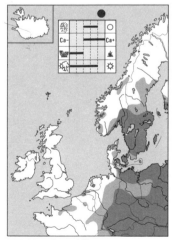

286 *Hepatica nobilis*
Hepatica

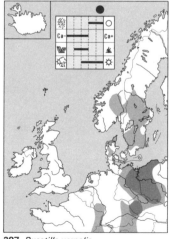

287 *Pusatilla vernalis*
Pale Pasque-flower

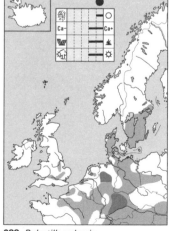

288 *Pulsatilla vulgaris*
Pasque-flower

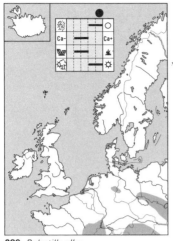

289 *Pulsatilla alba*
White Pasque-flower

290 *Pulsatilla pratensis*
Small Pasque-flower

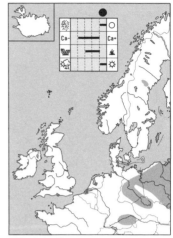

291 *Pulsatilla patens*
Eastern Pasque-flower

292 *Clematis recta*

293 *Clematis vitalba*
Traveller's Joy

294 *Clematis alpina*
Alpine Clematis

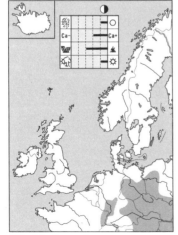

295 *Adonis vernalis*
Yellow Pheasant's-eye

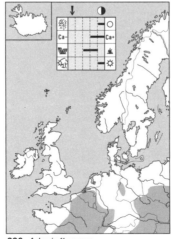

296 *Adonis flammea*
Large Pheasant's-eye

297 *Adonis aestivalis*
Summer Pheasant's-eye

Buttercup Family · Ranunculaceae

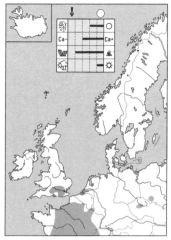

298 *Adonis annua*
Pheasant's-eye

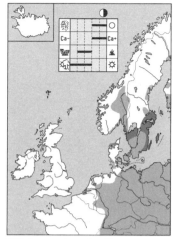

299 *Ranunculus polyanthemos*

300 *Ranunculus nemorosus*

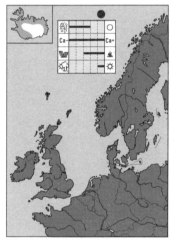

301 *Ranunculus repens*
Creeping Buttercup

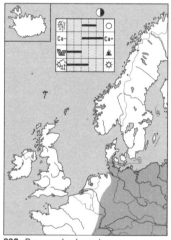

302 *Ranunculus lanuginosus*
Woolly Buttercup

303 *Ranunculus acris*
Meadow Buttercup

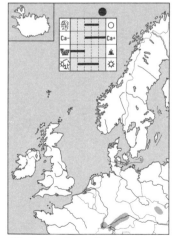

304 *Ranunculus montanus*

305 *Ranunculus oreophilus*

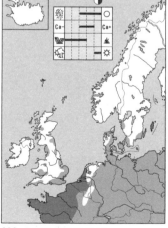

306 *Ranunculus sardous*
Hairy Buttercup

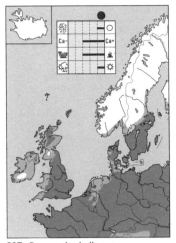

307 *Ranunculus bulbosus*
Bulbous Buttercup

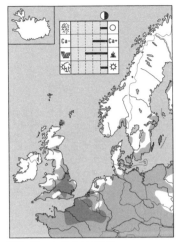

308 *Ranunculus arvensis*
Corn Buttercup

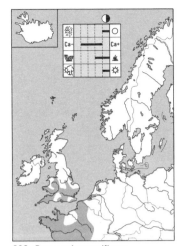

309 *Ranunculus parviflorus*
Small-flowered Buttercup

310 *Ranunculus illyricus*

311 *Ranunculus paludosus*
Jersey Buttercup

312 *Ranunculus pygmaeus*

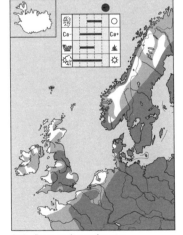

313 *Ranunculus auricomus*
Goldilocks Buttercup

314 *Ranunculus nivalis*

315 *Ranunculus sulphureus*

Buttercup Family · Ranunculaceae

316 *Ranunculus hyperboreus*

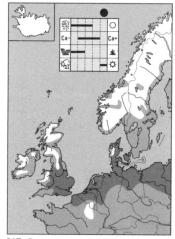

317 *Ranunculus sceleratus*
Celery-leaved Buttercup

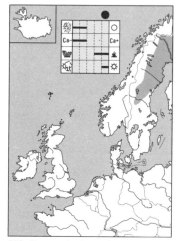

318 *Ranunculus lapponicus*

319 *Ranunculus cymbalaria*

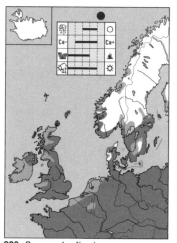

320 *Ranunculus ficaria*
Lesser Celandine

321 *Ranunculus aconitifolius*

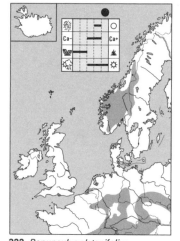

322 *Ranunculus platanifolius*
Large White Buttercup

323 *Ranunculus glacialis*
Glacier Buttercup

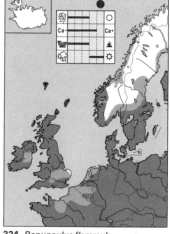

324 *Ranunculus flammula*
Lesser Spearwort

325 *Ranunculus reptans*
Creeping Spearwort

326 *Ranunculus lingua*
Greater Spearwort

327 *Ranunculus ophioglossifolius*
Adderstongue Spearwort

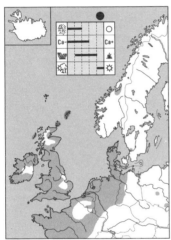

328 *Ranunculus hederaceus*
Ivy-leaved Buttercup

329 *Ranunculus omiophyllus*
Round-leaved Crowfoot

330 *Ranunculus tripartitus*
Three-lobed Crowfoot

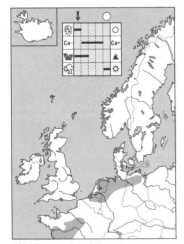

331 *Ranunculus ololeucos*

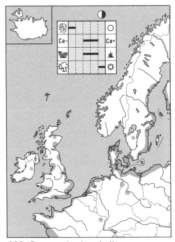

332 *Ranunculus baudotii*
Brackish Water Crowfoot

333 *Ranunculus peltatus*   N
Pond Water Crowfoot

59

Buttercup Family · Ranunculaceae

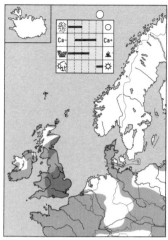

334 *Ranunculus aquatilis*
Common Water Crowfoot

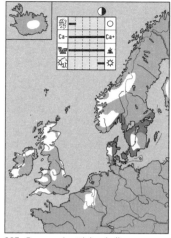

335 *Ranunculus trichophyllus*
Thread-leaved Water Crowfoot

336 *Ranunculus circinatus*
Fan-leaved Water Crowfoot

337 *Ranunculus fluitans*
River Water Crowfoot

338 *Aquilegia atrata*

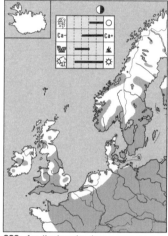

339 *Aquilegia vulgaris*
Columbine

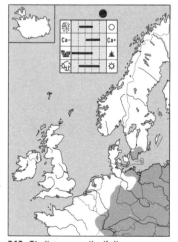

340 *Thalictrum aquilegifolium*
Greater Meadow-rue

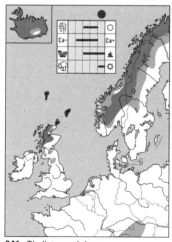

341 *Thalictrum alpinum*
Alpine Meadow-rue

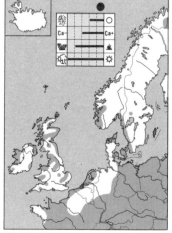

342 *Thalictrum minus*
Lesser Meadow-rue

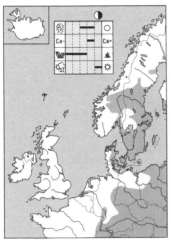

343 *Thalictrum simplex*
Small Meadow-rue

344 *Thalictrum lucidum*

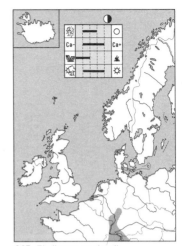

345 *Thalictrum morisonii*

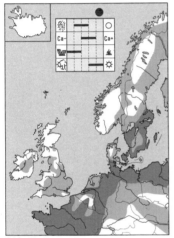

346 *Thalictrum flavum*
Common Meadow-rue

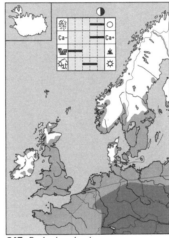

347 *Berberis vulgaris*
Barberry

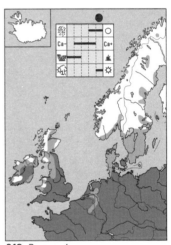

348 *Papaver rhoeas*
Common Poppy

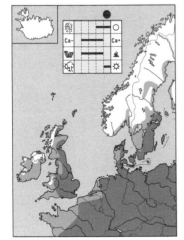

349 *Papaver dubium*
Long-headed Poppy

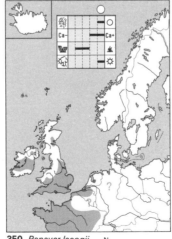

350 *Papaver lecoqii* N
Babington's Poppy

351 *Papaver argemone*
Prickly Poppy

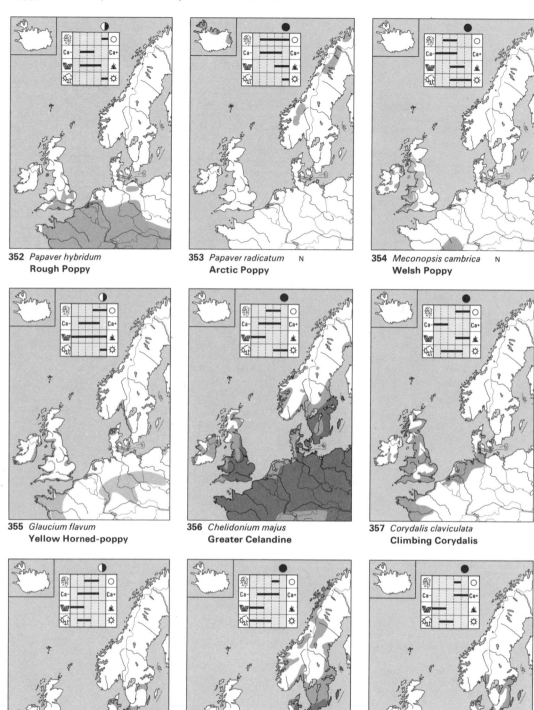

352 *Papaver hybridum*
Rough Poppy

353 *Papaver radicatum* N
Arctic Poppy

354 *Meconopsis cambrica* N
Welsh Poppy

355 *Glaucium flavum*
Yellow Horned-poppy

356 *Chelidonium majus*
Greater Celandine

357 *Corydalis claviculata*
Climbing Corydalis

358 *Corydalis bulbosa* N

359 *Corydalis intermedia*

360 *Corydalis pumila*

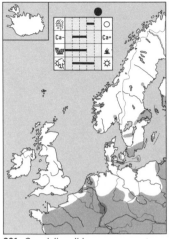

361 *Corydalis solida*   N
Bulbous Corydalis

362 *Fumaria occidentalis*

363 *Fumaria capreolata*
Ramping Fumitory

364 *Fumaria purpurea*

365 *Fumaria bastardii*

366 *Fumaria martinii*

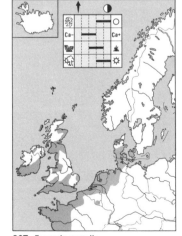

367 *Fumaria muralis*
Wall Fumitory

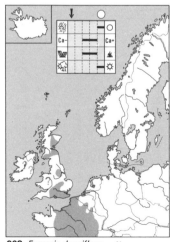

368 *Fumaria densiflora*   N

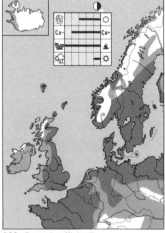

369 *Fumaria officinalis*
Common Fumitory

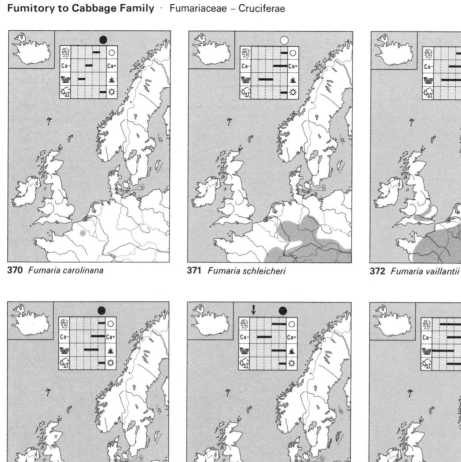

370 *Fumaria carolinana*

371 *Fumaria schleicheri*

372 *Fumaria vaillantii*

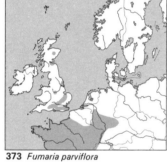

373 *Fumaria parviflora*
Small Fumitory

374 *Sisymbrium supinum*

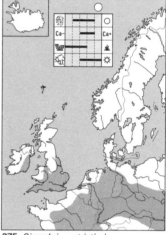

375 *Sisymbrium strictissimum*

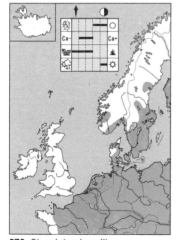

376 *Sisymbrium loeselii*
False London Rocket

377 *Sisymbrium austriacum*

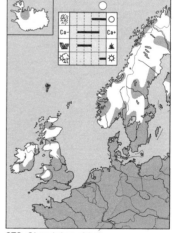

378 *Sisymbrium altissimum*
Tall Rocket

379 *Sisymbrium orientale*
Eastern Rocket

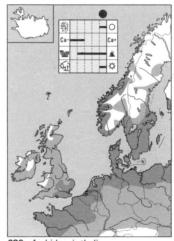

380 *Sisymbrium officinale*
Hedge Mustard

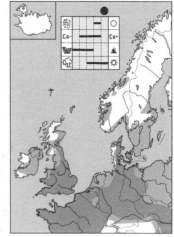

381 *Alliaria petiolata*
Jack-by-the-Hedge

382 *Descurainia sophia*   N
Flixweed

383 *Arabidopsis thaliana*
Thale Cress

384 *Arabidopsis suecica*

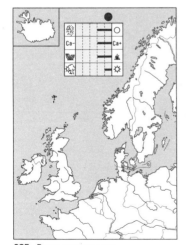

385 *Braya purpurascens*

386 *Braya linearis*

387 *Isatis tinctoria*
Woad

388 *Bunias orientalis* N
Warty Cabbage

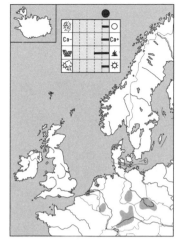

389 *Erysimum crepidifolium*

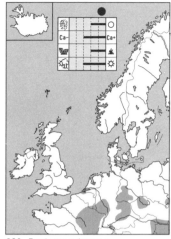

390 *Erysimum odoratum*

391 *Erysimum hieracifolium*

392 *Erysimum repandum*

393 *Erysimum cheiranthoides*
Treacle Mustard

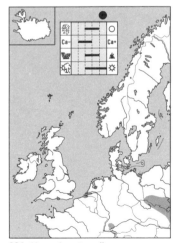

394 *Hesperis matronalis*
Dame's Violet

395 *Cheiranthus cheiri* N
Wallflower

396 *Matthiola incana*
Hoary Stock

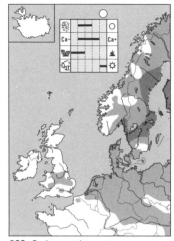

397 *Matthiola sinuata*
Sea Stock

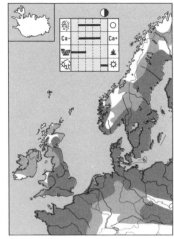

398 *Barbarea vulgaris*
Common Wintercress

399 *Barbarea stricta*   N
Small-flowered Wintercress

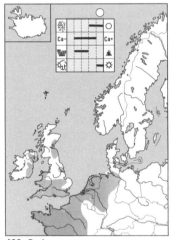

400 *Barbarea verna*
American Wintercress

401 *Barbarea intermedia*
Medium-flowered Wintercress

402 *Rorippa austriaca*
Austrian Yellowcress

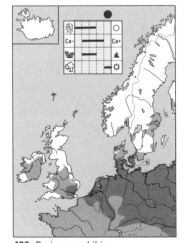

403 *Rorippa amphibia*
Great Yellowcress

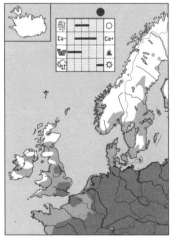

404 *Rorippa sylvestris*   N
Creeping Yellowcress

405 *Rorippa islandica*
Iceland Yellowcress

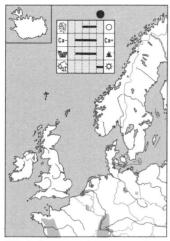

406 *Rorippa pyrenaica*

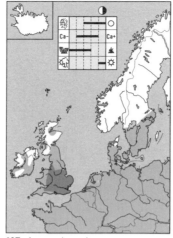

407 *Armoracia rusticana* N
Horseradish

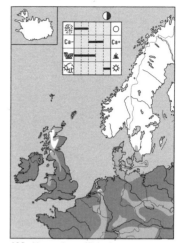

408 *Nasturtium officinale* N
Watercress

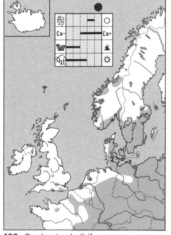

409 *Cardamine bulbifera*
Coralroot

410 *Cardamine heptaphylla*

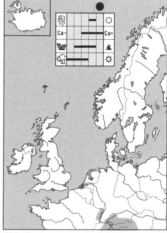

411 *Cardamine pentaphylla*

412 *Cardamine enneaphylla*

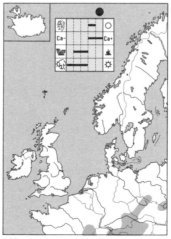

413 *Cardamine trifolia*

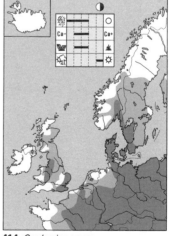

414 *Cardamine amara*
Large Bittercress

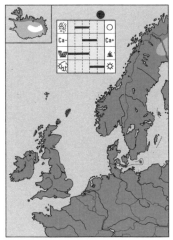

415 *Cardamine pratensis* N
Cuckoo Flower

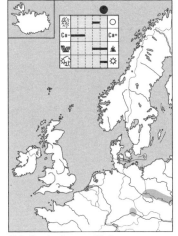

416 *Cardamine resedifolia*

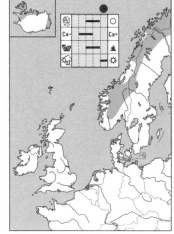

417 *Cardamine bellidifolia*

418 *Cardamine parviflora*

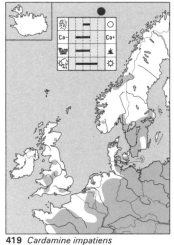

419 *Cardamine impatiens*
Narrow-leaved Bittercress

420 *Cardamine flexuosa*
Wavy Bittercress

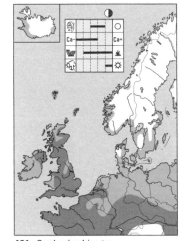

421 *Cardamine hirsuta*
Hairy Bittercress

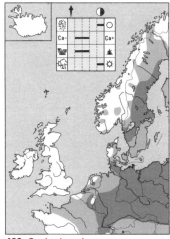

422 *Cardaminopsis arenosa*
Tall Rockcress

423 *Cardaminopsis petraea*
Northern Rockcress

Cabbage Family · Cruciferae

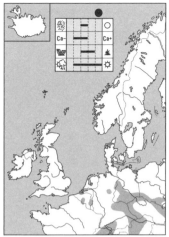

424 *Cardaminopsis halleri*

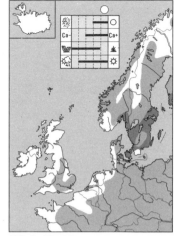

425 *Arabis glabra*
Tower Mustard

426 *Arabis pauciflora*

427 *Arabis hirsuta* N
Hairy Rockcress

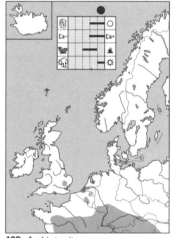

428 *Arabis turrita*
Towercress

429 *Arabis recta*
Annual Rockcress

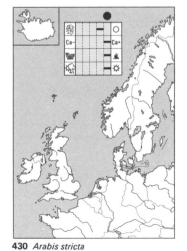

430 *Arabis stricta*
Bristol Rockcress

431 *Arabis alpina*
Alpine Rockcress

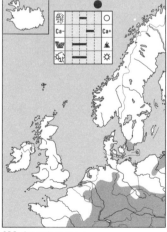

432 *Lunaria rediviva*
Perennial Honesty

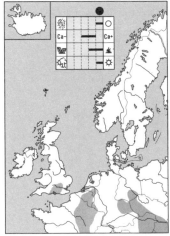

433 *Alyssum saxatile*
Golden Alyssum

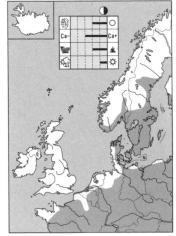

434 *Alyssum alyssoides*
Small Alison

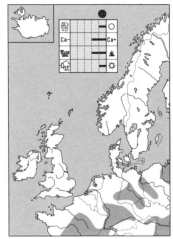

435 *Alyssum montanum*
Mountain Alison

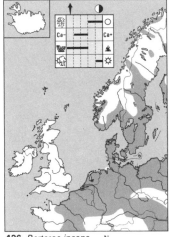

436 *Berteroa incana*   N
Hoary Alison

437 *Draba aizoides*
Yellow Whitlow-grass

438 *Draba alpina*

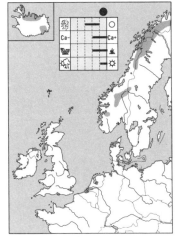

439 *Draba nivalis*

440 *Draba norvegica*
Rock Whitlow-grass

441 *Draba cacuminum*

Cabbage Family · Cruciferae

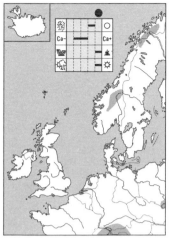

442 *Draba fladnizensis*

443 *Draba daurica*

444 *Draba cinerea*

445 *Draba incana*
Twisted Whitlow-grass

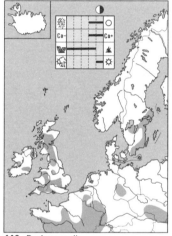

446 *Draba muralis*
Wall Whitlow-grass

447 *Draba nemorosa*

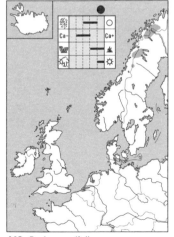

448 *Draba crassifolia*

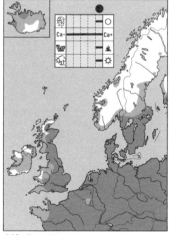

449 *Erophila verna*
Common Whitlow-grass

450 *Cochlearia officinalis* N
Common Scurvy-grass

72

451 *Cochlearia danica*
Early Scurvy-grass

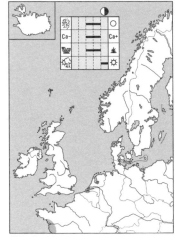

452 *Cochlearia aestuaria*

453 *Cochlearia anglica*
English Scurvy-grass

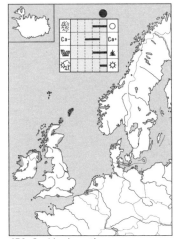

454 *Cochlearia scotica*
Scottish Scurvy-grass

455 *Kernera saxatilis*

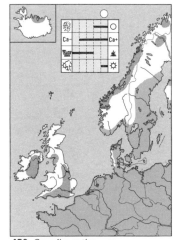

456 *Camelina sativa*   N
Gold of Pleasure

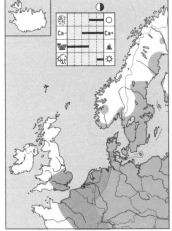

457 *Camelina microcarpa*

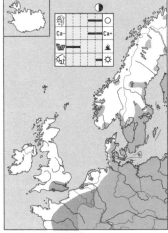

458 *Neslia paniculata*
Ball Mustard

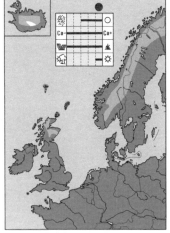

459 *Capsella bursa-pastoris*
Shepherd's Purse

73

Cabbage Family · Cruciferae

460 *Hymenolobus procumbens*

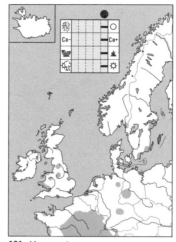

461 *Hornungia petraea*
Hutchinsia

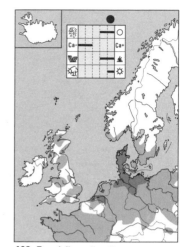

462 *Teesdalia nudicaulis*
Shepherd's Cress

463 *Thlaspi arvense*
Field Pennycress

464 *Thlaspi perfoliatum*
Perfoliate Pennycress

465 *Thlaspi alpestre*
Alpine Pennycress

466 *Thlaspi montanum*
Mountain Pennycress

467 *Iberis amara*   N
Wild Candytuft

468 *Biscutella laevigata*
Buckler Mustard

74

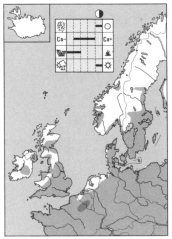

469 *Lepidium campestre*
Field Pepperwort

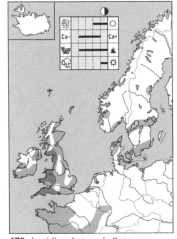

470 *Lepidium heterophyllum*
Smith's Pepperwort

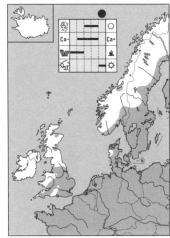

471 *Lepidium ruderale*
Narrow-leaved Pepperwort

472 *Lepidium latifolium*
Dittander

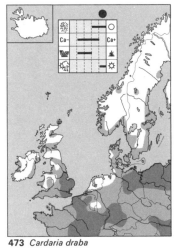

473 *Cardaria draba*
Hoary Cress

474 *Coronopus squamatus*
Swinecress

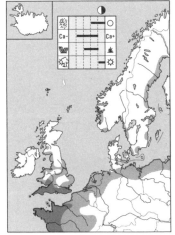

475 *Coronopus didymus*
Lesser Swinecress

476 *Subularia aquatica*
Awlwort

477 *Conringia orientalis*

75

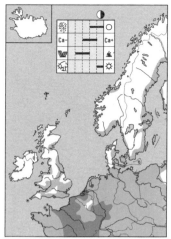

478 *Diplotaxis tenuifolia*
Perennial Wall Rocket

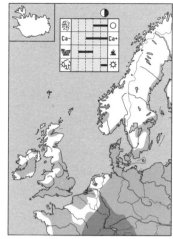

479 *Diplotaxis muralis*
Annual Wall Rocket

480 *Diplotaxis viminea*

481 *Brassica oleracea* N
Wild Cabbage

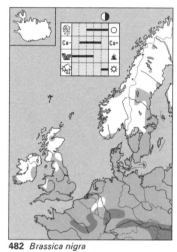

482 *Brassica nigra*
Black Mustard

483 *Brassica rapa*
Wild Turnip

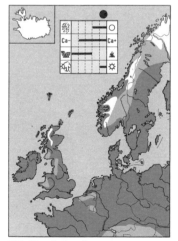

484 *Sinapis arvensis*
Charlock

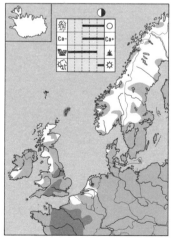

485 *Sinapis alba*
White Mustard

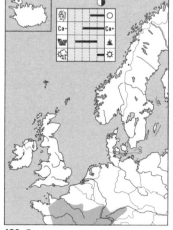

486 *Erucastrum nasturtiifolium*

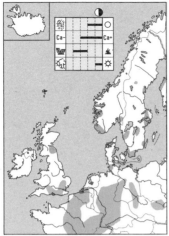

487 *Erucastrum gallicum*
Hairy Rocket

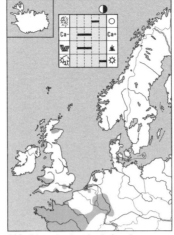

488 *Rhynchosinapis cheiranthos*
Wallflower Cabbage

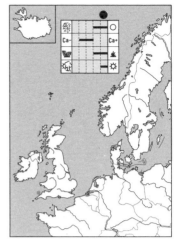

489 *Rhynchosinapis wrightii*
Lundy Cabbage

490 *Rhynchosinapis monensis*
Isle of Man Cabbage

491 *Cakile maritima*
Sea Rocket

492 *Cakile edentula*

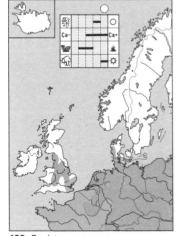

493 *Rapistrum rugosum*
Bastard Cabbage

494 *Crambe maritima*
Sea Kale

495 *Calepina irregularis*
White Ball Mustard

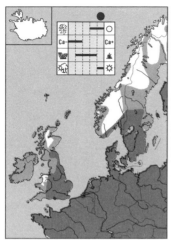

496 *Raphanus raphanistrum*
Wild Radish

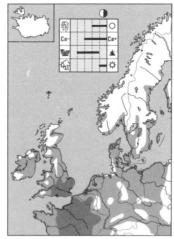

497 *Reseda luteola*
Weld

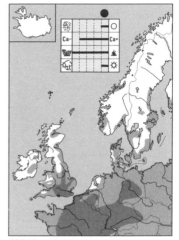

498 *Reseda lutea*
Wild Mignonette

499 *Sarracenia purpurea*
Pitcher Plant

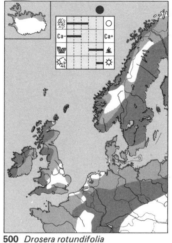

500 *Drosera rotundifolia*
Common Sundew

501 *Drosera intermedia*
Oblong-leaved Sundew

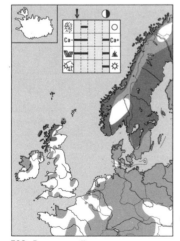

502 *Drosera anglica*
Great Sundew

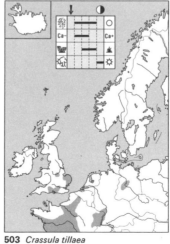

503 *Crassula tillaea*
Mossy Stonecrop

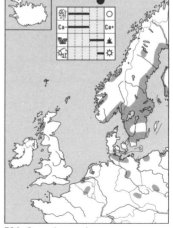

504 *Crassula aquatica*
Water Tillaea

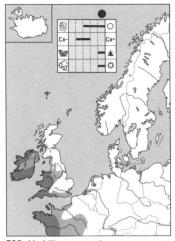

505 *Crassula vaillantii*

506 *Umbilicus rupestris*
Navelwort

507 *Jovibarba sobolifera*
Hen and Chickens Houseleek

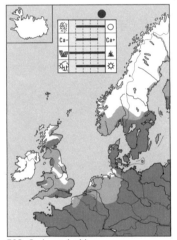

508 *Sedum telephium*
Orpine

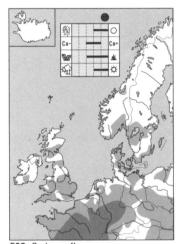

509 *Sedum reflexum*
Reflexed Stonecrop

510 *Sedum forsteranum*
Rock Stonecrop

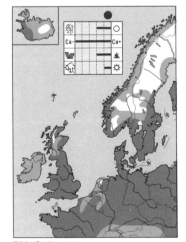

511 *Sedum acre*
Biting Stonecrop

512 *Sedum sexangulare*
Tasteless Stonecrop

513 *Sedum alpestre*
Alpine Stonecrop

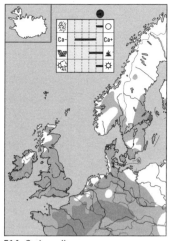

514 *Sedum album*
White Stonecrop

515 *Sedum anglicum*
English Stonecrop

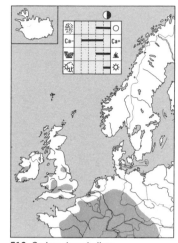

516 *Sedum dasyphyllum*
Thick-leaved Stonecrop

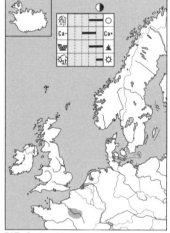

517 *Sedum hirsutum*

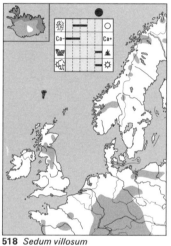

518 *Sedum villosum*
Hairy Stonecrop

519 *Sedum annuum*
Annual Stonecrop

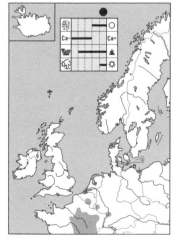

520 *Sedum rubens*

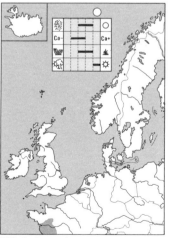

521 *Sedum andegavense*

522 *Sedum hispanicum*

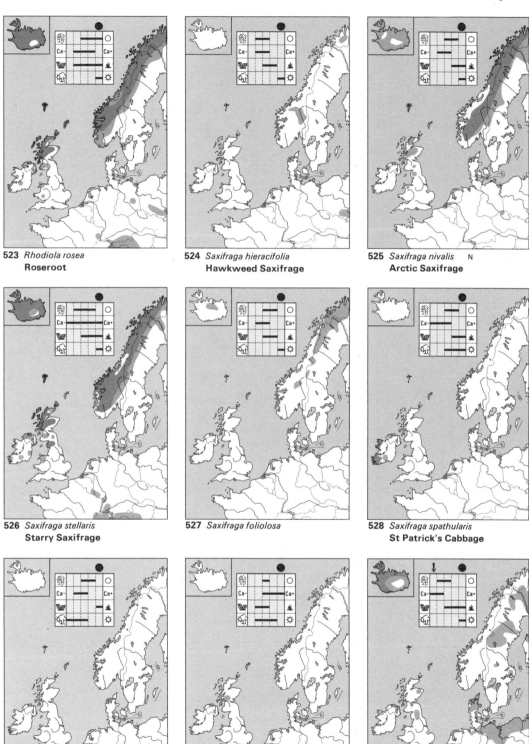

523 *Rhodiola rosea*
Roseroot

524 *Saxifraga hieracifolia*
Hawkweed Saxifrage

525 *Saxifraga nivalis*   N
Arctic Saxifrage

526 *Saxifraga stellaris*
Starry Saxifrage

527 *Saxifraga foliolosa*

528 *Saxifraga spathularis*
St Patrick's Cabbage

529 *Saxifraga hirsuta*
Kidney Saxifrage

530 *Saxifraga rotundifolia*

531 *Saxifraga hirculus*
Marsh Saxifrage

532 *Saxifraga tridactylites*
Rue-leaved Saxifrage

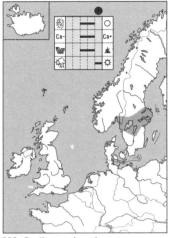

533 *Saxifraga osloensis*   N

534 *Saxifraga adscendens*

535 *Saxifraga aizoides*
Yellow Saxifrage

536 *Saxifraga caespitosa*
Tufted Saxifrage

537 *Saxifraga hartii*

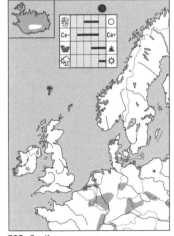

538 *Saxifraga rosacea*
Irish Saxifrage

539 *Saxifraga hypnoides*
Mossy Saxifrage

540 *Saxifraga granulata*
Meadow Saxifrage

541 *Saxifraga cernua*
Drooping Saxifrage

542 *Saxifraga rivularis*
Highland Saxifrage

543 *Saxifraga oppositifolia*
Purple Saxifrage

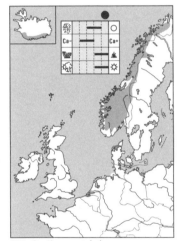

544 *Saxifraga cotyledon*

545 *Saxifraga paniculata*
Livelong Saxifrage

546 *Chrysoplenium oppositifolium*
Opposite-leaved Golden Saxifrage

547 *Chrysoplenium alternifolium* N
**Alternate-leaved Golden
Saxifrage**

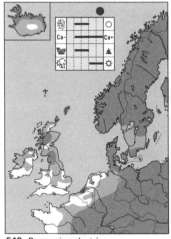

548 *Parnassia palustris*
Grass of Parnassus

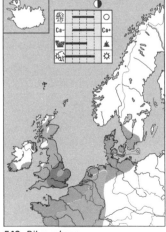

549 *Ribes rubrum*
Red Currant

550 *Ribes spicatum*

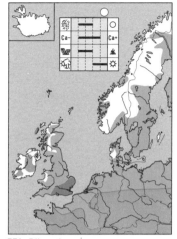

551 *Ribes nigrum*
Black Currant

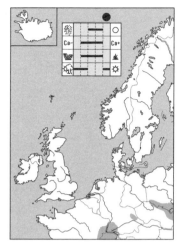

552 *Ribes petraeum*

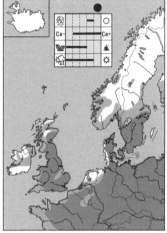

553 *Ribes uva-crispa*
Gooseberry

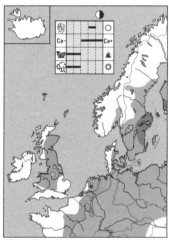

554 *Ribes alpinum*
Mountain Currant

555 *Aruncus dioicus*
Goatsbeard Spiraea

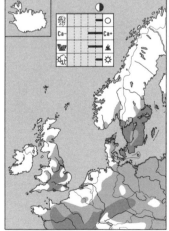

556 *Filipendula vulgaris*
Dropwort

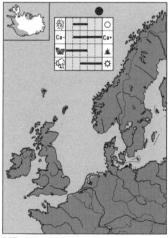

557 *Filipendula ulmaria*
Meadowsweet

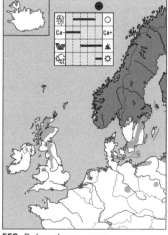

558 *Rubus chamaemorus*
Cloudberry

84

559 *Rubus arcticus*
Arctic Bramble

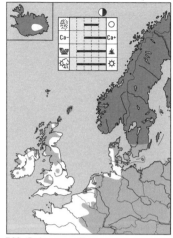

560 *Rubus saxatilis*
Stone Bramble

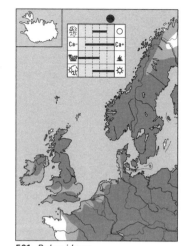

561 *Rubus idaeus*
Raspberry

562 *Rubus sect. Rubus subsect.*
caesii (caesius)
Dewberry

563 *Rubus sect. Rubus subsect. suberecti*
Bramble

564 *Rubus sect. Rubus subsect. silvatici*
Bramble

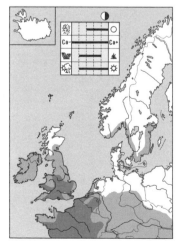

565 *Rubus sect. Rubus subsect. discolores*
Bramble

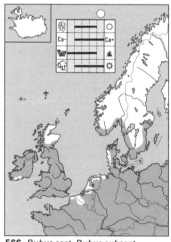

566 *Rubus sect. Rubus subsect.*
appendiculati
Bramble

567 *Rosa sempervirens*

85

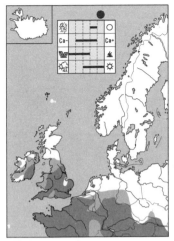

568 *Rosa arvensis*
Field Rose

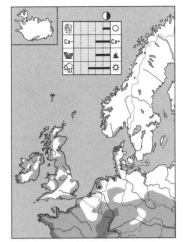

569 *Rosa pimpinellifolia*
Burnet Rose

570 *Rosa acicularis*

571 *Rosa majalis*

572 *Rosa vosegiaca*   N

573 *Rosa pendulina*

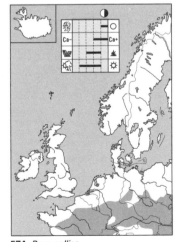

574 *Rosa gallica*
Provence Rose

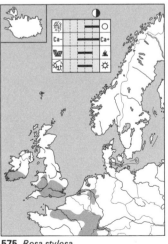

575 *Rosa stylosa*

576 *Rosa jundzilii*

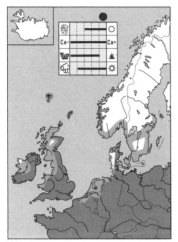

577 *Rosa canina*   N
Dog Rose

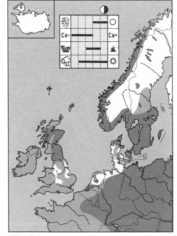

578 *Rosa tomentosa*   N
Downy Rose

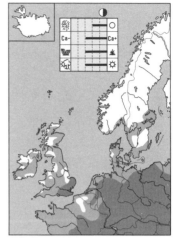

579 *Rosa rubiginosa*   N
Sweet Briar

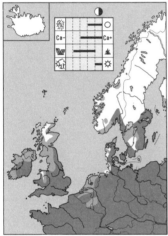

580 *Agrimonia eupatoria*
Agrimony

581 *Agrimonia procera*
Fragrant Agrimony

582 *Aremonia agrimonoides*
Bastard Agrimony

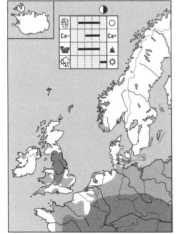

583 *Sanguisorba officinalis*
Great Burnet

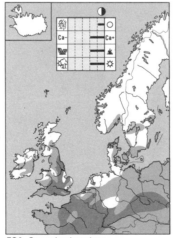

584 *Sanguisorba minor*
Salad Burnet

585 *Dryas octopetala*
Mountain Avens

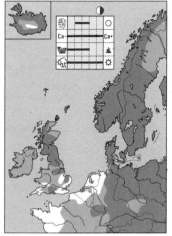

586 *Geum rivale*
Water Avens

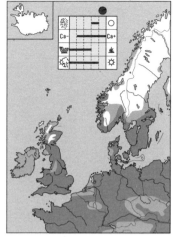

587 *Geum urbanum*
Herb Bennet

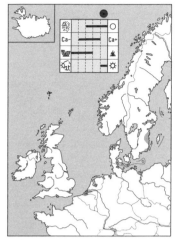

588 *Geum hispidum*

589 *Potentilla fruticosa*
Shrubby Cinquefoil

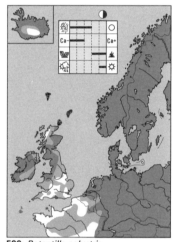

590 *Potentilla palustris*
Marsh Cinquefoil

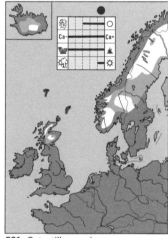

591 *Potentilla anserina*
Silverweed

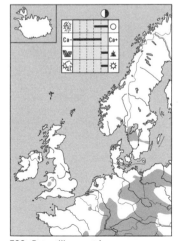

592 *Potentilla rupestris*
Rock Cinquefoil

593 *Potentilla multifida*

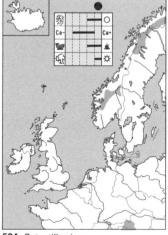

594 *Potentilla nivea*

595 *Potentilla chamissonis*   N

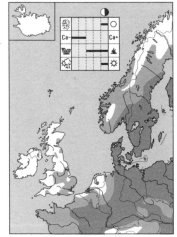

596 *Potentilla argentea*
Hoary Cinquefoil

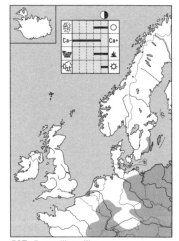

597 *Potentilla collina agg.*

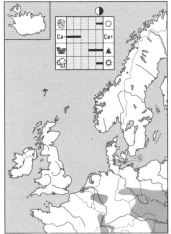

598 *Potentilla inclinata*

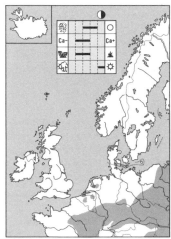

599 *Potentilla supina*

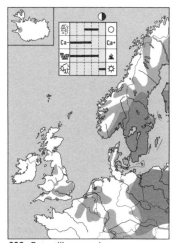

600 *Potentilla norvegica*
Norwegian Cinquefoil

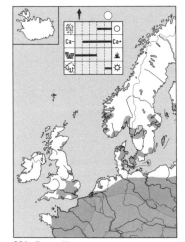

601 *Potentilla recta*
Sulphur Cinquefoil

602 *Potentilla thuringiaca*

603 *Potentilla hyparctica*

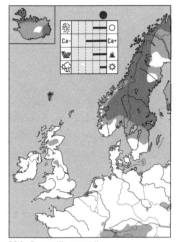

604 *Potentilla crantzii*
Alpine Cinquefoil

605 *Potentilla aurea*

606 *Potentilla heptaphylla*

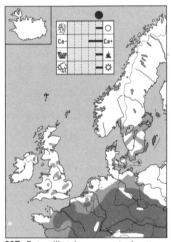

607 *Potentilla tabernaemontani* N
Spring Cinquefoil

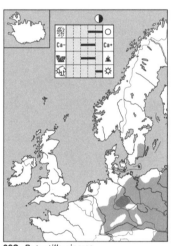

608 *Potentilla cinerea*
Grey Cinquefoil

609 *Potentilla erecta*
Tormentil

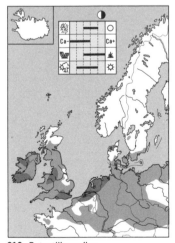

610 *Potentilla anglica*
Trailing Tormentil

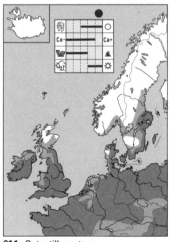

611 *Potentilla reptans*
Creeping Cinquefoil

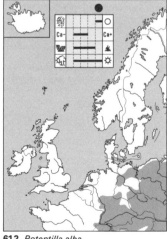

612 *Potentilla alba*
White Cinquefoil

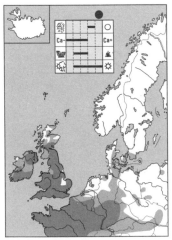

613 *Potentilla sterilis*
Barren Strawberry

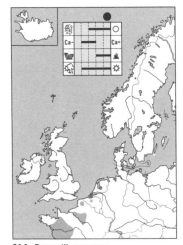

614 *Potentilla montana*

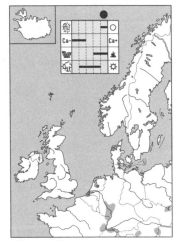

615 *Potentilla micrantha*
Pink Barren Strawberry

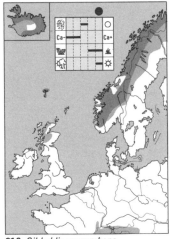

616 *Sibbaldia procumbens*
Sibbaldia

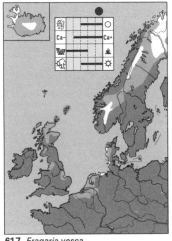

617 *Fragaria vesca*
Wild Strawberry

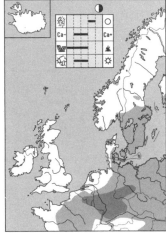

618 *Fragaria moschata*
Hautbois Strawberry

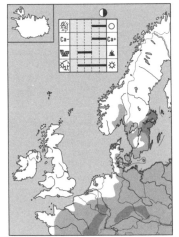

619 *Fragaria viridis*

620 *Alchemilla alpina*
Alpine Lady's Mantle

621 *Alchemilla pallens*

622 *Alchemilla hoppeana*

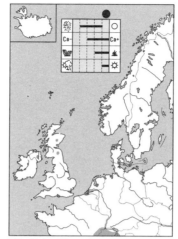

623 *Alchemilla conjuncta*

624 *Alchemilla faeroensis*

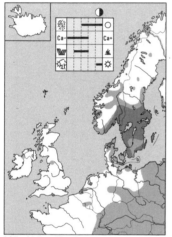

625 *Alchemilla glaucescens*

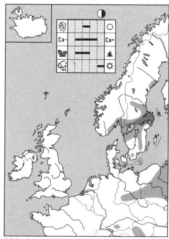

626 *Alchemilla plicata*

627 *Alchemilla propinqua*

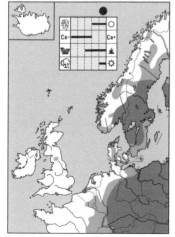

628 *Alchemilla monticola*

629 *Alchemilla crinita*

630 *Alchemilla strigulosa*

631 *Alchemilla subglobosa*

632 *Alchemilla sarmatica*

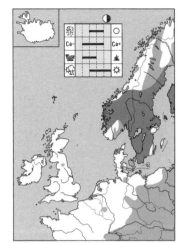

633 *Alchemilla subcrenata*

634 *Alchemilla cymatophylla*

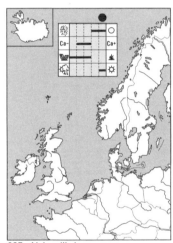

635 *Alchemilla heptagona*

636 *Alchemilla acutiloba*

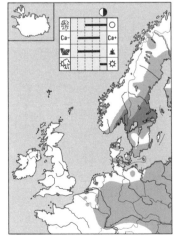

637 *Alchemilla gracilis*

638 *Alchemilla xanthochlora*
Lady's Mantle

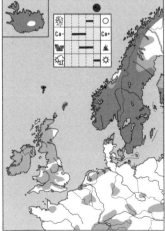

639 *Alchemilla filicaulis*

93

Rose Family · Rosaceae

640 *Alchemilla minima*

641 *Alchemilla glomerulans*

642 *Alchemilla nebulosa*

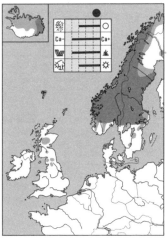

643 *Alchemilla wichurae*

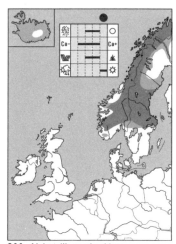

644 *Alchemilla murbeckiana*

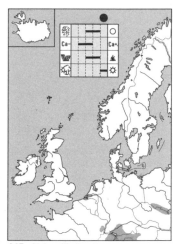

645 *Alchemilla lineata*

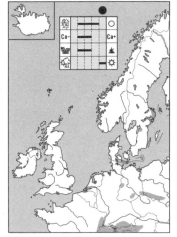

646 *Alchemilla obtusa*

647 *Alchemilla glabra*
Lady's Mantle

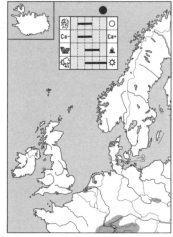

648 *Alchemilla coriacea*

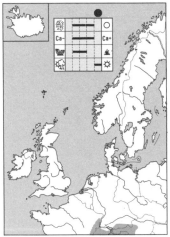

649 *Alchemilla incisa*

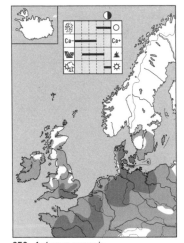

650 *Aphanes arvensis*
Parsley Piert

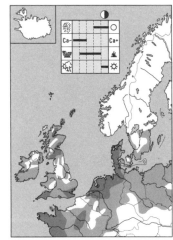

651 *Aphanes microcarpa*

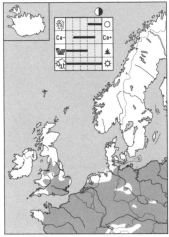

652 *Pyrus pyraster*
Wild Pear

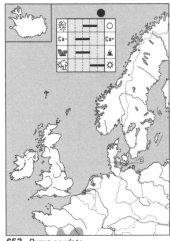

653 *Pyrus cordata*
Plymouth Pear

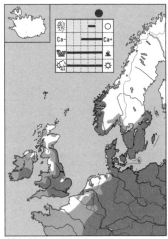

654 *Malus sylvestris*   N
Crab Apple

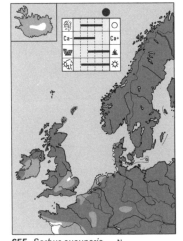

655 *Sorbus aucuparia*   N
Rowan

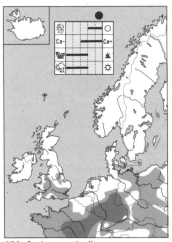

656 *Sorbus torminalis*
Service Tree

657 *Sorbus chamaemespilus*

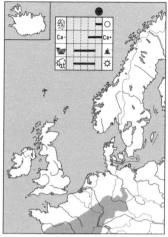

658 *Sorbus domestica*

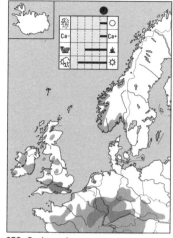

659 *Sorbus aria* N
Whitebeam

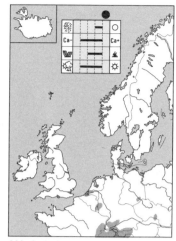

660 *Sorbus mougeotii*

661 *Sorbus hybrida*
Broad-leaved Whitebeam

662 *Sorbus meinichii*

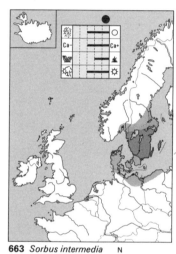

663 *Sorbus intermedia* N
Swedish Whitebeam

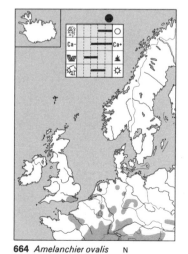

664 *Amelanchier ovalis* N
Amelanchier

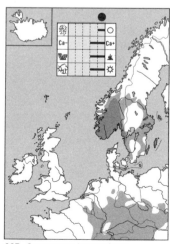

665 *Cotoneaster integerrimus*
Wild Cotoneaster

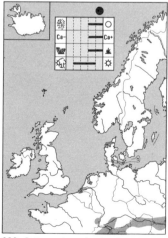

666 *Cotoneaster nebrodensis*

667 *Cotoneaster niger*

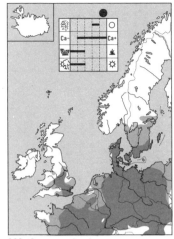

668 *Crataegus laevigata*
Midland Hawthorn

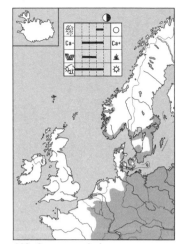

669 *Crataegus calycina*

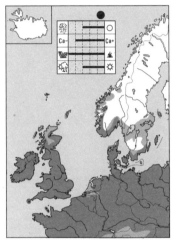

670 *Crataegus monogyna*
Hawthorn

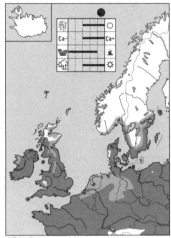

671 *Prunus spinosa*
Blackthorn

672 *Prunus fruticosa*

673 *Prunus avium*
Wild Cherry

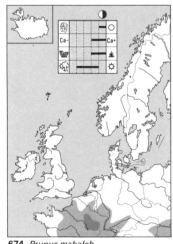

674 *Prunus mahaleb*
St Lucie's Cherry

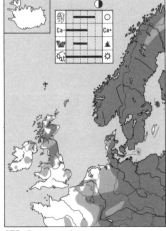

675 *Prunus padus*
Bird Cherry

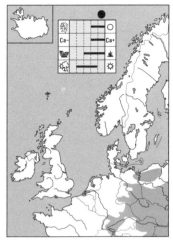

676 *Lembotropis nigricans*

677 *Cytisus scoparius*
Broom

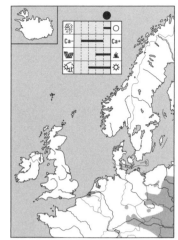

678 *Chamaecytisus ratisbonensis*

679 *Chamaecytisus supinus*
Clustered Broom

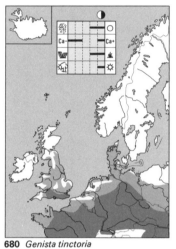

680 *Genista tinctoria*
Dyer's Greenweed

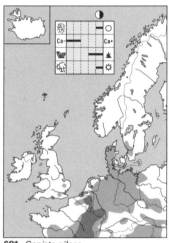

681 *Genista pilosa*
Hairy Greenweed

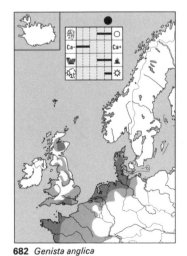

682 *Genista anglica*
Petty Whin

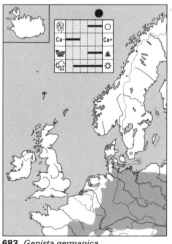

683 *Genista germanica*
German Greenweed

684 *Ulex europaeus*
Gorse

685 *Ulex minor*
Dwarf Gorse

686 *Ulex gallii*
Western Gorse

687 *Chamaespartium saggitale*
Winged Broom

688 *Colutea arborescens*
Bladder Senna

689 *Astragalus cicer*
Wild Lentil

690 *Astragalus danicus*
Purple Milk-vetch

691 *Astragalus frigidus*
Yellow Alpine Milk-vetch

692 *Astragalus penduliflorus*

693 *Astragalus alpinus*
Alpine Milk-vetch

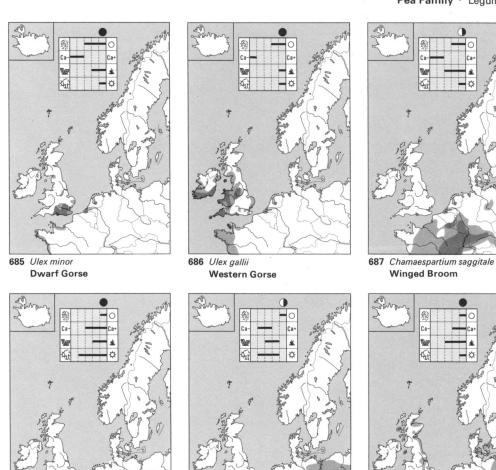

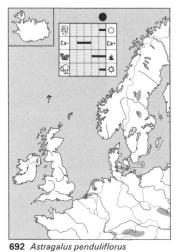

99

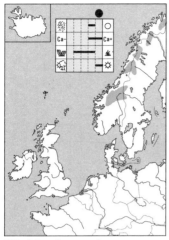

694 *Astragalus norvegicus*

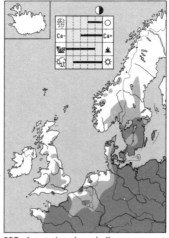

695 *Astragalus glycyphyllos*
Wild Liquorice

696 *Astragalus exscapus*

697 *Astragalus arenarius*

698 *Astragalus baioniensis*

699 *Oxytropis lapponica*
Northern Milk-vetch

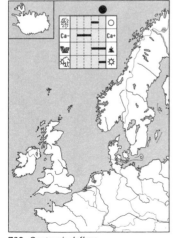

700 *Oxytropis deflexa*

701 *Oxytropis campestris*
Yellow Milk-vetch

702 *Oxytropis halleri*
Mountain Milk-vetch

703 *Oxytropis pilosa*
Hairy Milk-vetch

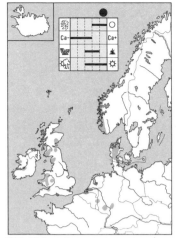

704 *Vicia orobus*
Upright Vetch

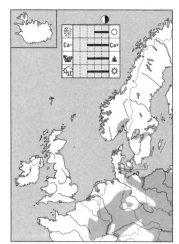

705 *Vicia pisiformis*

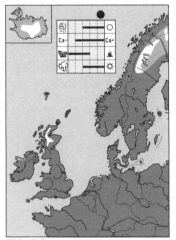

706 *Vicia cracca*
Tufted Vetch

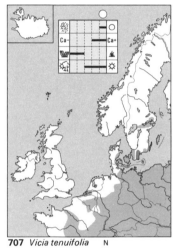

707 *Vicia tenuifolia* N
Fine-leaved Vetch

708 *Vicia cassubica*
Danzig Vetch

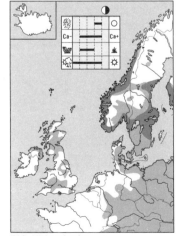

709 *Vicia sylvatica*
Wood Vetch

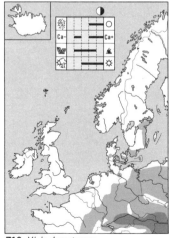

710 *Vicia dumetorum*

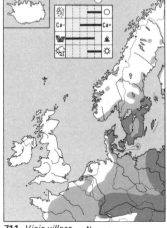

711 *Vicia villosa* N
Fodder Vetch

101

712 *Vicia hirsuta*
Hairy Tare

713 *Vicia tenuissima*
Slender Tare

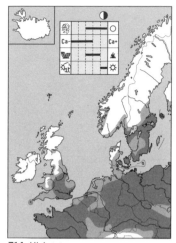

714 *Vicia tetrasperma*
Smooth Tare

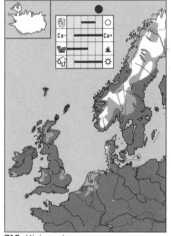

715 *Vicia sepium*
Bush Vetch

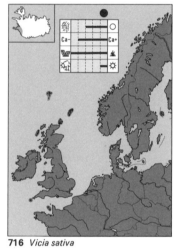

716 *Vicia sativa*
Common Vetch

717 *Vicia lathyroides*
Spring Vetch

718 *Vicia lutea*
Yellow Vetch

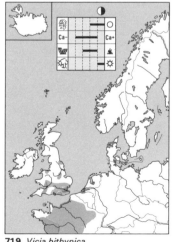

719 *Vicia bithynica*
Bithynian Vetch

720 *Vicia narbonensis*

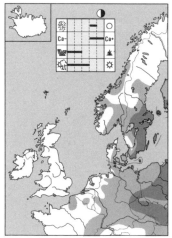

721 *Lathyrus vernus*
Spring Pea

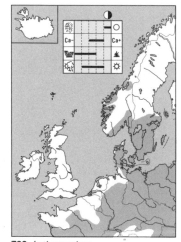

722 *Lathyrus niger*
Black Pea

723 *Lathyrus japonicus*
Sea Pea

724 *Lathyrus pannonicus*

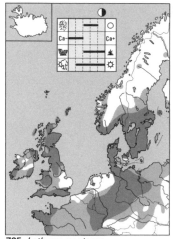

725 *Lathyrus montanus*
Bitter Vetchling

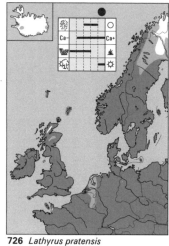

726 *Lathyrus pratensis*
Meadow Vetchling

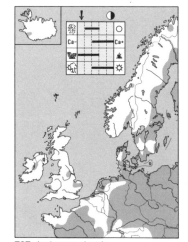

727 *Lathyrus palustris*
Marsh Pea

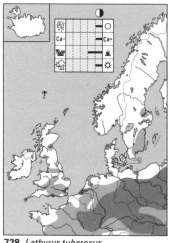

728 *Lathyrus tuberosus*
Tuberous Pea

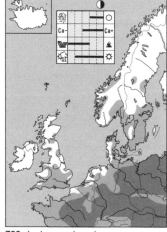

729 *Lathyrus sylvestris*
Narrow-leaved Everlasting Pea

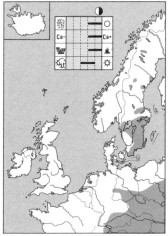

730 *Lathyrus latifolius* N
Broad-leaved Everlasting Pea

731 *Lathyrus sphaericus*

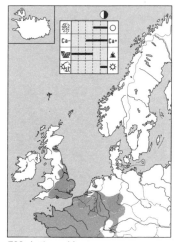

732 *Lathyrus hirsutus*
Hairy Vetchling

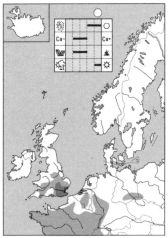

733 *Lathyrus nissolia*
Grass Vetchling

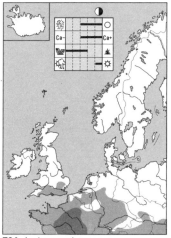

734 *Lathyrus aphaca*
Yellow Vetchling

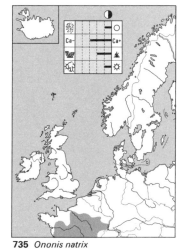

735 *Ononis natrix*
Large Yellow Rest-harrow

736 *Ononis reclinata*
Small Rest-harrow

737 *Ononis pusilla*

738 *Ononis spinosa*
Spiny Rest-harrow

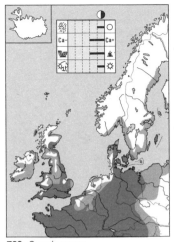

739 *Ononis repens*
Rest-harrow

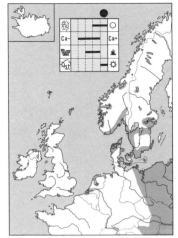

740 *Ononis arvensis*

741 *Melilotus dentata*

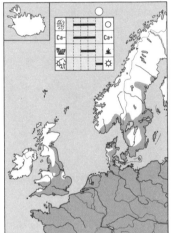

742 *Melilotus altissima*
Tall Melilot

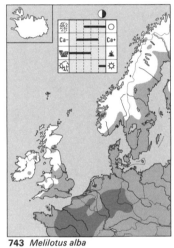

743 *Melilotus alba*
White Melilot

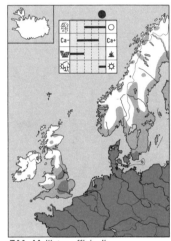

744 *Melilotus officinalis*
Ribbed Melilot

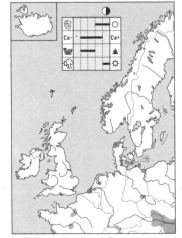

745 *Trigonella monspeliaca*

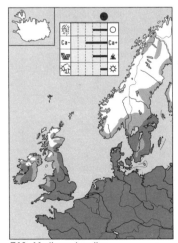

746 *Medicago lupulina*
Black Medick

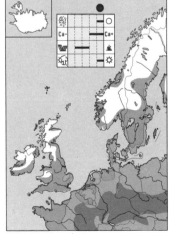

747 *Medicago sativa* N
Lucerne

105

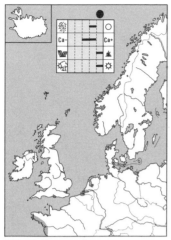

748 *Medicago marina*

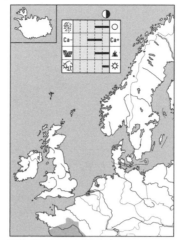

749 *Medicago orbicularis*

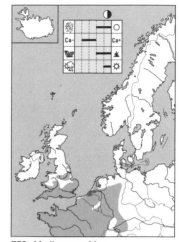

750 *Medicago arabica*
Spotted Medick

751 *Medicago polymorpha*
Toothed Medick

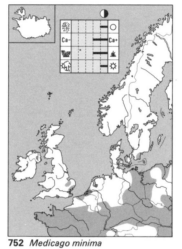

752 *Medicago minima*
Bur Medick

753 *Trifolium ornithopodioides* N
Fenugreek

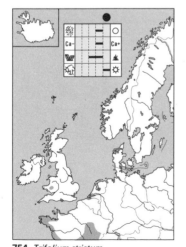

754 *Trifolium strictum*
Upright Clover

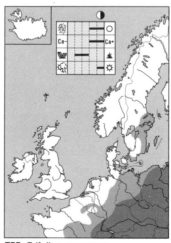

755 *Trifolium montanum*
Mountain Clover

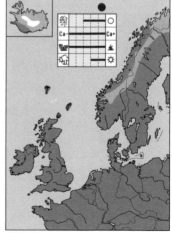

756 *Trifolium repens*
White Clover

106

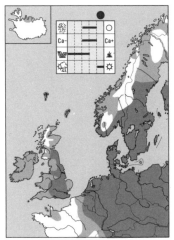

757 *Trifolium hybridum*
Alsike Clover

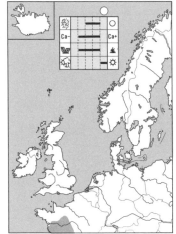

758 *Trifolium michelianum*

759 *Trifolium retusum*

760 *Trifolium glomeratum*
Clustered Clover

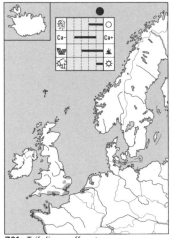

761 *Trifolium suffocatum*
Suffocated Clover

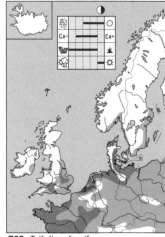

762 *Trifolium fragiferum*
Strawberry Clover

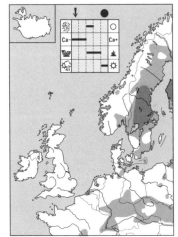

763 *Trifolium spadiceum*

764 *Trifolium aureum* N
Large Hop Trefoil

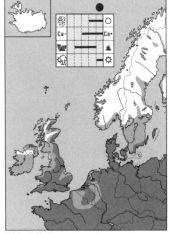

765 *Trifolium campestre*
Hop Trefoil

107

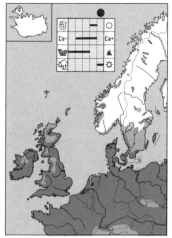

766 *Trifolium dubium*
Lesser Trefoil

767 *Trifolium micranthum*
Slender Trefoil

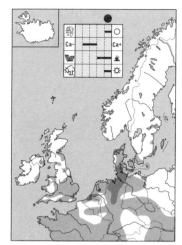

768 *Trifolium striatum*
Knotted Clover

769 *Trifolium arvense*
Haresfoot Clover

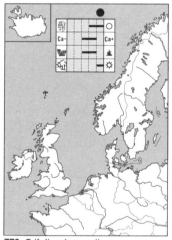

770 *Trifolium bocconii*
Twin-flowered Clover

771 *Trifolium scabrum*
Rough Clover

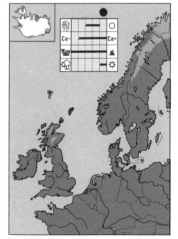

772 *Trifolium pratense*
Red Clover

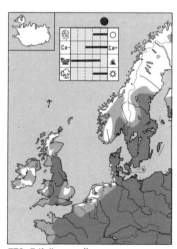

773 *Trifolium medium*
Zigzag Clover

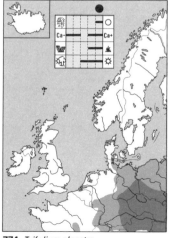

774 *Trifolium alpestre*
Mountain Zigzag Clover

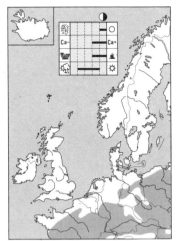

775 *Trifolium rubens*

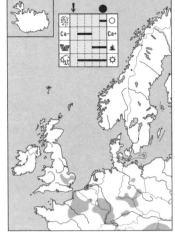

776 *Trifolium ochroleucon*
Sulphur Clover

777 *Trifolium squamosum*
Sea Clover

778 *Trifolium subterraneum*
Burrowing Clover

779 *Dorycnium pentaphyllum*

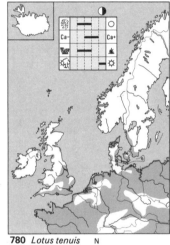

780 *Lotus tenuis*   N
Narrow-leaved Birdsfoot Trefoil

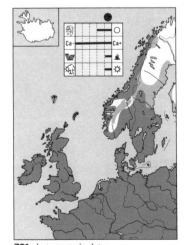

781 *Lotus corniculatus*
Birdsfoot Trefoil

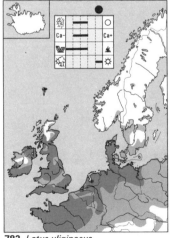

782 *Lotus uliginosus*
Greater Birdsfoot Trefoil

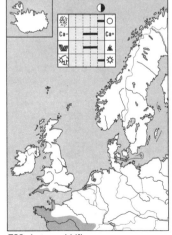

783 *Lotus subbiflorus*
Hairy Birdsfoot Trefoil

109

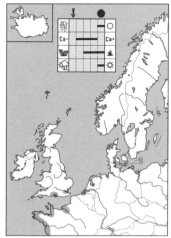

784 *Lotus angustissimus*
Slender Birdsfoot Trefoil

785 *Tetragonolobus maritimus*
Dragon's Teeth

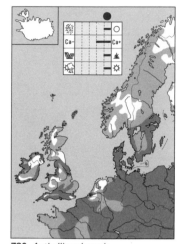

786 *Anthyllis vulneraria*
Kidney Vetch

787 *Ornithopus perpusillus*
Birdsfoot

788 *Ornithopus pinnatus*
Orange Birdsfoot

789 *Ornithopus compressus*

790 *Coronilla emerus*
Scorpion Senna

791 *Coronilla vaginalis*
Small Scorpion Vetch

792 *Coronilla minima*

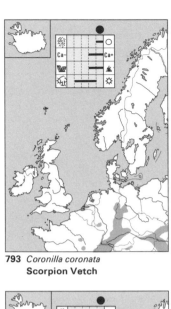

793 *Coronilla coronata*
Scorpion Vetch

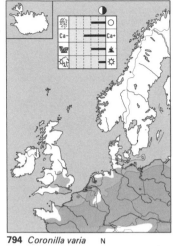

794 *Coronilla varia*   N
Crown Vetch

795 *Hippocrepis comosa*
Horseshoe Vetch

796 *Onobrychis arenaria*

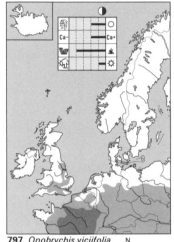

797 *Onobrychis viciifolia*   N
Sainfoin

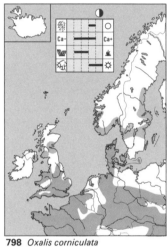

798 *Oxalis corniculata*
Yellow Oxalis

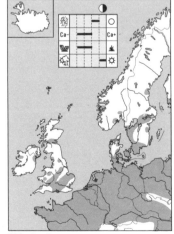

799 *Oxalis europaea*
Upright Yellow Oxalis

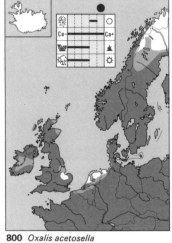

800 *Oxalis acetosella*
Wood Sorrel

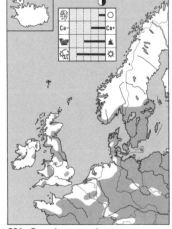

801 *Geranium sanguineum*
Bloody Cranesbill

Geranium Family · Geraniaceae

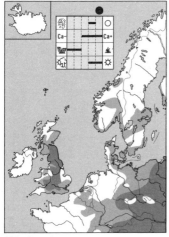

802 *Geranium pratense*
Meadow Cranesbill

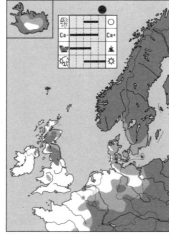

803 *Geranium sylvaticum*
Wood Cranesbill

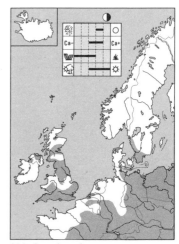

804 *Geranium phaeum*
Dusky Cranesbill

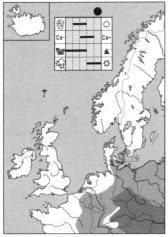

805 *Geranium palustre*
Marsh Cranesbill

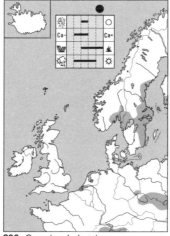

806 *Geranium bohemicum*

807 *Geranium lanuginosum*

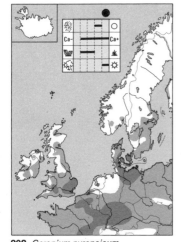

808 *Geranium pyrenaicum*
Hedgerow Cranesbill

809 *Geranium rotundifolium*
Round-leaved Cranesbill

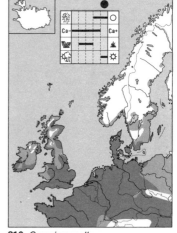

810 *Geranium molle*
Dovesfoot Cranesbill

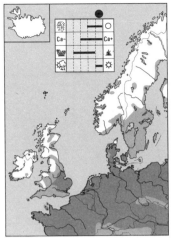

811 *Geranium pusillum*
Small-flowered Cranesbill

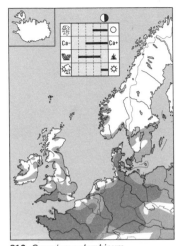

812 *Geranium columbinum*
Long-stalked Cranesbill

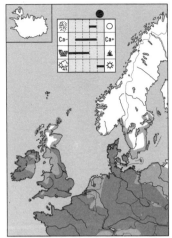

813 *Geranium dissectum*
Cut-leaved Cranesbill

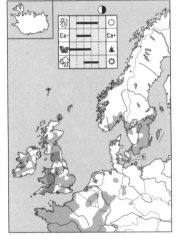

814 *Geranium lucidum*
Shining Cranesbill

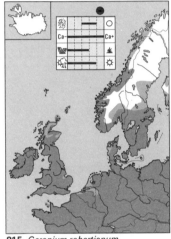

815 *Geranium robertianum*
Herb Robert

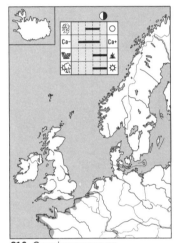

816 *Geranium purpureum*
Little Robin

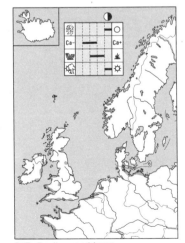

817 *Erodium maritimum*
Sea Storksbill

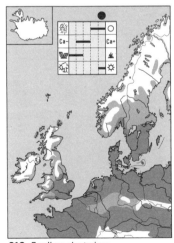

818 *Erodium cicutarium*
Common Storksbill

819 *Tribulus terrestris*
Small Caltrop

820 *Linum perenne*
Perennial Flax

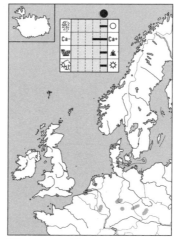

821 *Linum austriacum*

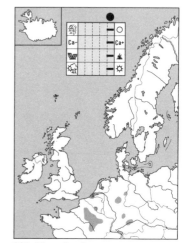

822 *Linum leonii*

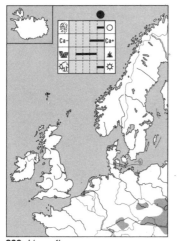

823 *Linum flavum*
Yellow Flax

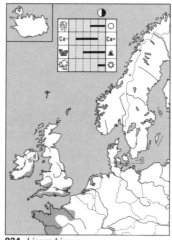

824 *Linum bienne*
Pale Flax

825 *Linum viscosum*

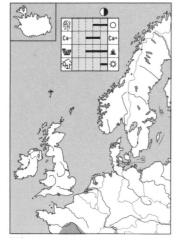

826 *Linum trigynum*

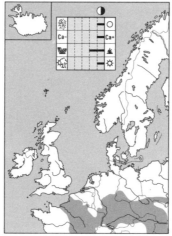

827 *Linum tenuifolium*

828 *Linum suffruticosum*
White Flax

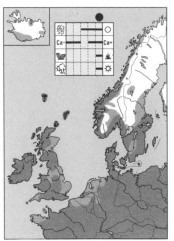

829 *Linum catharticum*
Purging Flax

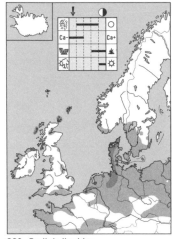

830 *Radiola linoides*
Allseed

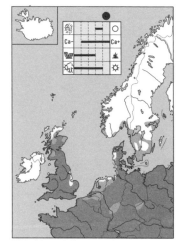

831 *Mercurialis perenne*
Dog's Mercury

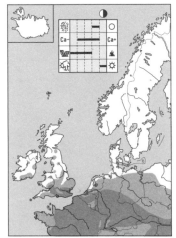

832 *Mercurialis annua*
Annual Mercury

833 *Mercurialis ovata*

834 *Euphorbia peplis*
Purple Spurge

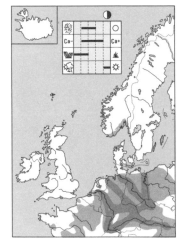

835 *Euphorbia palustris*
Marsh Spurge

836 *Euphorbia hyberna*
Irish Spurge

837 *Euphorbia dulcis*
Sweet Spurge

115

Spurge Family · Euphorbiaceae

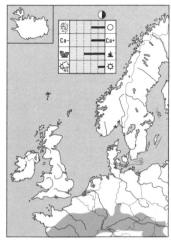

838 *Euphorbia brittingeri*

839 *Euphorbia platyphyllos*
Broad-leaved Spurge

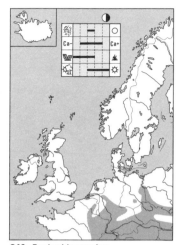

840 *Euphorbia serrulata*
Upright Spurge

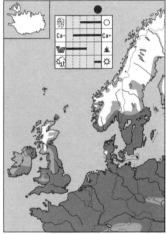

841 *Euphorbia helioscopia*
Sun Spurge

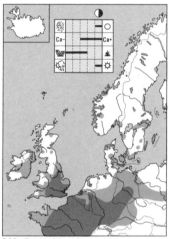

842 *Euphorbia exigua* N
Dwarf Spurge

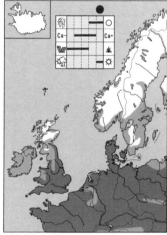

843 *Euphorbia peplus*
Petty Spurge

844 *Euphorbia portlandica*
Portland Spurge

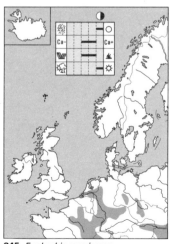

845 *Euphorbia seguierana*

846 *Euphorbia paralias*
Sea Spurge

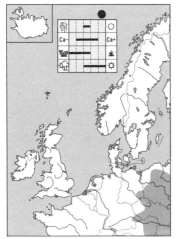

847 *Euphorbia lucida*

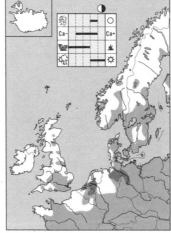

848 *Euphorbia esula*
Leafy Spurge

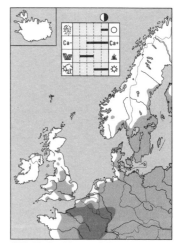

849 *Euphorbia cyparissias*   N
Cypress Spurge

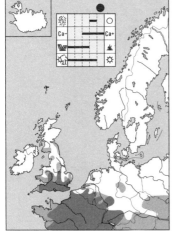

850 *Euphorbia amygdaloides*
Wood Spurge

851 *Dictamnus albus*
Burning Bush

852 *Polygala chamaebuxus*
Shrubby Milkwort

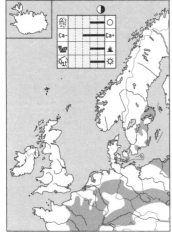

853 *Polygala comosa*
Tufted Milkwort

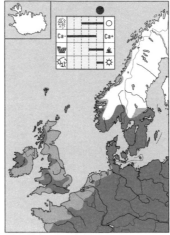

854 *Polygala vulgaris*
Common Milkwort

855 *Polygala serpyllifolia*
Heath Milkwort

856 *Polygala calcarea*
Chalk Milkwort

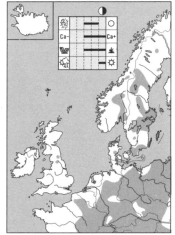

857 *Polygala amarella*
Dwarf Milkwort

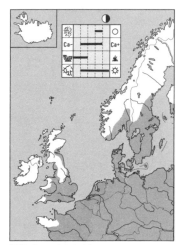

858 *Acer platanoides*   N
Norway Maple

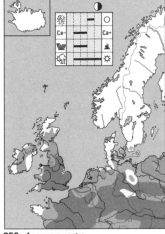

859 *Acer campestre*
Field Maple

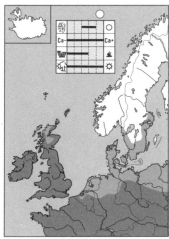

860 *Acer pseudoplatanus*   N
Sycamore

861 *Acer monspessulanum*   N
Montpelier Maple

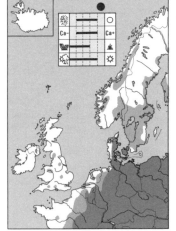

862 *Impatiens noli-tangere*   N
Touch-me-not Balsam

863 *Impatiens capensis*
Orange Balsam

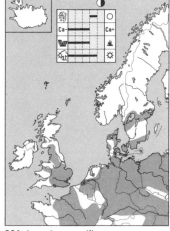

864 *Impatiens parviflora*
Small Balsam

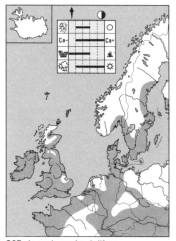

865 *Impatiens glandulifera*
Himalayan Balsam

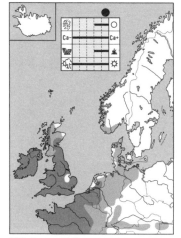

866 *Ilex aquifolium* N
Holly

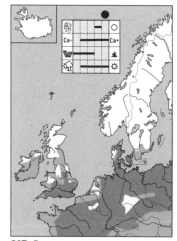

867 *Euonymus europaeus*
Spindle-tree

868 *Euonymus latifolius*

869 *Staphylea pinnata*
Bladder-nut

870 *Buxus sempervirens* N
Box

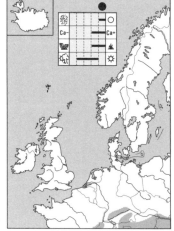

871 *Rhamnus saxatilis*

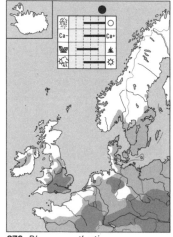

872 *Rhamnus catharticus*
Buckthorn

873 *Frangula alnus*
Alder Buckthorn

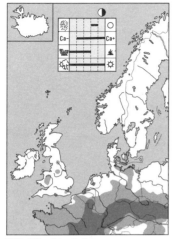

874 *Tilia platyphyllos*
Large-leaved Lime

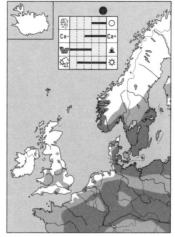

875 *Tilia cordata*
Small-leaved Lime

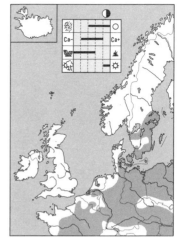

876 *Malva alcea*

877 *Malva moschata*
Musk Mallow

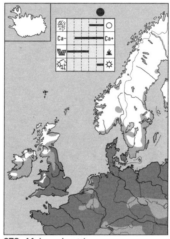

878 *Malva sylvestris*
Common Mallow

879 *Malva pusilla*
Small Mallow

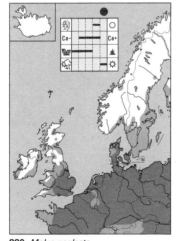

880 *Malva neglecta*
Dwarf Mallow

881 *Lavatera cretica*
Smaller Tree Mallow

882 *Lavatera arborea*
Tree Mallow

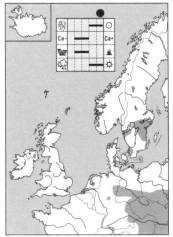

883 *Lavatera thuringiaca*

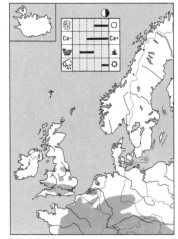

884 *Althaea hirsuta*
Rough Mallow

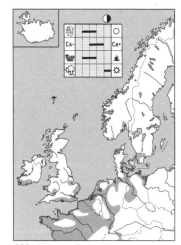

885 *Althaea officinalis*
Marsh Mallow

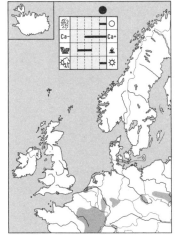

886 *Thymelaea passerina*
Annual Thymelaea

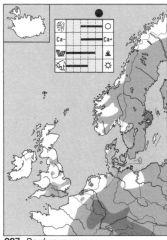

887 *Daphne mezereon*
Mezereon

888 *Daphne laureola*
Spurge Laurel

889 *Hippophae rhamnoides*   N
Sea Buckthorn

890 *Hypericum androsaemum*
Tutsan

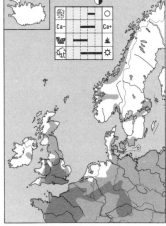

891 *Hypericum hirsutum*
Hairy St John's Wort

892 *Hypericum pulchrum*
Slender St John's Wort

893 *Hypericum montanum*
Pale St John's Wort

894 *Hypericum elodes*
Marsh St John's Wort

895 *Hypericum linariifolium*
Flax-leaved St John's Wort

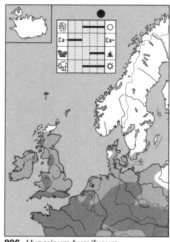

896 *Hypericum humifusum*
Trailing St John's Wort

897 *Hypericum tetrapterum*
Square-stalked St John's Wort

898 *Hypericum undulatum*
Wavy St John's Wort

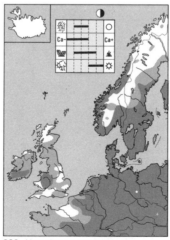

899 *Hypericum maculatum*
Imperforate St John's Wort

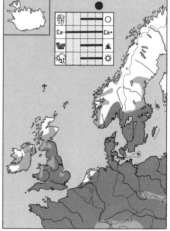

900 *Hypericum perforatum*
Perforate St John's Wort

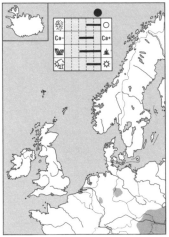

901 *Hypericum elegans*

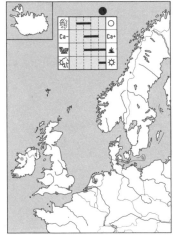

902 *Hypericum canadense*
Irish St John's Wort

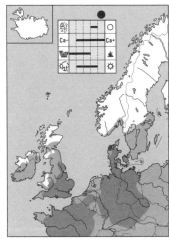

903 *Viola odorata*
Sweet Violet

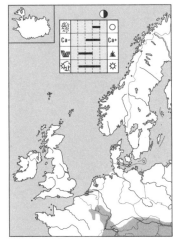

904 *Viola alba*
White Violet

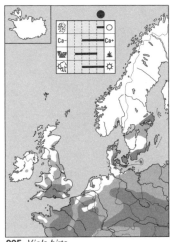

905 *Viola hirta*
Hairy Violet

906 *Viola collina*

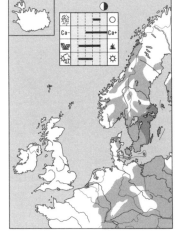

907 *Viola mirabilis*

908 *Viola rupestris*
Teesdale Violet

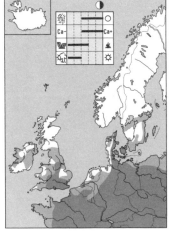

909 *Viola reichenbachiana*
Early Dog Violet

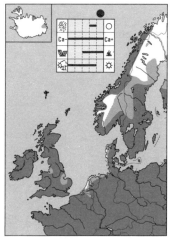

910 *Viola riviniana*
Common Dog Violet

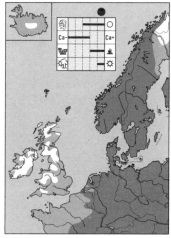

911 *Viola canina*
Heath Dog Violet

912 *Viola lactea*
Pale Dog Violet

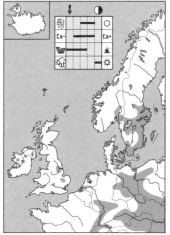

913 *Viola persicifolia*
Fen Violet

914 *Viola pumila*
Meadow Violet

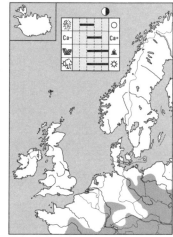

915 *Viola elatior*

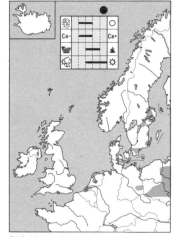

916 *Viola uliginosa*

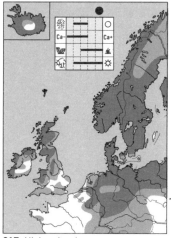

917 *Viola palustris*
Marsh Violet

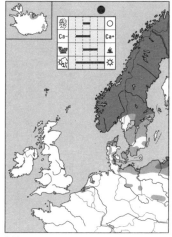

918 *Viola epipsila*

919 *Viola selkirkii*
Northern Violet

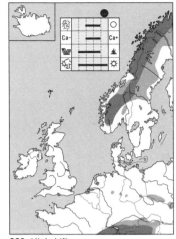

920 *Viola biflora*
Yellow Wood Violet

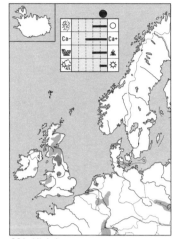

921 *Viola lutea*
Mountain Pansy

922 *Viola hispida*

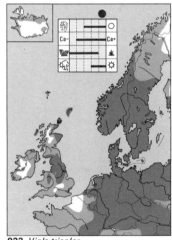

923 *Viola tricolor*
Wild Pansy

924 *Viola arvensis*
Field Pansy

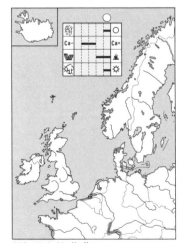

925 *Viola kitaibeliana*
Dwarf Pansy

926 *Tuberaria guttata*
Spotted Rock-rose

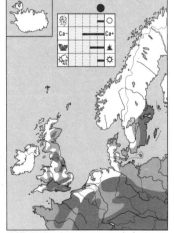

927 *Helianthemum nummularium*
Common Rock-rose

928 *Helianthemum appeninum*
White Rockrose

929 *Helianthemum oelandicum*

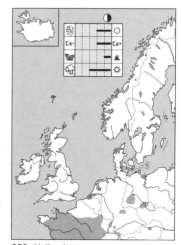

930 *Helianthemum canum*
Hoary Rockrose

931 *Fumana procumbens*
Common fumana

932 *Tamarix gallica*
Tamarisk

933 *Myricaria germanica*

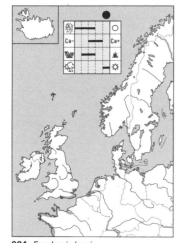

934 *Frankenia laevis*
Sea-heath

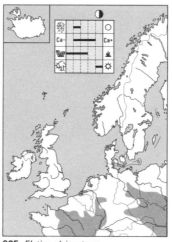

935 *Elatine alsinastrum*
Waterwort

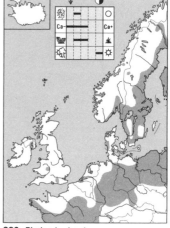

936 *Elatine hydropiper*

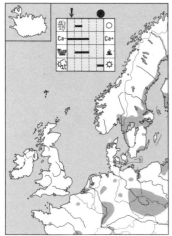

937 *Elatine triandra*

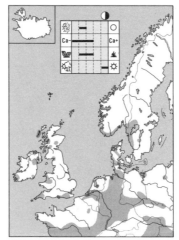

938 *Elatine hexandra*

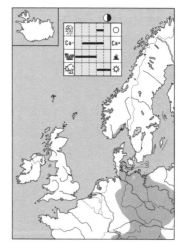

939 *Bryonia alba*

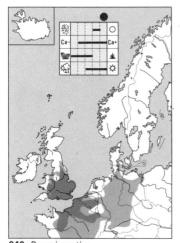

940 *Bryonia cretica*
White Bryony

941 *Lythrum salicaria*
Purple Loosestrife

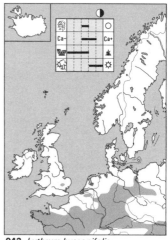

942 *Lythrum hyssopifolia*
Grass Poly

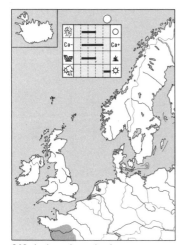

943 *Lythrum borysthenicum*

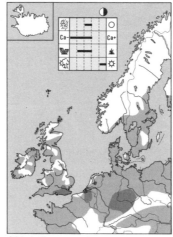

944 *Lythrum portula*
Water Purslane

945 *Trapa natans*
Water Chestnut

Willowherb Family · Onagraceae

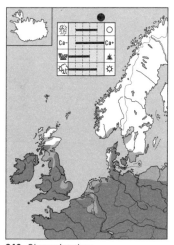

946 *Circaea lutetiana*
Enchanter's Nightshade

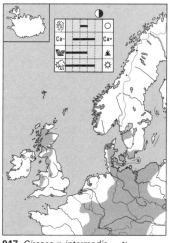

947 *Circaea × intermedia*   N
Upland Enchanter's Nightshade

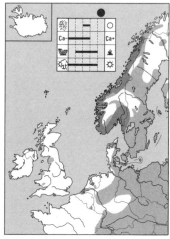

948 *Circaea alpina*
Alpine Enchanter's Nightshade

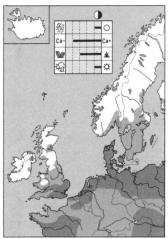

949 *Oenothera biennis*   N
Common Evening Primrose

950 *Oenothera muricata agg.*   N
Small-flowered Evening Primrose

951 *Ludwigia palustris*
Hampshire Purslane

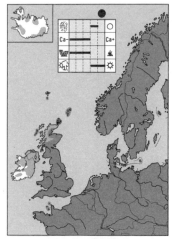

952 *Epilobium angustifolium*
Rosebay Willowherb

953 *Epilobium latifolium*
River Beauty

954 *Epilobium dodonaei*

128

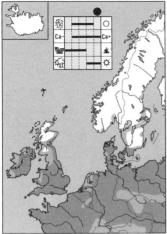

955 *Epilobium hirsutum*
Great Willowherb

956 *Epilobium parviflorum*
Hoary Willowherb

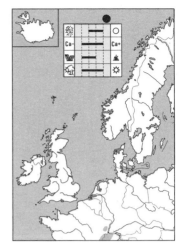

957 *Epilobium duriaei*

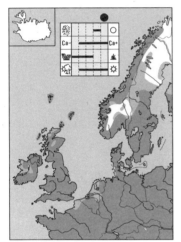

958 *Epilobium montanum*
Broad-leaved Willowherb

959 *Epilobium collinum*

960 *Epilobium lanceolatum*
Spear-leaved Willowherb

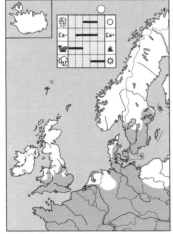

961 *Epilobium tetragonum* N
Square-stemmed Willowherb

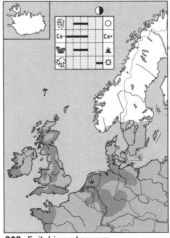

962 *Epilobium obscurum*
Short-fruited Willowherb

963 *Epilobium roseum*
Pale Willowherb

Willowherb Family · Onagraceae

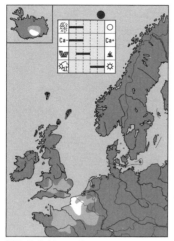

964 *Epilobium palustre*
Marsh Willowherb

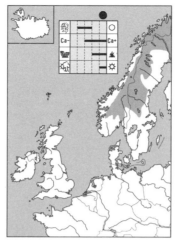

965 *Epilobium davuricum*

966 *Epilobium nutans*

967 *Epilobium anagallidifolium*
Alpine Willowherb

968 *Epilobium hornemanii*

969 *Epilobium lactiflorum*

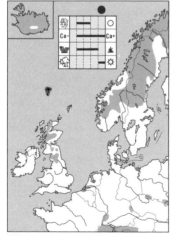

970 *Epilobium alsinifolium*
Chickweed Willowherb

971 *Epilobium glandulosum*

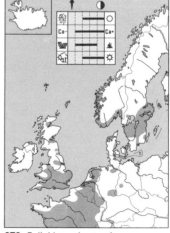

972 *Epilobium adenocaulon*
American Willowherb

973 *Epilobium brunnescens*
New Zealand Willowherb

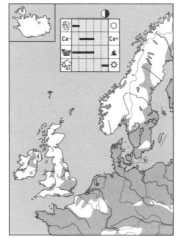

974 *Myriophyllum verticillatum*
Whorled Water Milfoil

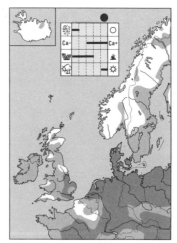

975 *Myriophyllum spicatum*
Spiked Water Milfoil

976 *Myriophyllum alterniflorum*

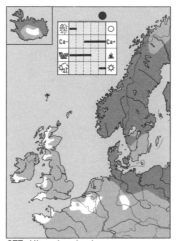

977 *Hippuris vulgaris*
Marestail

978 *Hippuris tetraphylla*

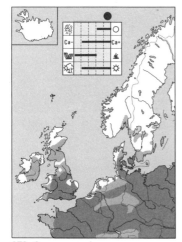

979 *Cornus sanguinea*
Dogwood

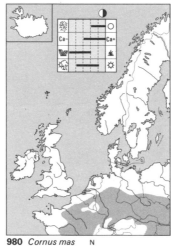

980 *Cornus mas* N
Cornelian Cherry

981 *Cornus suecica*
Dwarf Cornel

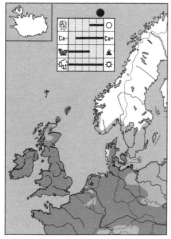

982 *Hedera helix*
Ivy

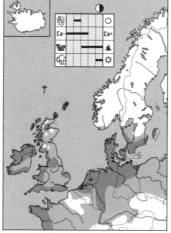

983 *Hydrocotyle vulgaris*
Marsh Pennywort

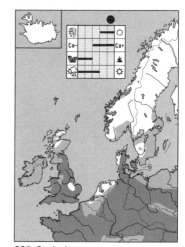

984 *Sanicula europaea*
Sanicle

985 *Astrantia major*   N
Astrantia

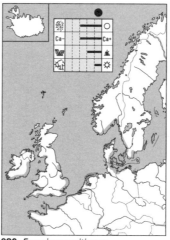

986 *Eryngium maritimum*
Sea Holly

987 *Eryngium campestre*
Field Eryngo

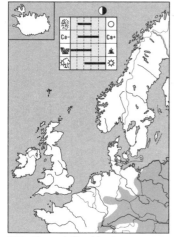

988 *Chaerophyllum hirsutum*

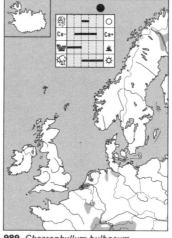

989 *Chaerophyllum bulbosum*

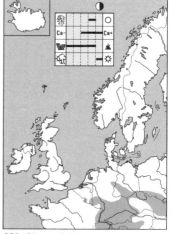

990 *Chaerophyllum aureum*
Golden Chervil

991 *Chaerophyllum temulentum*
Rough Chervil

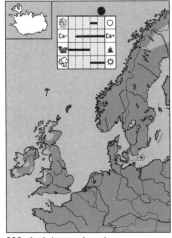

992 *Anthriscus sylvestris*
Cow Parsley

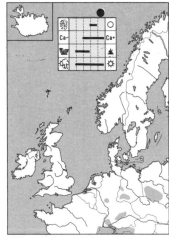

993 *Anthriscus nitida*

994 *Anthriscus caucalis*
Bur Chervil

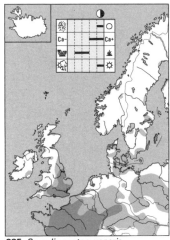

995 *Scandix pecten-veneris*
Shepherd's Needle

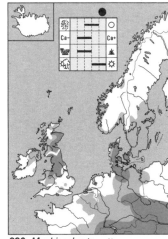

996 *Myrrhis odorata* N
Sweet Cicely

997 *Smyrnium olusatrum*
Alexanders

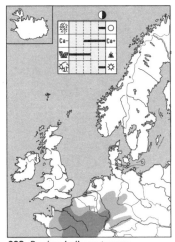

998 *Bunium bulbocastaneum*
Great Pignut

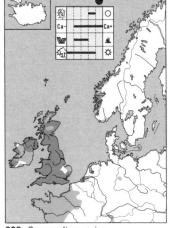

999 *Conopodium majus*
Pignut

133

Carrot Family · Umbelliferae

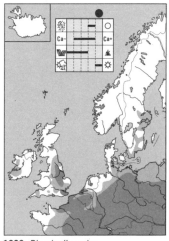

1000 *Pimpinella major*
Greater Burnet Saxifrage

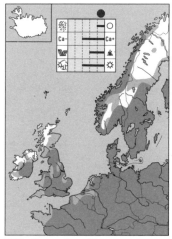

1001 *Pimpinella saxifraga*
Burnet Saxifrage

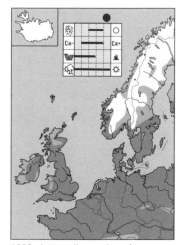

1002 *Aegopodium podagraria*   N
Ground Elder

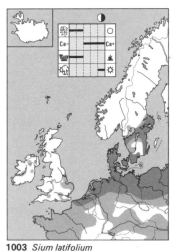

1003 *Sium latifolium*
Greater Water-parsnip

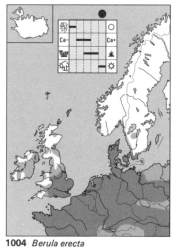

1004 *Berula erecta*
Lesser Water-parsnip

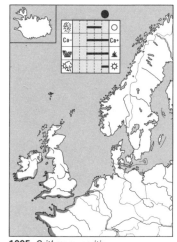

1005 *Crithmum maritimum*
Rock Samphire

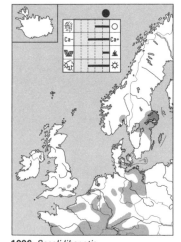

1006 *Seseli libanotis*
Moon Carrot

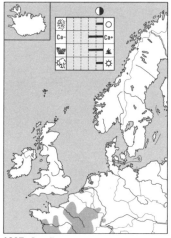

1007 *Seseli montanum*

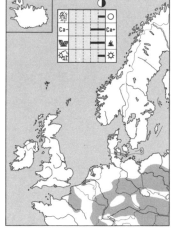

1008 *Seseli annuum*

134

1009 *Seseli hippomarathrum*

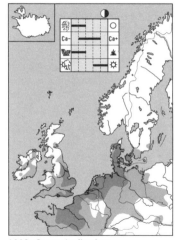

1010 *Oenanthe fistulosa*
Tubular Water Dropwort

1011 *Oenanthe pimpinelloides*
Corky-fruited Water Dropwort

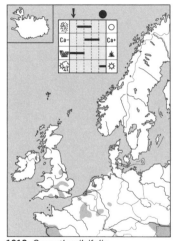

1012 *Oenanthe silaifolia*
Narrow-leaved Water Dropwort

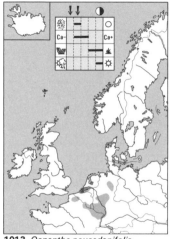

1013 *Oenanthe peucedanifolia*

1014 *Oenanthe lachenalii*
Parsley Water Dropwort

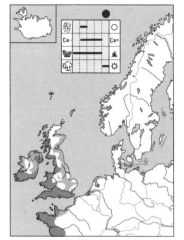

1015 *Oenanthe crocata*
Hemlock Water Dropwort

1016 *Oenanthe fluviatilis*
River Water Dropwort

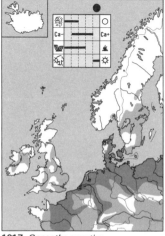

1017 *Oenanthe aquatica*
Fine-leaved Water Dropwort

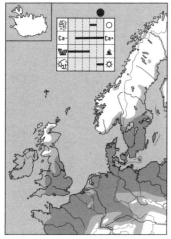

1018 *Aethusa cynapium*
Fool's Parsley

1019 *Athamanta cretensis*

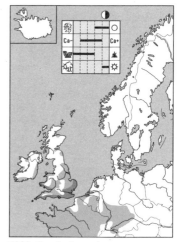

1020 *Foeniculum vulgare*
Fennel

1021 *Silaum silaus*
Pepper Saxifrage

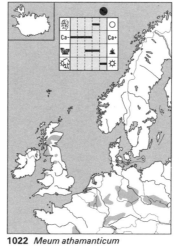

1022 *Meum athamanticum*
Spignel

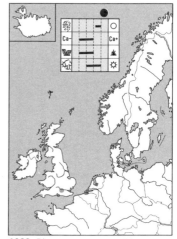

1023 *Physospermum cornubiense*
Bladder-seed

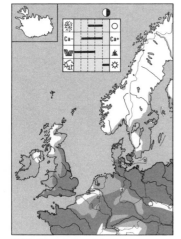

1024 *Conium maculatum*
Hemlock

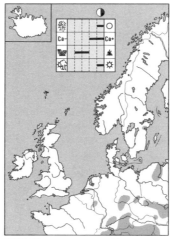

1025 *Pleurospermum austriacum*

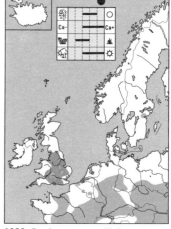

1026 *Bupleurum rotundifolium*
Thorow-wax

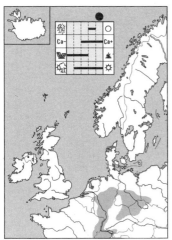

1027 *Bupleurum longifolium*

1028 *Bupleurum baldense*
Small Hare's-ear

1029 *Bupleurum gerardi*

1030 *Bupleurum tenuissimum*
Slender Hare's-ear

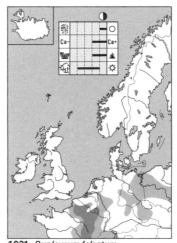

1031 *Bupleurum falcatum*
Sickle Hare's-ear

1032 *Trinia glauca*
Honewort

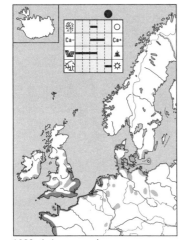

1033 *Apium graveolens*
Wild Celery

1034 *Apium nodiflorum*
Fool's Watercress

1035 *Apium repens*
Creeping Marshwort

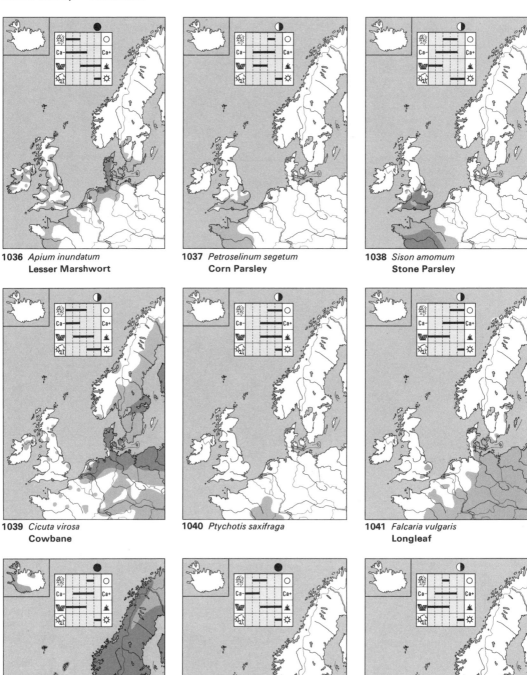

1036 *Apium inundatum*
Lesser Marshwort

1037 *Petroselinum segetum*
Corn Parsley

1038 *Sison amomum*
Stone Parsley

1039 *Cicuta virosa*
Cowbane

1040 *Ptychotis saxifraga*

1041 *Falcaria vulgaris*
Longleaf

1042 *Carum carvi*
Caraway

1043 *Carum verticillatum*
Whorled Caraway

1044 *Cnidium dubium*
Cnidium

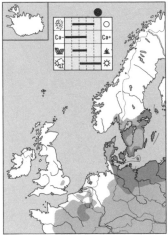

1045 *Selinum carvifolia*
Cambridge Milk Parsley

1046 *Selinum pyrenaum*

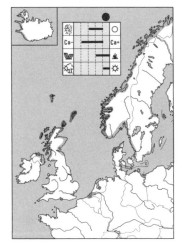

1047 *Ligusticum scoticum*
Scots Lovage

1048 *Ligusticum mutellinum*

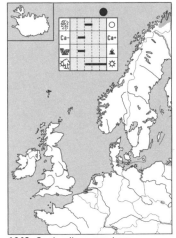

1049 *Conioselinum tataricum*

1050 *Angelica palustris*

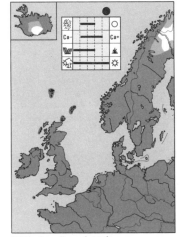

1051 *Angelica sylvestris*
Angelica

1052 *Angelica archangelica*
Garden Angelica

1053 *Peucedanum officinale*
Hog's Fennel

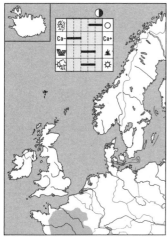

1054 *Peucedanum gallicum*

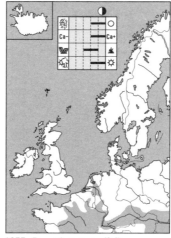

1055 *Peucedanum carvifolia*

1056 *Peucedanum alsaticum*

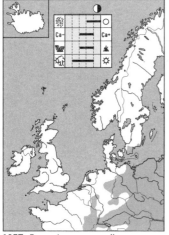

1057 *Peucedanum oreoselinum*

1058 *Peucedanum palustre*
Milk Parsley

1059 *Peucedanum lancifolium*

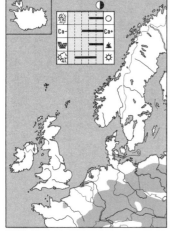

1060 *Peucedanum cervaria*

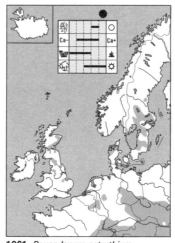

1061 *Peucedanum ostruthium*
Masterwort

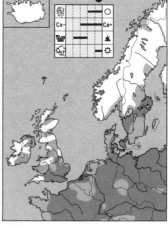

1062 *Pastinaca sativa*
Wild Parsnip

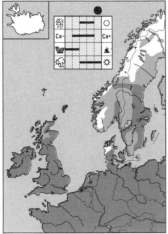

1063 *Heracleum sphondylium*
Hogweed

1064 *Tordylium maximum*
Hartwort

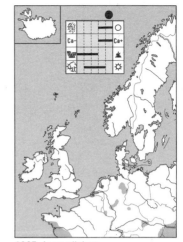

1065 *Laser trilobum*

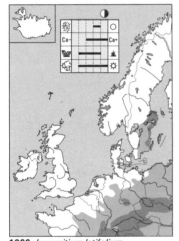

1066 *Laserpitium latifolium*
Sermountain

1067 *Laserpitium prutenicum*

1068 *Laserpitium siler*

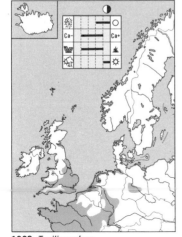

1069 *Torilis nodosa*
Knotted Bur Parsley

1070 *Torilis arvensis*
Spreading Bur Parsley

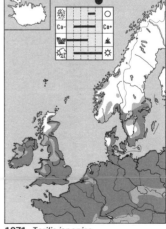

1071 *Torilis japonica*
Upright Hedge Parsley

1072 *Caucalis platycarpos*
Small Bur Parsley

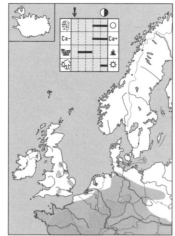

1073 *Turgenia latifolia*
Greater Bur Parsley

1074 *Orlaya grandiflora*

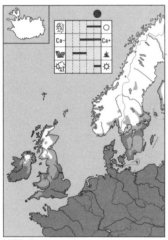

1075 *Daucus carota*
Wild Carrot

1076 *Chimaphila umbellata*
Umbellate Wintergreen

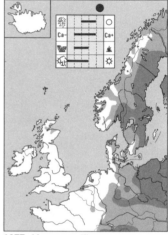

1077 *Moneses uniflora*
One-flowered Wintergreen

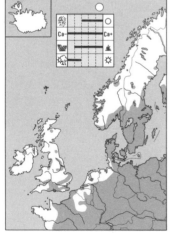

1078 *Monotropa hypopitys agg.*
Yellow Birdsnest

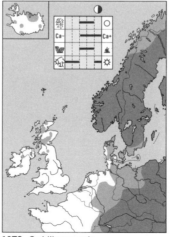

1079 *Orthilia secunda*
Toothed Wintergreen

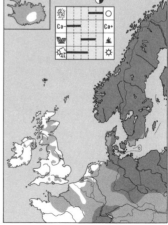

1080 *Pyrola minor*
Common Wintergreen

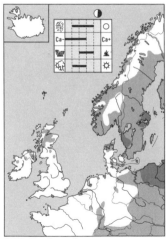

1081 *Pyrola media*
Intermediate Wintergreen

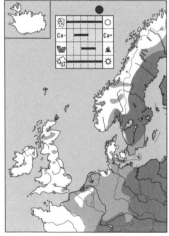

1082 *Pyrola rotundifolia*
Round-leaved Wintergreen

1083 *Pyrola norvegica*

1084 *Pyrola grandiflora*

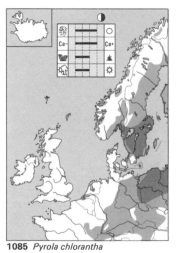

1085 *Pyrola chlorantha*
Yellow Wintergreen

1086 *Diapensia lapponica*
Diapensia

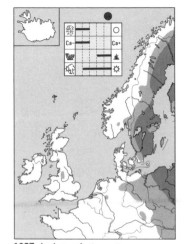

1087 *Ledum palustre* N
Labrador Tea

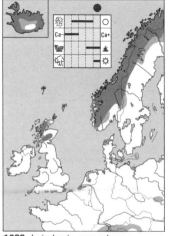

1088 *Loiseleuria procumbens*
Wild Azalea

1089 *Rhododendron lapponicum*
Arctic Rhododendron

143

Heath Family · Ericaceae

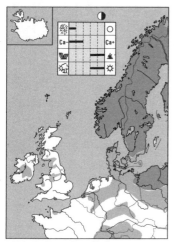

1090 *Andromeda polifolia*
Bog Rosemary

1091 *Chamaedaphne calyculata*
Leatherleaf

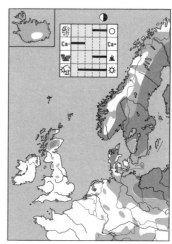

1092 *Arctostaphylos uva-ursi*
Alpine Bearberry

1093 *Arctous alpina*
Black Bearberry

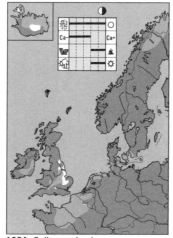

1094 *Calluna vulgaris*
Heather

1095 *Erica herbacea*

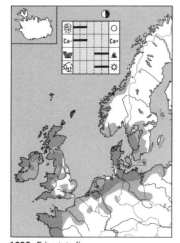

1096 *Erica tetralix*
Cross-leaved Heath

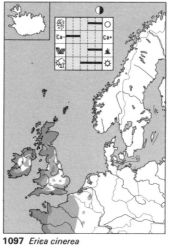

1097 *Erica cinerea*
Bell Heather

1098 *Erica erigena*
Irish Heath

1099 *Erica mackaiana*
Mackay's Heath

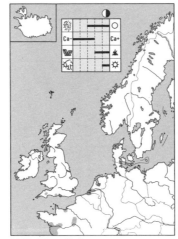

1100 *Erica ciliaris*
Dorset Heath

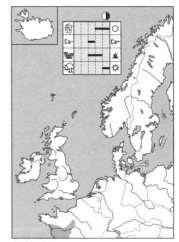

1101 *Erica vagans*
Cornish Heath

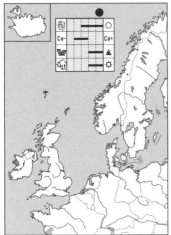

1102 *Daboecia cantabrica*
St Dabeoc's Heath

1103 *Vaccinium vitis-idaea*
Cowberry

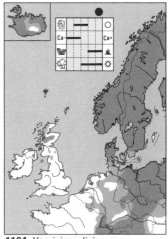

1104 *Vaccinium uliginosum*
Northern Bilberry

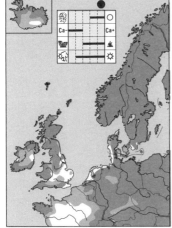

1105 *Vaccinium myrtillus*
Bilberry

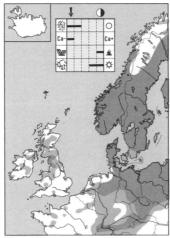

1106 *Vaccinium oxycoccus*
Cranberry

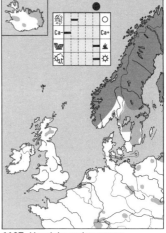

1107 *Vaccinium microcarpus*
Small Cranberry

145

1108 *Phyllodoce caerulea*
Mountain Heath

1109 *Cassiope hypnoides*
Cassiope

1110 *Cassiope tetragona*

1111 *Arbutus unedo*
Strawberry Tree

1112 *Empetrum nigrum*
Crowberry

1113 *Empetrum hermaphroditum*
Mountain Crowberry

1114 *Anagallis tenella*
Bog Pimpernel

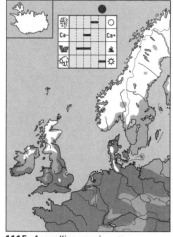

1115 *Anagallis arvensis*   N
Scarlet Pimpernel

1116 *Anagallis minima*
Chaffweed

146

1117 *Androsace maxima*

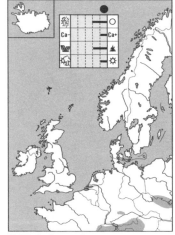

1118 *Androsace lactea*

1119 *Androsace septentrionalis*
Northern Androsace

1120 *Androsace elongata*

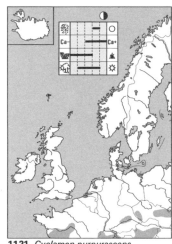

1121 *Cyclamen purpurascens*
Cyclamen

1122 *Glaux maritima*
Sea Milkwort

1123 *Hottonia palustris*
Water Violet

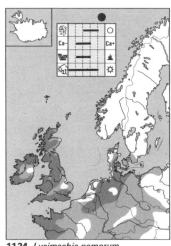

1124 *Lysimachia nemorum*
Yellow Pimpernel

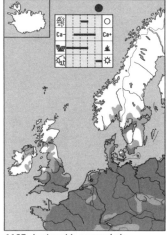

1125 *Lysimachia nummularia*
Creeping Jenny

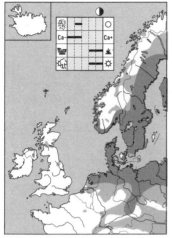

1126 *Lysimachia thyrsiflora*
Tufted Loosestrife

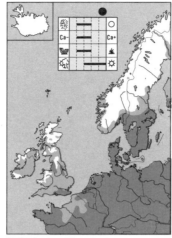

1127 *Lysimachia vulgaris*
Yellow Loosestrife

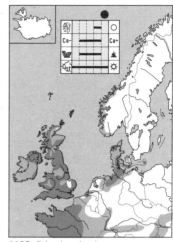

1128 *Primula vulgaris*
Primrose

1129 *Primula veris*
Cowslip

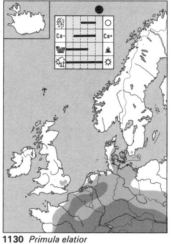

1130 *Primula elatior*
Oxlip

1131 *Primula farinosa*
Birdseye Primrose

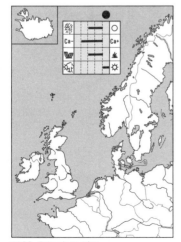

1132 *Primula scotica*
Scottish Primrose

1133 *Primula scandinavica*

1134 *Primula stricta*

1135 *Primula auricula*
Auricula

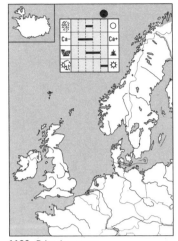

1136 *Primula nutans*

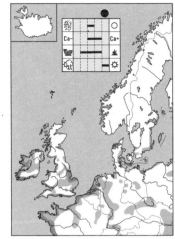

1137 *Samolus valerandi*
Brookweed

1138 *Soldanella montana*

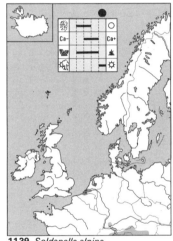

1139 *Soldanella alpina*
Alpine Snowbell

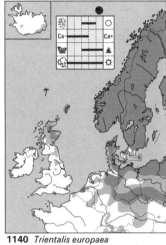

1140 *Trientalis europaea*
Chickweed Wintergreen

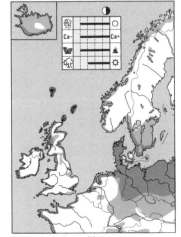

1141 *Armeria maritima*   N
Thrift

1142 *Armeria alliacea*
Jersey Thrift

1143 *Limonium vulgare*
Common Sea-lavender

1144 *Limonium humile*
Lax-flowered Sea-lavender

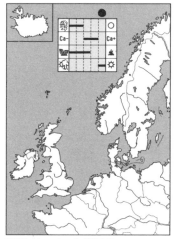

1145 *Limonium bellidifolium*
Matted Sea-lavender

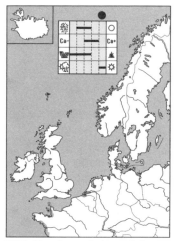

1146 *Limonium auriculae-ursifolium*

1147 *Limonium binervosum* N
Rock Sea-lavender

1148 *Limonium recurvum*

1149 *Limonium transwallianum*

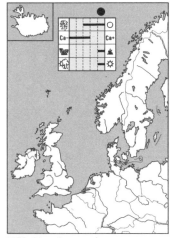

1150 *Limonium paradoxum*

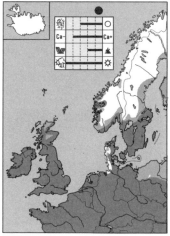

1151 *Fraxinus excelsior* N
Ash

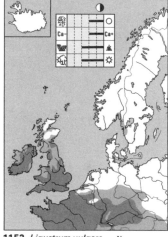

1152 *Ligustrum vulgare* N
Privet

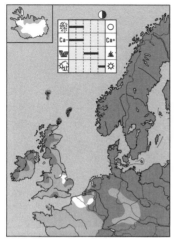

1153 *Menyanthes trifoliata*
Bogbean

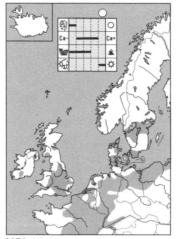

1154 *Nymphoides peltata*   N
Fringed Water-lily

1155 *Vinca minor*
Lesser Periwinkle

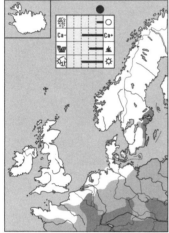

1156 *Vincetoxicum hirundinaria*
Vincetoxicum

1157 *Blackstonia perfoliata*   N
Yellow-wort

1158 *Centaurium tenuiflorum*
Slender Centaury

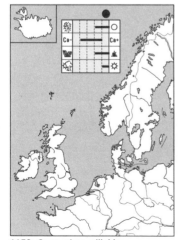

1159 *Centaurium scilloides*
Perennial Centaury

1160 *Centaurium littorale*
Seaside Centaury

1161 *Centaurium pulchellum*
Lesser Centaury

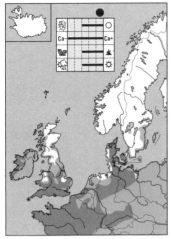

1162 *Centaurium erythraea*
Common Centaury

1163 *Lomatogonium rotatum*

1164 *Cicendia filiformis*
Yellow Centaury

1165 *Exaculum pusillum*
Guernsey Centaury

1166 *Gentiana nivalis*
Alpine Gentian

1167 *Gentiana utriculosa*
Bladder Gentian

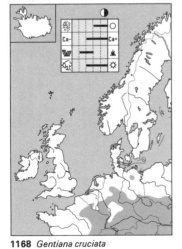

1168 *Gentiana cruciata*
Cross Gentian

1169 *Gentiana verna*
Spring Gentian

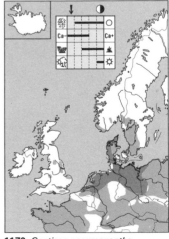

1170 *Gentiana pneumonanthe*
Marsh Gentian

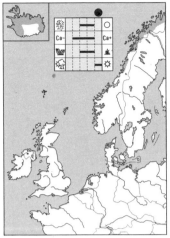

1171 *Gentiana detonsa*

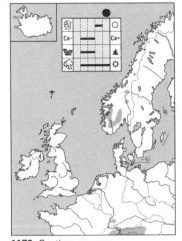

1172 *Gentiana purpurea*
Purple Gentian

1173 *Gentiana lutea*
Great Yellow Gentian

1174 *Gentiana asclepiadea*
Willow Gentian

1175 *Gentianella campestris*   N
Field Gentian

1176 *Gentianella austriaca*
Austrian Gentian

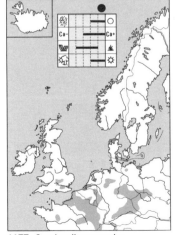

1177 *Gentianella germanica*
Chiltern Gentian

1178 *Gentianella amarella*
Autumn Gentian

1179 *Gentianella anglica*
Early Gentian

153

1180 *Gentianella aspera*

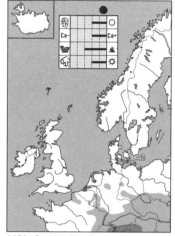

1181 *Gentianella ciliata*
Fringed Gentian

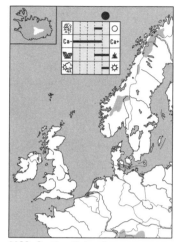

1182 *Gentianella tenella*
Slender Gentian

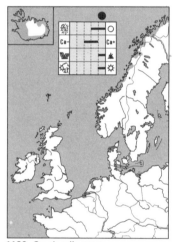

1183 *Gentianella aurea*
Northern Gentian

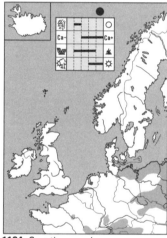

1184 *Swertia perennis*
Marsh Felwort

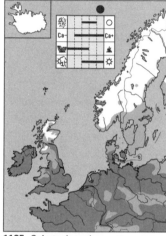

1185 *Calystegia sepium*   N
Hedge Bindweed

1186 *Calystegia soldanella*
Sea Bindweed

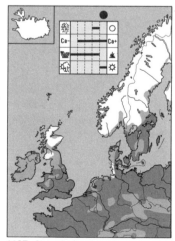

1187 *Convolvulus arvensis*
Field Bindweed

1188 *Cuscuta epilinum*
Flax Dodder

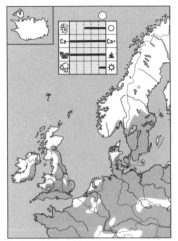

1189 *Cuscuta epithymum*
Common Dodder

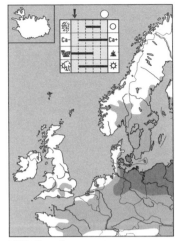

1190 *Cuscuta europaea*
Greater Dodder

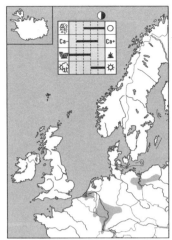

1191 *Cuscuta gronovii*

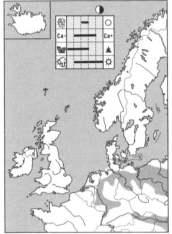

1192 *Cuscuta lupuliformis*

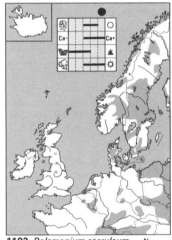

1193 *Polemonium caeruleum* N
Jacob's Ladder

1194 *Polemonium acutiflorum*

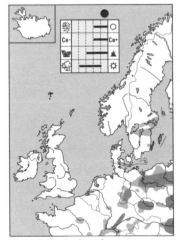

1195 *Asperula tinctoria*
Dyer's Woodruff

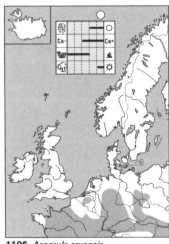

1196 *Asperula arvensis*
Blue Woodruff

1197 *Asperula odorata*
Woodruff

Bedstraw Family · Rubiaceae

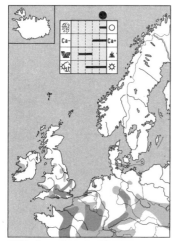

1198 *Asperula cynanchica*
Squinancywort

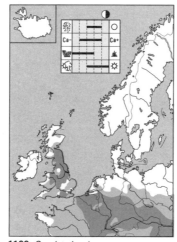

1199 *Cruciata laevipes*
Crosswort

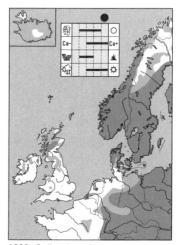

1200 *Galium boreale*
Northern Bedstraw

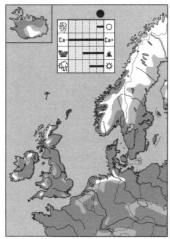

1201 *Galium verum*
Lady's Bedstraw

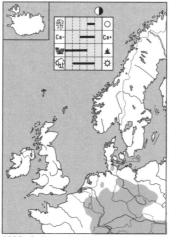

1202 *Galium sylvaticum*

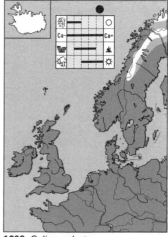

1203 *Galium palustre*
Marsh Bedstraw

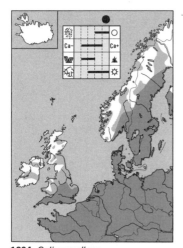

1204 *Galium mollugo*
Hedge Bedstraw

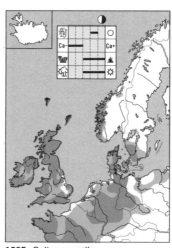

1205 *Galium saxatile*
Heath Bedstraw

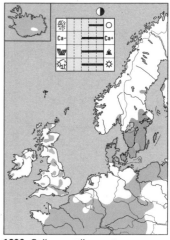

1206 *Galium pumilum* N
Slender Bedstraw

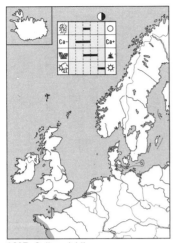

1207 *Galium debile*
Slender Marsh Bedstraw

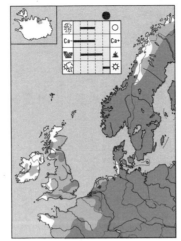

1208 *Galium uliginosum*
Fen Bedstraw

1209 *Galium tricornutum*
Corn Cleavers

1210 *Galium parisiense*
Wall Bedstraw

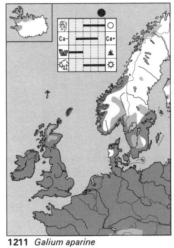

1211 *Galium aparine*
Common Cleavers

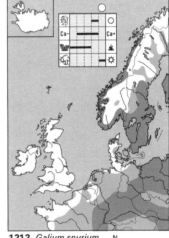

1212 *Galium spurium*   N
False Cleavers

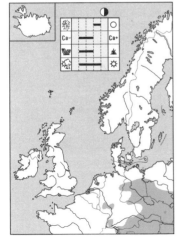

1213 *Galium rotundifolium*

1214 *Galium glaucum*

1215 *Galium trifidum*

1216 *Galium triflorum*

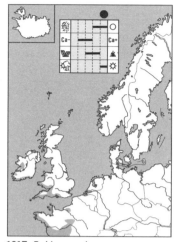

1217 *Rubia peregrina*
Wild Madder

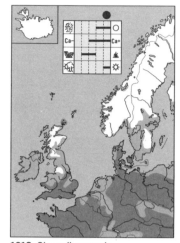

1218 *Sherardia arvensis*
Field Madder

1219 *Heliotropium europaeum*
Heliotrope

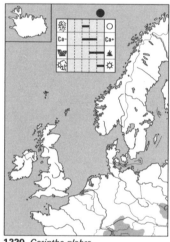

1220 *Cerinthe glabra*

1221 *Cerinthe minor*
Lesser Honeywort

1222 *Onosma arenaria*

1223 *Echium plantagineum*
Purple Viper's Bugloss

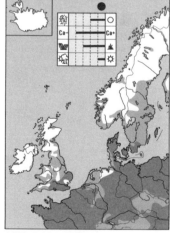

1224 *Echium vulgare*
Viper's Bugloss

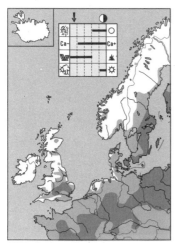

1225 *Buglossoides arvense*
Corn Gromwell

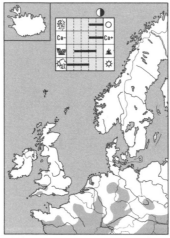

1226 *Buglossoides purpuro-caeruleum*
Purple Gromwell

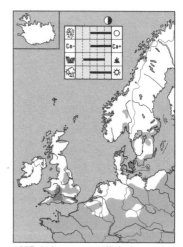

1227 *Lithospermum officinale*
Common Gromwell

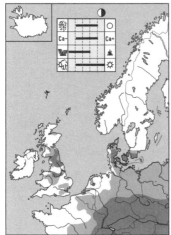

1228 *Myosotis sylvatica*
Wood Forgetmenot

1229 *Myosotis decumbens*   N

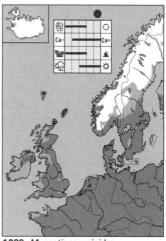

1230 *Myosotis scorpioides*
Water Forgetmenot

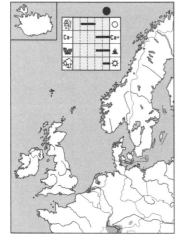

1231 *Myosotis caespititia*

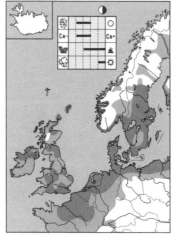

1232 *Myosotis laxa*   N
Tufted Forgetmenot

1233 *Myosotis stolonifera*   N
Pale Forgetmenot

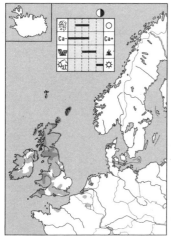

1234 *Myosotis secunda*
Creeping Forgetmenot

1235 *Myosotis sicula*
Jersey Forgetmenot

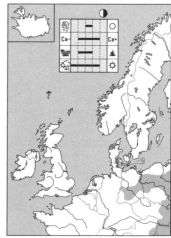

1236 *Myosotis sparsiflora*

1237 *Myosotis alpestris*
Alpine Forgetmenot

1238 *Myosotis arvensis*
Field Forgetmenot

1239 *Myosotis ramosissima*
Early Forgetmenot

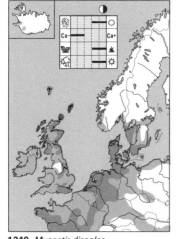

1240 *Myosotis discolor*
Changing Forgetmenot

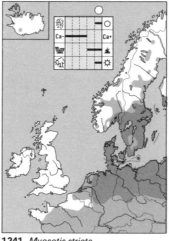

1241 *Myosotis stricta*

1242 *Mertensia maritima*
Oyster Plant

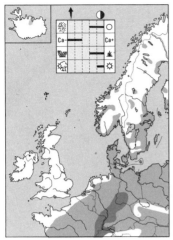

1243 *Lappula squarrosa*
Bur Forgetmenot

1244 *Lappula deflexa*

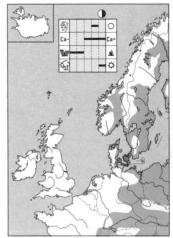

1245 *Asperugo procumbens*   N
Madwort

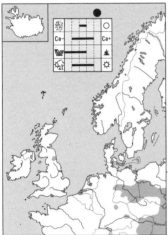

1246 *Omphalodes scorpioides*

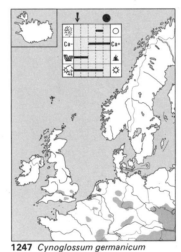

1247 *Cynoglossum germanicum*
Green Houndstongue

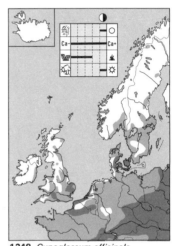

1248 *Cynoglossum officinale*
Houndstongue

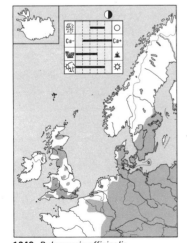

1249 *Pulmonaria officinalis*
Lungwort

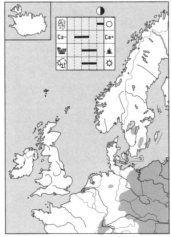

1250 *Pulmonaria angustifolia*

1251 *Pulmonaria longifolia*   N
Narrow-leaved Lungwort

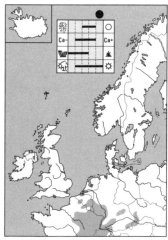

1252 *Pulmonaria montana*

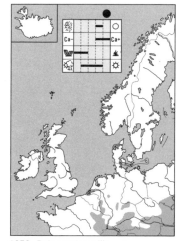

1253 *Pulmonaria mollis* N

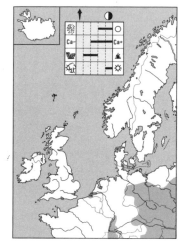

1254 *Nonea pulla*
Nonea

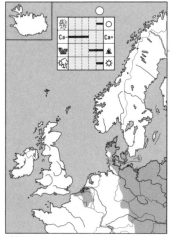

1255 *Anchusa officinalis* N
Alkanet

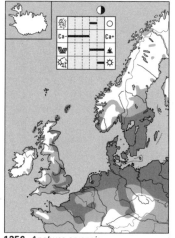

1256 *Anchusa arvensis*
Bugloss

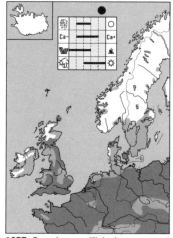

1257 *Symphytum officinale*
Common Comfrey

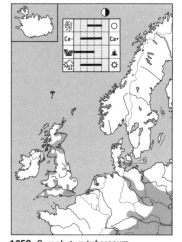

1258 *Symphytum tuberosum*
Tuberous Comfrey

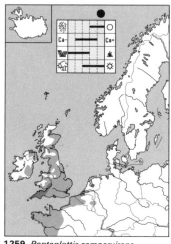

1259 *Pentaglottis sempervirens*
Green Alkanet

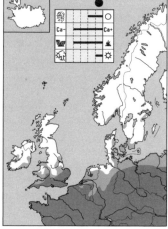

1260 *Verbena officinalis*
Vervain

1261 *Callitriche obtusangula*

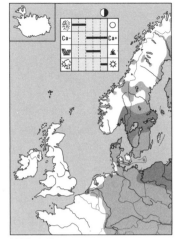

1262 *Callitriche cophocarpa*

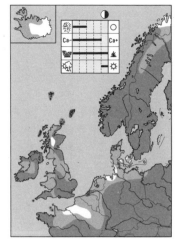

1263 *Callitriche stagnalis* N
Water Starwort

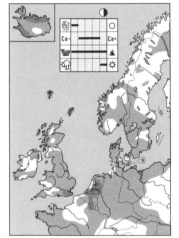

1264 *Callitriche hamulata*

1265 *Callitriche hermaphroditica* N

1266 *Ajuga genevensis*
Blue Bugle

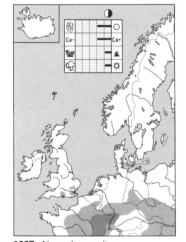

1267 *Ajuga chamaepitys*
Ground Pine

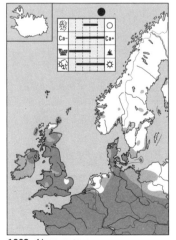

1268 *Ajuga reptans*
Bugle

1269 *Ajuga pyramidalis*
Pyramidal Bugle

1270 *Teucrium botrys*
Cut-leaved Germander

1271 *Teucrium scorodonia*
Wood Sage

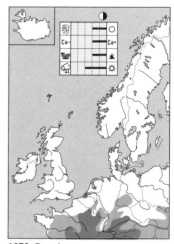

1272 *Teucrium montanum*
Mountain Germander

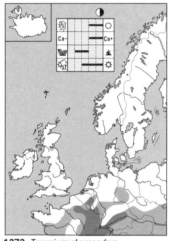

1273 *Teucrium chamaedrys*
Wall Germander

1274 *Teucrium scordium*
Water Germander

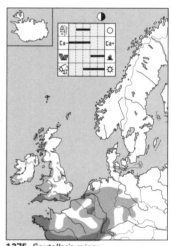

1275 *Scutellaria minor*
Lesser Skullcap

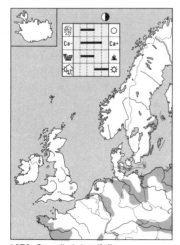

1276 *Scutellaria hastifolia*
Spear-leaved Skullcap

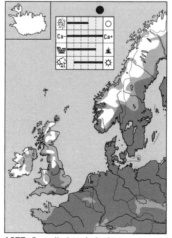

1277 *Scutellaria galericulata*
Skullcap

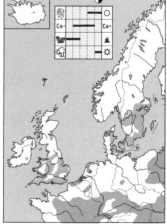

1278 *Marrubium vulgare*
White Horehound

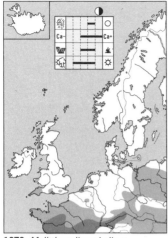

1279 *Melittis melissophyllum*
Bastard Balm

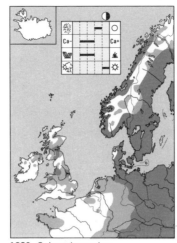

1280 *Galeopsis speciosa*
Large-flowered Hemp-nettle

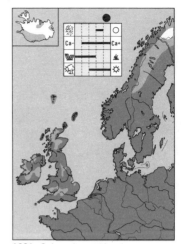

1281 *Galeopsis tetrahit*   N
Common Hemp-nettle

1282 *Galeopsis pubescens*

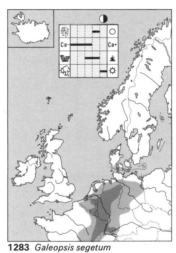

1283 *Galeopsis segetum*
Downy Hemp-nettle

1284 *Galeopsis ladanum*

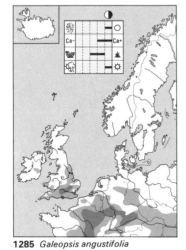

1285 *Galeopsis angustifolia*
Red Hemp-nettle

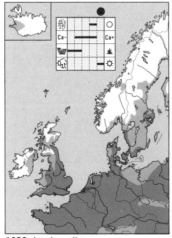

1286 *Lamium album*
White Dead-nettle

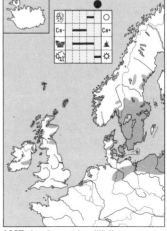

1287 *Lamium molucellifolium*

165

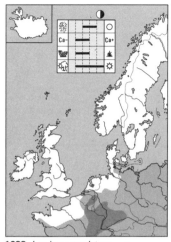

1288 *Lamium maculatum* N
Spotted Dead-nettle

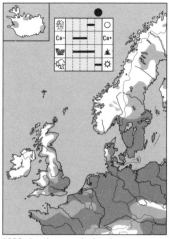

1289 *Lamium amplexicaule*
Henbit Dead-nettle

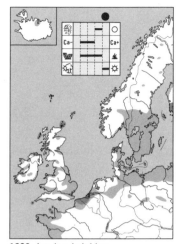

1290 *Lamium hybridum*
Cut-leaved Dead-nettle

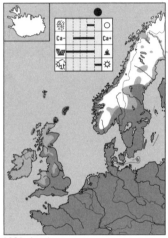

1291 *Lamium purpureum*
Red Dead-nettle

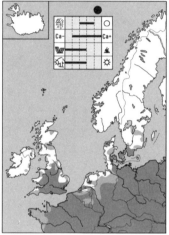

1292 *Lamiastrum galeobdolon*
Yellow Archangel

1293 *Leonurus marrubiastrum*
False Motherwort

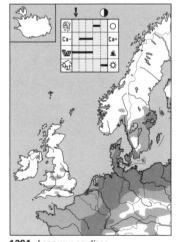

1294 *Leonurus cardiaca*
Motherwort

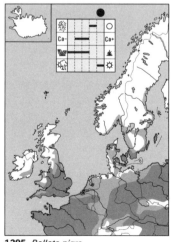

1295 *Ballota nigra*
Black Horehound

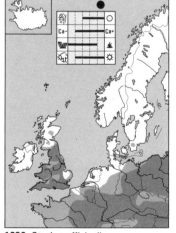

1296 *Stachys officinalis*
Betony

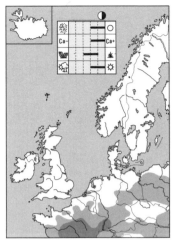

1297 *Stachys recta*
Yellow Woundwort

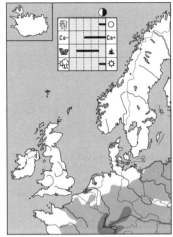

1298 *Stachys annua*
Annual Woundwort

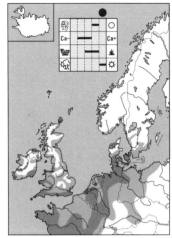

1299 *Stachys arvensis*
Field Woundwort

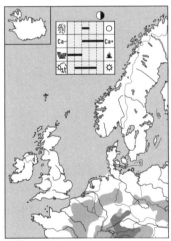

1300 *Stachys alpina*
Limestone Woundwort

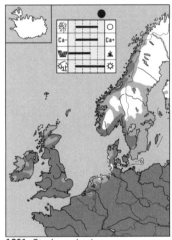

1301 *Stachys sylvatica*
Hedge Woundwort

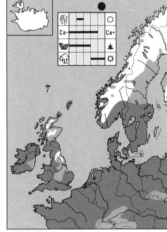

1302 *Stachys palustris*
Marsh Woundwort

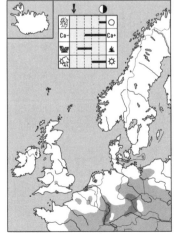

1303 *Stachys germanica*
Downy Woundwort

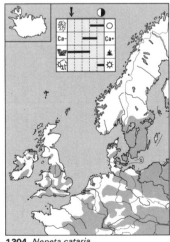

1304 *Nepeta cataria*
Catmint

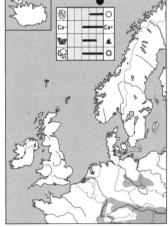

1305 *Nepeta nuda*
Hairless Catmint

167

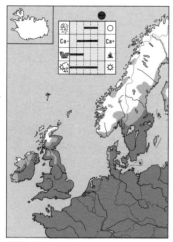

1306 *Glechoma hederacea*
Ground Ivy

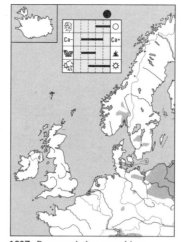

1307 *Dracocephalum ruyschiana*

1308 *Prunella grandiflora*
Large Self-heal

1309 *Prunella laciniata*
Cut-leaved Self-heal

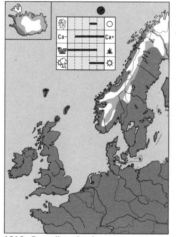

1310 *Prunella vulgaris*
Self-heal

1311 *Acinos arvensis*
Basil Thyme

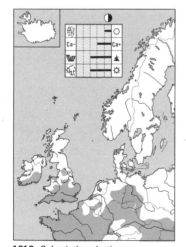

1312 *Calamintha sylvatica*
Common Calamint

1313 *Calamintha nepeta*
Lesser Calamint

1314 *Clinopodium vulgare*
Wild Basil

168

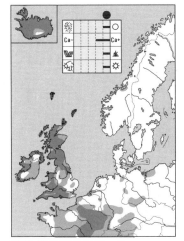

1315 *Origanum vulgare*
Marjoram

1316 *Thymus praecox* N

1317 *Thymus serpyllum*
Wild Thyme

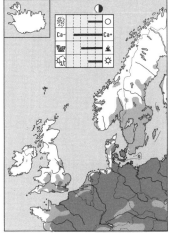

1318 *Thymus pulegioides* N
Large Thyme

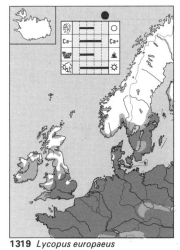

1319 *Lycopus europaeus*
Gypsywort

1320 *Lycopus exaltatus*

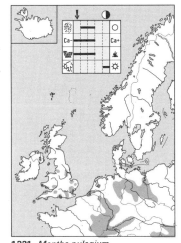

1321 *Mentha pulegium*
Pennyroyal

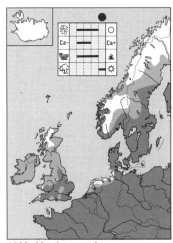

1322 *Mentha arvensis*
Corn Mint

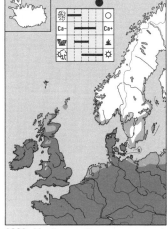

1323 *Mentha aquatica*
Water Mint

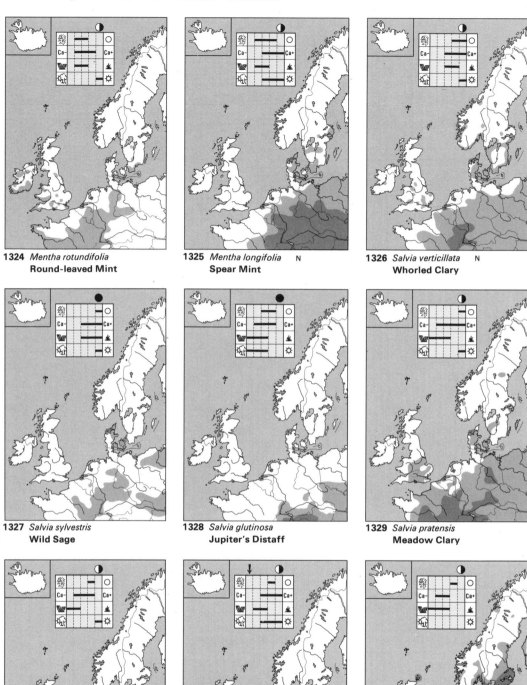

1324 *Mentha rotundifolia*
Round-leaved Mint

1325 *Mentha longifolia* N
Spear Mint

1326 *Salvia verticillata* N
Whorled Clary

1327 *Salvia sylvestris*
Wild Sage

1328 *Salvia glutinosa*
Jupiter's Distaff

1329 *Salvia pratensis*
Meadow Clary

1330 *Salvia verbenaca*

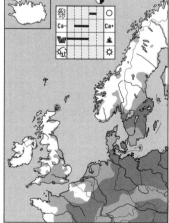

1331 *Atropa bella-donna*
Deadly Nightshade

1332 *Hyoscyamus niger*
Henbane

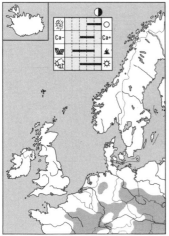

1333 *Physalis alkekengi*

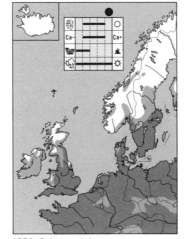

1334 *Solanum dulcamara*
Bittersweet

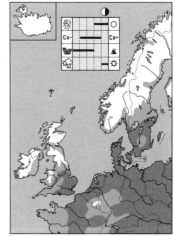

1335 *Solanum nigrum*
Black Nightshade

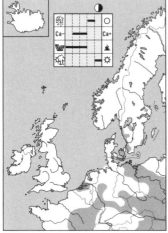

1336 *Solanum luteum*
Hairy Nightshade

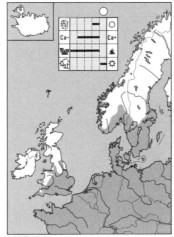

1337 *Datura stramonium*   N
Thorn-apple

1338 *Gratiola officinalis*
Gratiola

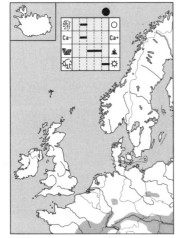

1339 *Lindernia procumbens*

1340 *Limosella australis*
Welsh Mudwort

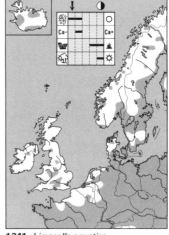

1341 *Limosella aquatica*
Mudwort

1342 *Mimulus guttatus*
Monkey Flower

1343 *Mimulus luteus*
Blood-drop Emlets

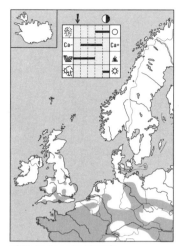

1344 *Verbascum blattaria*
Moth Mullein

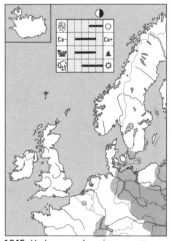

1345 *Verbascum phoeniceum* N
Purple Mullein

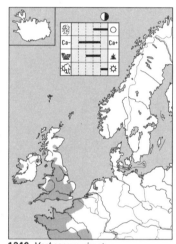

1346 *Verbascum virgatum*
Twiggy Mullein

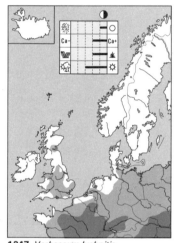

1347 *Verbascum lychnitis*
White Mullein

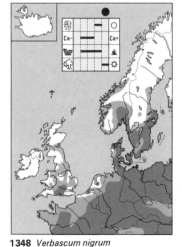

1348 *Verbascum nigrum*
Dark Mullein

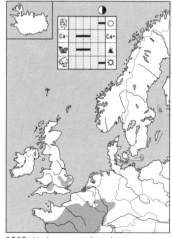

1349 *Verbascum pulverulentum*
Hoary Mullein

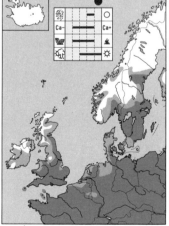

1350 *Verbascum thapsus*
Great Mullein

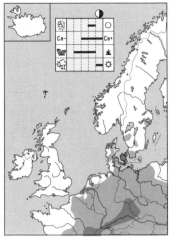

1351 *Verbascum densiflorum*

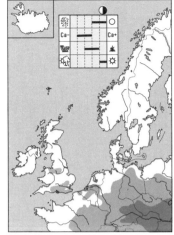

1352 *Verbascum phlomoides*
Orange Mullein

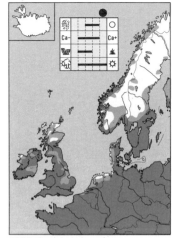

1353 *Scrophularia nodosa*
Common Figwort

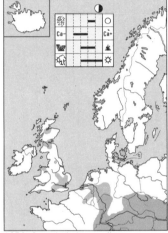

1354 *Scrophularia vernalis*
Yellow Figwort

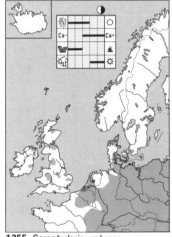

1355 *Scrophularia umbrosa* N
Green Figwort

1356 *Scrophularia scorodonia*
Balm-leaved Figwort

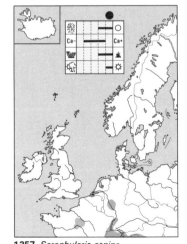

1357 *Scrophularia canina*
French Figwort

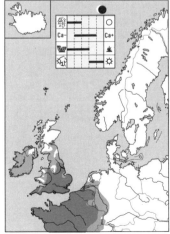

1358 *Scrophularia auriculata* N
Water Figwort

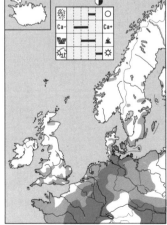

1359 *Misopates orontium*
Lesser Snapdragon

1360 *Anarrhinum bellidifolium*
Daisy-leaved Toadflax

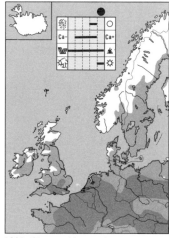

1361 *Chaenorrhinum minus*
Small Toadflax

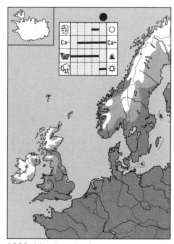

1362 *Linaria vulgaris*
Common Toadflax

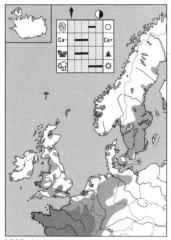

1363 *Linaria repens*
Pale Toadflax

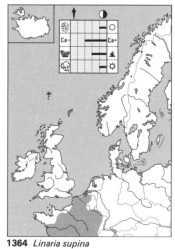

1364 *Linaria supina*
Prostrate Toadflax

1365 *Linaria arvensis*

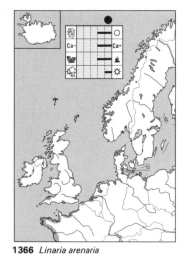

1366 *Linaria arenaria*
Sand Toadflax

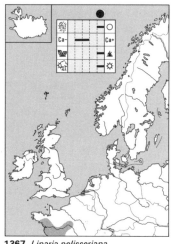

1367 *Linaria pelisseriana*
Jersey Toadflax

1368 *Linaria alpina*
Alpine Toadflax

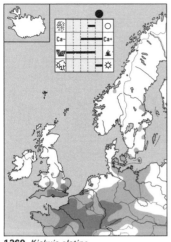

1369 *Kickxia elatine*
Sharp-leaved Fluellen

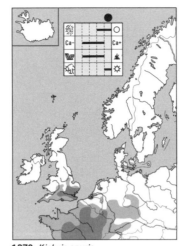

1370 *Kickxia spuria*
Round-leaved Fluellen

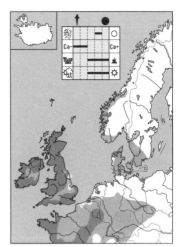

1371 *Digitalis purpurea*
Foxglove

1372 *Digitalis lutea*
Small Yellow Foxglove

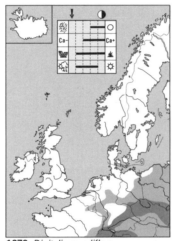

1373 *Digitalis grandiflora*
Large Yellow Foxglove

1374 *Erinus alpinus*
Fairy Foxglove

1375 *Veronica alpina*
Alpine Speedwell

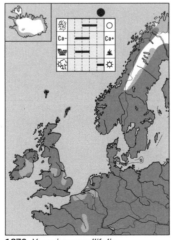

1376 *Veronica serpyllifolia*
Thyme-leaved Speedwell

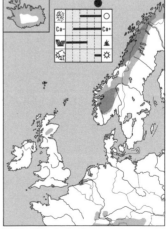

1377 *Veronica fruticans*
Rock Speedwell

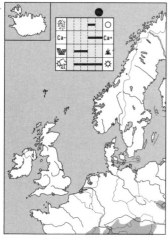

1378 *Veronica urticifolia*

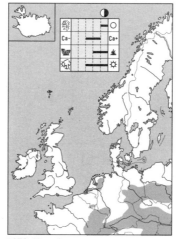

1379 *Veronica prostrata*

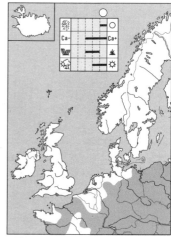

1380 *Veronica austriaca* N

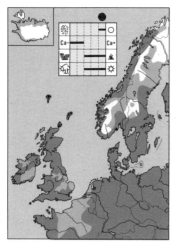

1381 *Veronica officinalis*
Heath Speedwell

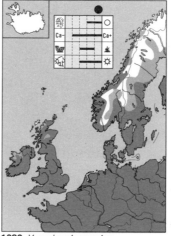

1382 *Veronica chamaedrys*
Germander Speedwell

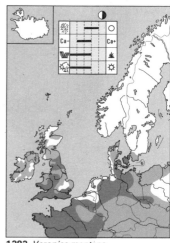

1383 *Veronica montana*
Wood Speedwell

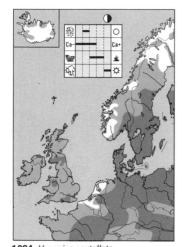

1384 *Veronica scutellata*
Marsh Speedwell

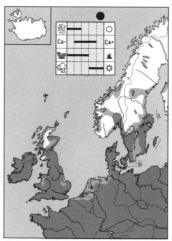

1385 *Veronica beccabunga*
Brooklime

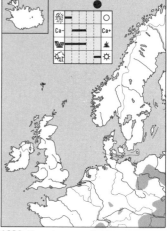

1386 *Veronica anagalloides*

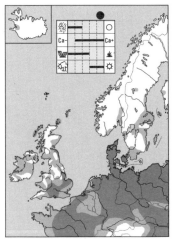

1387 *Veronica anagallis-aquatica*
Water Speedwell

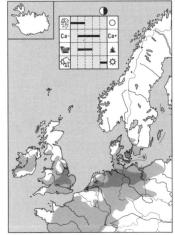

1388 *Veronica catenata*
Pink Water Speedwell

1389 *Veronica acinifolia*
French Speedwell

1390 *Veronica praecox*
Breckland Speedwell

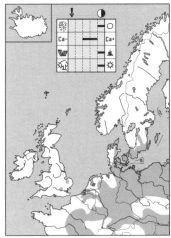

1391 *Veronica triphyllos*
Fingered Speedwell

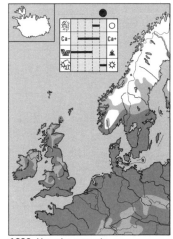

1392 *Veronica arvensis*
Wall Speedwell

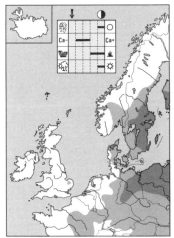

1393 *Veronica verna*
Spring Speedwell

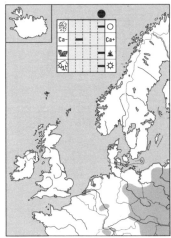

1394 *Veronica dillenii*

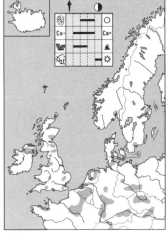

1395 *Veronica peregrina*
American Speedwell

177

Figwort Family · Scrophulariaceae

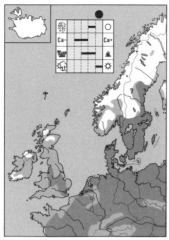

1396 *Veronica agrestis*
Green Field Speedwell

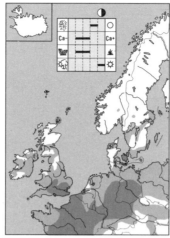

1397 *Veronica polita*
Grey Field Speedwell

1398 *Veronica opaca*

1399 *Veronica persica*
Common Field Speedwell

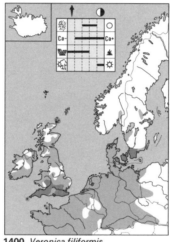

1400 *Veronica filiformis*
Slender Speedwell

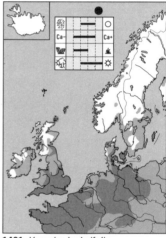

1401 *Veronica hederifolia*
Ivy-leaved Speedwell

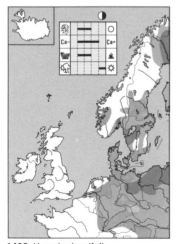

1402 *Veronica longifolia*

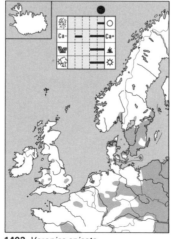

1403 *Veronica spicata*
Spiked Speedwell

1404 *Sibthorpia europaea*
Cornish Moneywort

1405 *Melampyrum cristatum*
Crested Cow-wheat

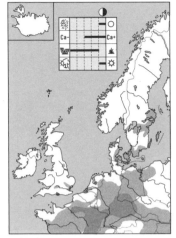

1406 *Melampyrum arvense*
Field Cow-wheat

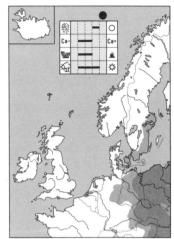

1407 *Melampyrum nemorosum*

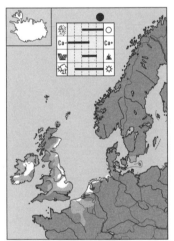

1408 *Melampyrum pratense*
Common Cow-wheat

1409 *Melampyrum sylvaticum*
Small Cow-wheat

1410 *Euphrasia rostkoviana*   N
Eyebright

1411 *Euphrasia rivularis*
Eyebright

1412 *Euphrasia anglica*
Eyebright

1413 *Euphrasia vigursii*
Eyebright

1414 *Euphrasia hirtella*
Eyebright

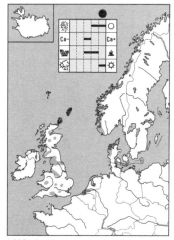

1415 *Euphrasia arctica*
Eyebright

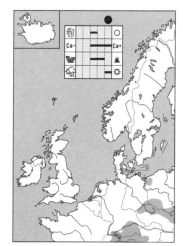

1416 *Euphrasia picta*
Eyebright

1417 *Euphrasia tetraquetra*
Eyebright

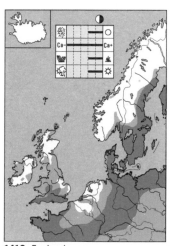

1418 *Euphrasia nemorosa*
Eyebright

1419 *Euphrasia pseudo-kerneri*
Eyebright

1420 *Euphrasia confusa*
Eyebright

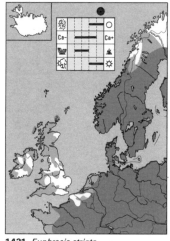

1421 *Euphrasia stricta*
Eyebright

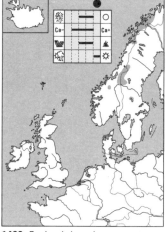

1422 *Euphrasia hyperborea*
Eyebright

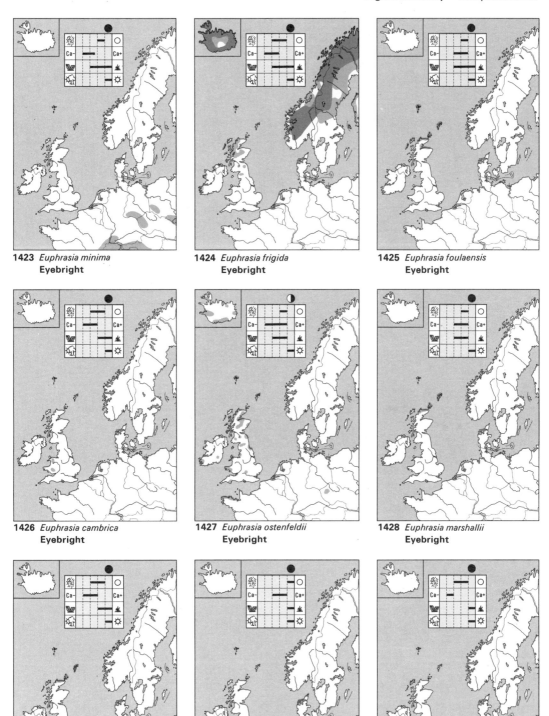

1423 *Euphrasia minima*
Eyebright

1424 *Euphrasia frigida*
Eyebright

1425 *Euphrasia foulaensis*
Eyebright

1426 *Euphrasia cambrica*
Eyebright

1427 *Euphrasia ostenfeldii*
Eyebright

1428 *Euphrasia marshallii*
Eyebright

1429 *Euphrasia rotundifolia*
Eyebright

1430 *Euphrasia dunensis*
Eyebright

1431 *Euphrasia campbelliae*
Eyebright

Figwort Family · Scrophulariaceae

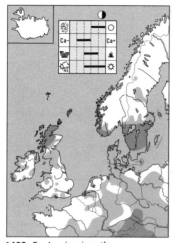

1432 *Euphrasia micrantha*
Eyebright

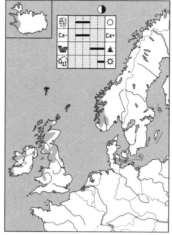

1433 *Euphrasia scottica*
Eyebright

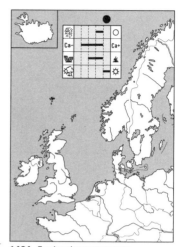

1434 *Euphrasia atropurpurea*
Eyebright

1435 *Euphrasia bottnica*
Eyebright

1436 *Euphrasia salisburgensis*
Irish Eyebright

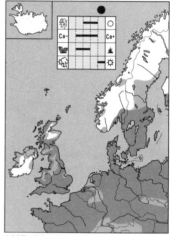

1437 *Odontites verna*
Red Bartsia

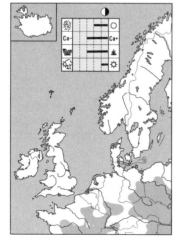

1438 *Odontites lutea*
Yellow Odontites

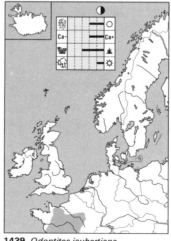

1439 *Odontites jaubertiana*

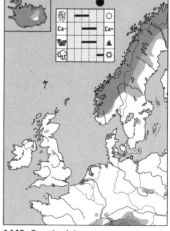

1440 *Bartsia alpina*
Alpine Bartsia

182

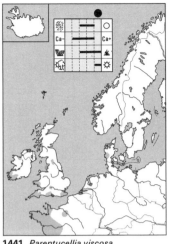

1441 *Parentucellia viscosa*
Yellow Bartsia

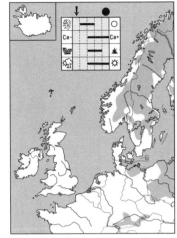

1442 *Pedicularis sceptrum-carolinum*
Moor-king

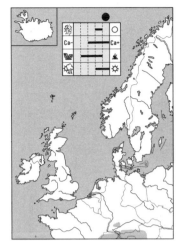

1443 *Pedicularis foliosa*
Leafy Lousewort

1444 *Pedicularis hirsuta*

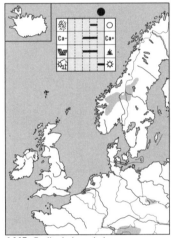

1445 *Pedicularis oederi*

1446 *Pedicularis flammea*

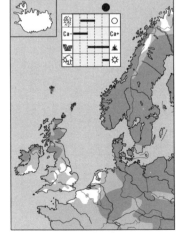

1447 *Pedicularis palustris*
Marsh Lousewort

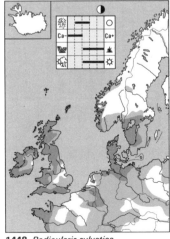

1448 *Pedicularis sylvatica*
Lousewort

1449 *Pedicularis lapponica*

1450 *Rhinanthus groenlandicus*

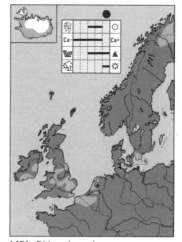

1451 *Rhinanthus minor*
Yellow Rattle

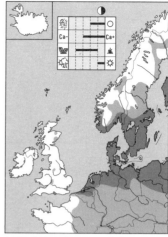

1452 *Rhinanthus angustifolius*

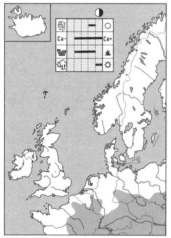

1453 *Rhinanthus alectorolophus*

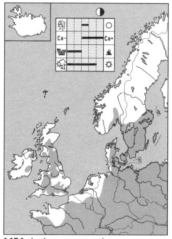

1454 *Lathraea squamaria*
Toothwort

1455 *Lathraea clandestina*
Purple Toothwort

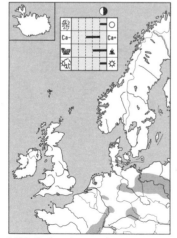

1456 *Orobanche arenaria*

1457 *Orobanche purpurea*
Purple Broomrape

1458 *Orobanche caerulescens*

1459 *Orobanche alba*

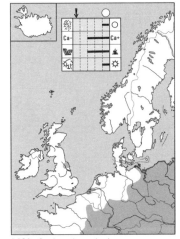

1460 *Orobanche reticulata*
Thistle Broomrape

1461 *Orobanche amethystea*

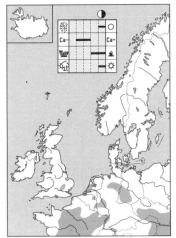

1462 *Orobanche loricata*
Ox-tongue Broomrape

1463 *Orobanche minor*
Common Broomrape

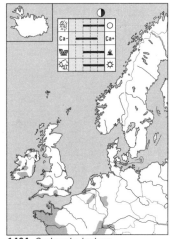

1464 *Orobanche hederae*
Ivy Broomrape

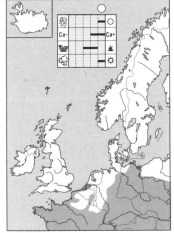

1465 *Orobanche caryophyllacea*
Clove-scented Broomrape

1466 *Orobanche teucrii*

1467 *Orobanche elatior*
Knapweed Broomrape

185

1468 *Orobanche alsatica*

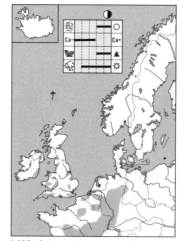

1469 *Orobanche rapum-genistae*
Greater Broomrape

1470 *Orobanche gracilis*

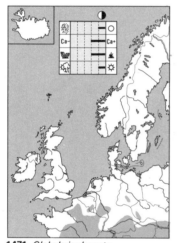

1471 *Globularia elongata*
Globularia

1472 *Pinguicula grandiflora*
Large-flowered Butterwort

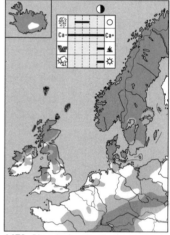

1473 *Pinguicula vulgaris*
Common Butterwort

1474 *Pinguicula alpina*
Alpine Butterwort

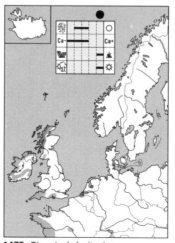

1475 *Pinguicula lusitanica*
Pale Butterwort

1476 *Pinguicula villosa*

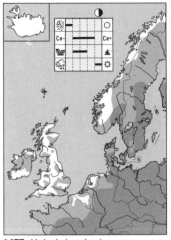

1477 *Utricularia vulgaris* N
Greater Bladderwort

1478 *Utricularia minor* N
Lesser Bladderwort

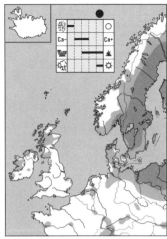

1479 *Utricularia intermedia* N
Intermediate Bladderwort

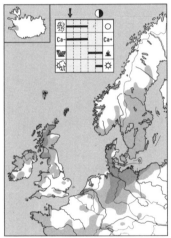

1480 *Littorella uniflora*
Shoreweed

1481 *Plantago coronopus*
Buckshorn Plantain

1482 *Plantago maritima*
Sea Plantain

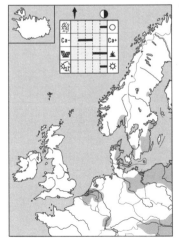

1483 *Plantago indica* N
Branched Plantain

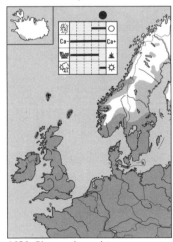

1484 *Plantago lanceolata*
Ribwort Plantain

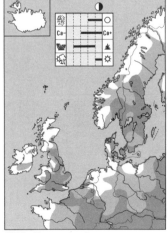

1485 *Plantago media*
Hoary Plantain

187

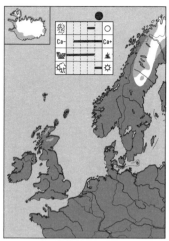

1486 *Plantago major*
Greater Plantain

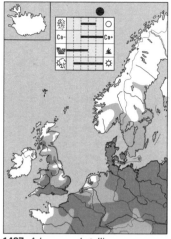

1487 *Adoxa moschatellina*
Moschatel

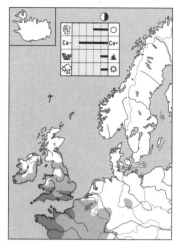

1488 *Centranthus ruber*   N
Red Valerian

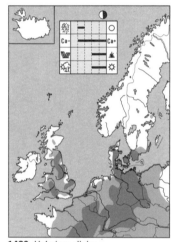

1489 *Valeriana dioica*
Marsh Valerian

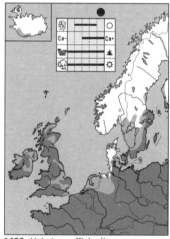

1490 *Valeriana officinalis*
Common Valerian

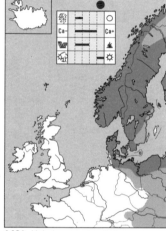

1491 *Valeriana sambucifolia*

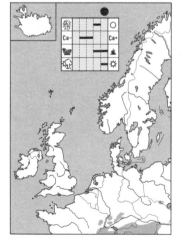

1492 *Valeriana tripteris*

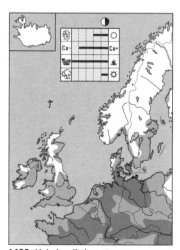

1493 *Valerianella locusta agg.*
Cornsalad

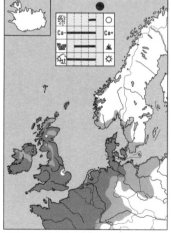

1494 *Lonicera periclymenum*
Honeysuckle

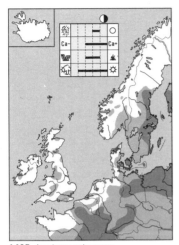

1495 *Lonicera xylosteum*
Fly Honeysuckle

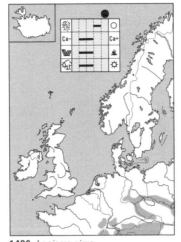

1496 *Lonicera nigra*
Black-berried Honeysuckle

1497 *Lonicera alpigena*

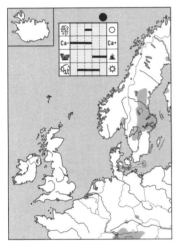

1498 *Lonicera caerulea*
Blue Honeysuckle

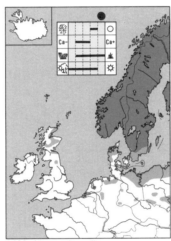

1499 *Linnaea borealis*
Twinflower

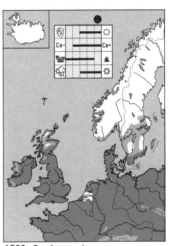

1500 *Sambucus nigra*
Elder

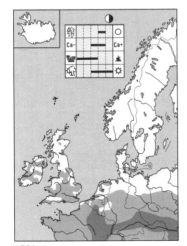

1501 *Sambucus ebulus*
Dwarf Elder

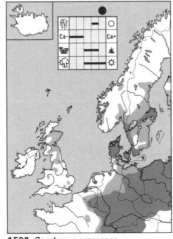

1502 *Sambucus racemosa*
Red-berried Elder

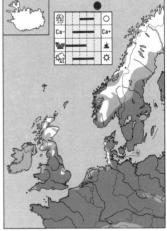

1503 *Viburnum opulus*
Guelder Rose

189

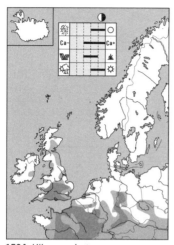

1504 *Viburnum lantana*
Wayfaring Tree

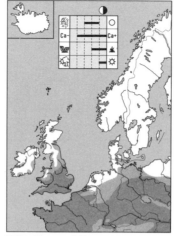

1505 *Dipsacus fullonum*
Teasel

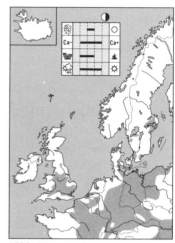

1506 *Dipsacus pilosus*
Small Teasel

1507 *Dipsacus laciniatus*

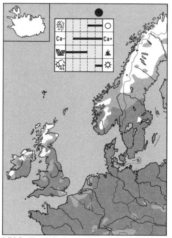

1508 *Knautia arvensis*
Field Scabious

1509 *Knautia sylvatica*
Wood Scabious

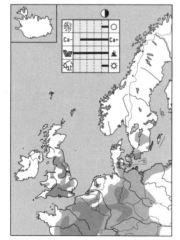

1510 *Scabiosa columbaria*
Small Scabious

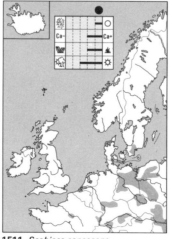

1511 *Scabiosa canescens*

1512 *Scabiosa ochroleuca*
Yellow Scabious

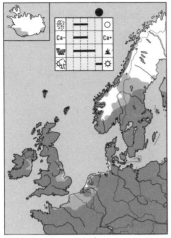

1513 *Succisa pratensis*
Devilsbit Scabious

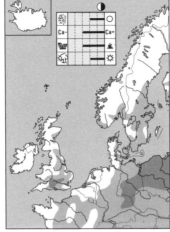

1514 *Campanula glomerata*
Clustered Bellflower

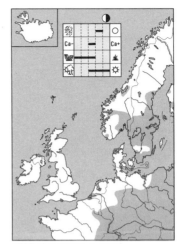

1515 *Campanula cervicaria*

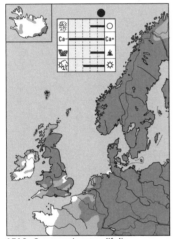

1516 *Campanula rotundifolia*
Harebell

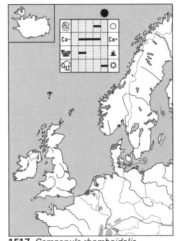

1517 *Campanula rhomboidalis*

1518 *Campanula cochlearifolia*

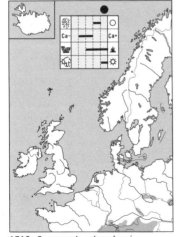

1519 *Campanula scheuchzeri*

1520 *Campanula baumgartenii*

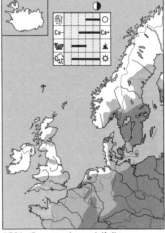

1521 *Campanula persicifolia*
Peach-leaved Bellflower

Bellflower Family · Campanulaceae

1522 *Campanula rapunculus*
Rampion Bellflower

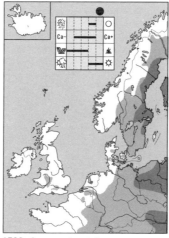

1523 *Campanula patula*
Spreading Bellflower

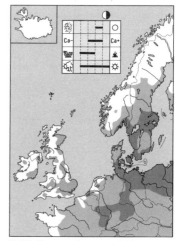

1524 *Campanula rapunculoides*
Creeping Bellflower

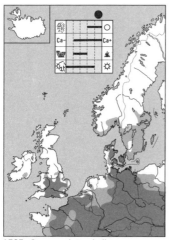

1525 *Campanula trachelium*
Nettle-leaved Bellflower

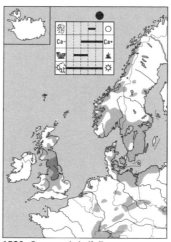

1526 *Campanula latifolia*
Giant Bellflower

1527 *Campanula barbata*
Bearded Bellflower

1528 *Campanula uniflora*

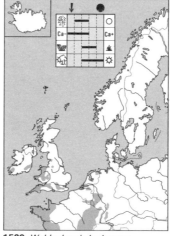

1529 *Wahlenbergia hederacea*
Ivy-leaved Bellflower

1530 *Legousia speculum-veneris*
Large Venus's Looking Glass

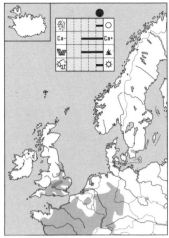

1531 *Legousia hybrida*
Venus's Looking Glass

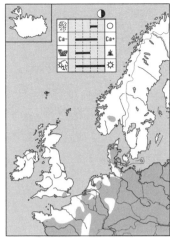

1532 *Phyteuma spicatum*
Spiked Rampion

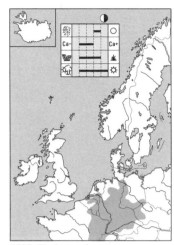

1533 *Phyteuma nigrum*

1534 *Phyteuma tenerum*
Round-headed Rampion

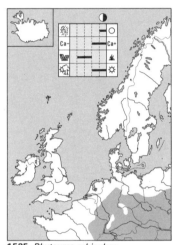

1535 *Phyteuma orbiculare*

1536 *Jasione perennis*

1537 *Jasione montana*
Sheepsbit Scabious

1538 *Lobelia dortmanna*
Water Lobelia

1539 *Lobelia urens*
Heath Lobelia

Daisy Family · Compositae

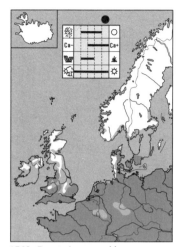

1540 *Eupatorium cannabinum*
Hemp Agrimony

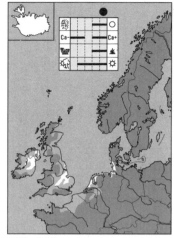

1541 *Solidago virgaurea*
Golden-rod

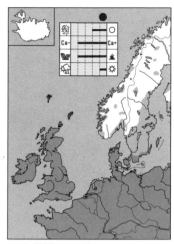

1542 *Bellis perennis*
Daisy

1543 *Bellidiastrum michelii*

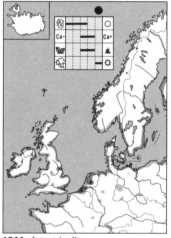

1544 *Aster tripolium*
Sea Aster

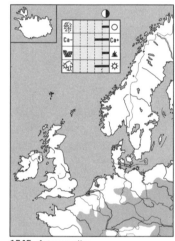

1545 *Aster amellus*

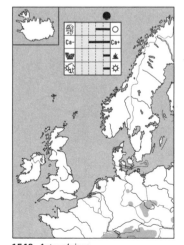

1546 *Aster alpinus*

1547 *Aster sibiricus*

1548 *Crinitaria linosyris*
Goldilocks

194

1549 *Erigeron borealis*
Alpine Fleabane

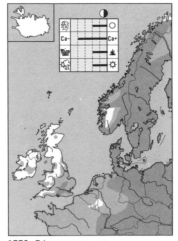

1550 *Erigeron acer*   N
Blue Fleabane

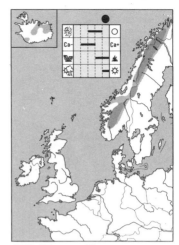

1551 *Erigeron uniflorus*

1552 *Erigeron unalaschense*

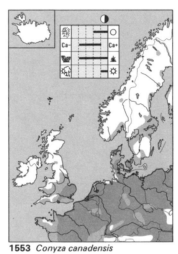

1553 *Conyza canadensis*
Canadian Fleabane

1554 *Filago lutescens*
Red-tipped Cudweed

1555 *Filago pyramidata*
Broad-leaved Cudweed

1556 *Filago vulgaris*
Common Cudweed

1557 *Filago gallica*
Narrow-leaved Cudweed

1558 *Filago minima*
Small Cudweed

1559 *Filago arvensis*

1560 *Micropus erectus*
Micropus

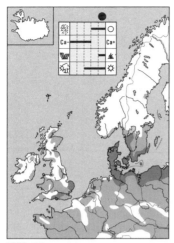

1561 *Gnaphalium sylvaticum*
Heath Cudweed

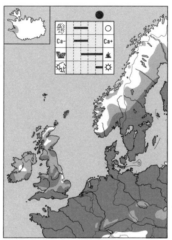

1562 *Gnaphalium uliginosum*
Marsh Cudweed

1563 *Gnaphalium luteo-album*
Jersey Cudweed

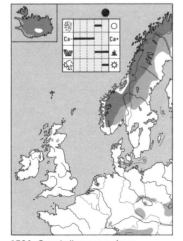

1564 *Gnaphalium norvegicum*
Highland Cudweed

1565 *Gnaphalium supinum*
Dwarf Cudweed

1566 *Gnaphalium undulatum*
Cape Cudweed

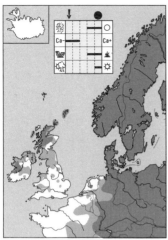

1567 *Antennaria dioica*
Mountain Everlasting

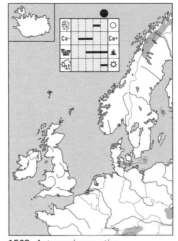

1568 *Antennaria carpatica*

1569 *Antennaria alpina* N

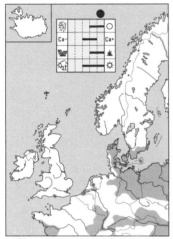

1570 *Helichrysum arenarium*
Helichrysum

1571 *Inula hirta*

1572 *Inula conyza*
Ploughman's Spikenard

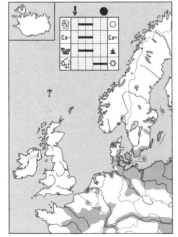

1573 *Inula brittanica*

1574 *Inula salicina*
Irish Fleabane

1575 *Inula crithmoides*
Golden Samphire

1576 *Inula helvetica*

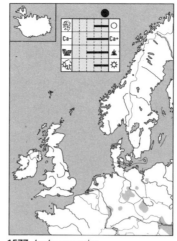

1577 *Inula germanica*

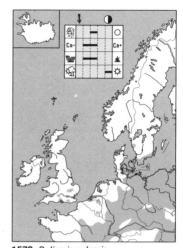

1578 *Pulicaria vulgaris*
Small Fleabane

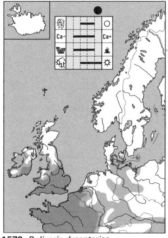

1579 *Pulicaria dysenterica*
Common Fleabane

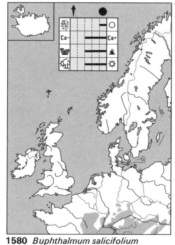

1580 *Buphthalmum salicifolium*
Yellow Ox-eye

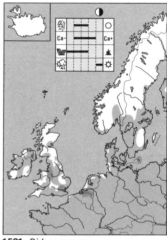

1581 *Bidens cernua*
Nodding Bur-marigold

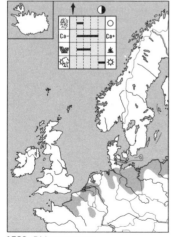

1582 *Bidens connata*

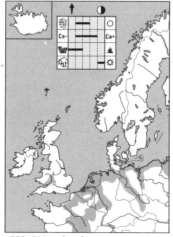

1583 *Bidens frondosa*
Beggar Ticks

1584 *Bidens radiata*

198

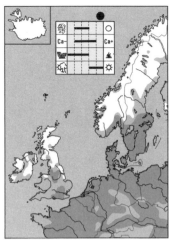

1585 *Bidens tripartita*
Trifid Bur-marigold

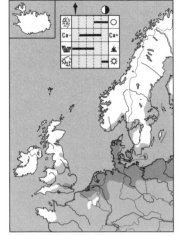

1586 *Galinsoga parviflora*
Gallant Soldier

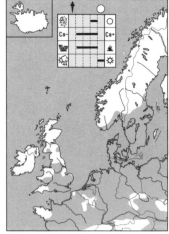

1587 *Galinsoga ciliata*
Shaggy Soldier

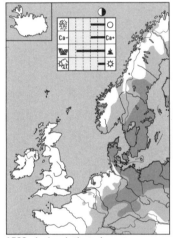

1588 *Anthemis tinctoria* N
Yellow Chamomile

1589 *Anthemis austriaca*

1590 *Anthemis arvensis*
Corn Chamomile

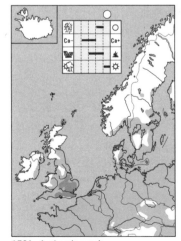

1591 *Anthemis cotula*
Stinking Chamomile

1592 *Chamaemelum nobile*
Lawn Chamomile

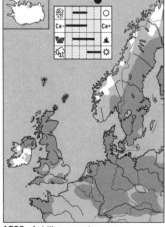

1593 *Achillea ptarmica* N
Sneezewort

199

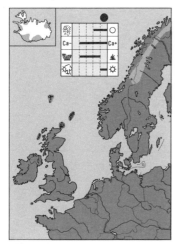

1594 *Achillea millefolium*
Yarrow

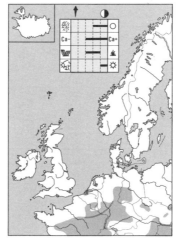

1595 *Achillea nobilis*

1596 *Achillea setacea*

1597 *Achillea collina*

1598 *Achillea pannonica*

1599 *Otanthus maritimus*
Cottonweed

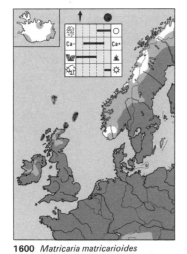

1600 *Matricaria matricarioides*
Pineapple Mayweed

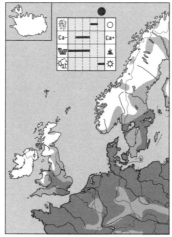

1601 *Matricaria recutita*
Scented Mayweed

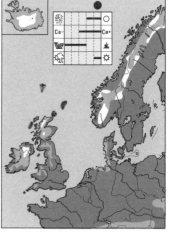

1602 *Tripleurospermum maritimum agg.*   N
Sea Mayweed

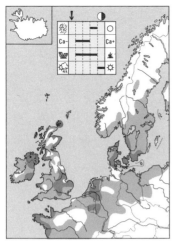

1603 *Chrysanthemum segetum*
Corn Marigold

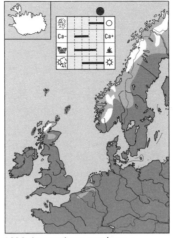

1604 *Leucanthemum vulgare*
Ox-eye Daisy

1605 *Tanacetum corymbosum*

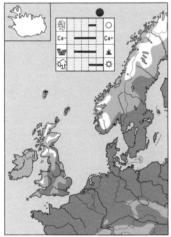

1606 *Tanacetum vulgare*
Tansy

1607 *Cotula coronopifolia*
Buttonweed

1608 *Artemisia absinthium*
Wormwood

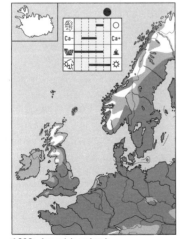

1609 *Artemisia vulgaris*
Mugwort

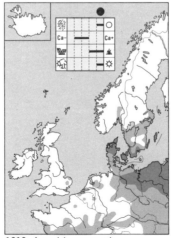

1610 *Artemisia campestris*
Field Wormwood

1611 *Artemisia maritima*
Sea Wormwood

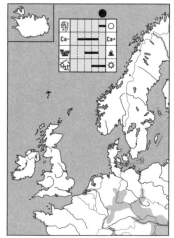

1612 *Artemisia pontica*

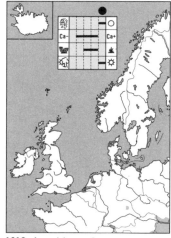

1613 *Artemisia austriaca*

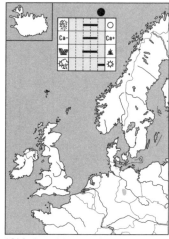

1614 *Artemisia rupestris*

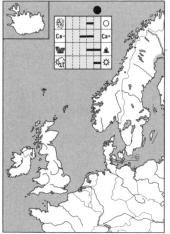

1615 *Artemisia borealis*

1616 *Artemisia laciniata*

1617 *Artemisia norvegica*
Scottish Wormwood

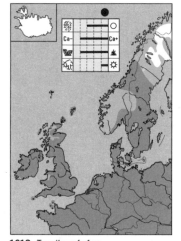

1618 *Tussilago farfara*
Coltsfoot

1619 *Petasites fragrans*
Winter Heliotrope

1620 *Petasites hybridus*
Butterbur

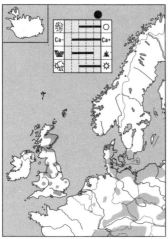

1621 *Petasites albus*
White Butterbur

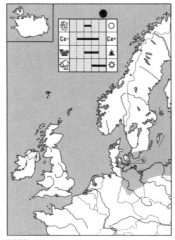

1622 *Petasites spurius*

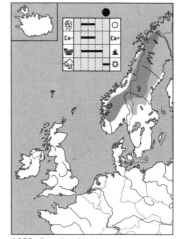

1623 *Petasites frigidus*

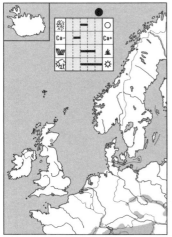

1624 *Homogyne alpina*
Purple Coltsfoot

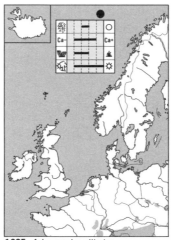

1625 *Adenostyles alliariae*

1626 *Arnica montana*
Arnica

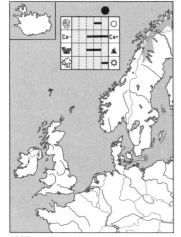

1627 *Arnica alpina*

1628 *Doronicum pardalianches*
Leopardsbane

1629 *Doronicum plantagineum*
Green Leopardsbane

1630 *Senecio spathulifolius*

1631 *Senecio integrifolius*
Field Fleawort

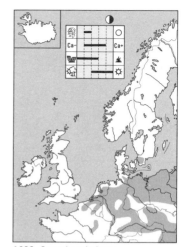

1632 *Senecio paludosus*
Fen Ragwort

1633 *Senecio fluviatilis*
Broad-leaved Ragwort

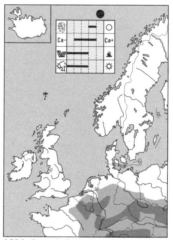

1634 *Senecio fuchsii* N
Alpine Ragwort

1635 *Senecio nemorensis*

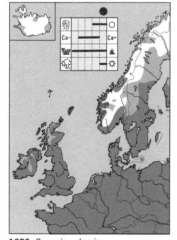

1636 *Senecio vulgaris*
Groundsel

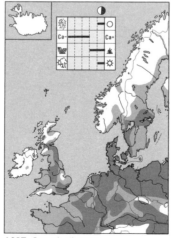

1637 *Senecio viscosus*
Sticky Groundsel

1638 *Senecio sylvaticus*
Heath Groundsel

204

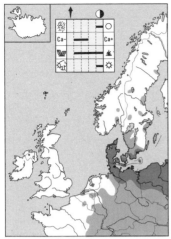

1639 *Senecio vernalis*

1640 *Senecio cineraria*
Silver Ragwort

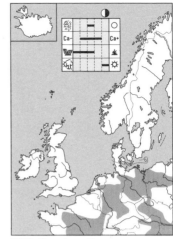

1641 *Senecio erraticus*

1642 *Senecio squalidus* N
Oxford Ragwort

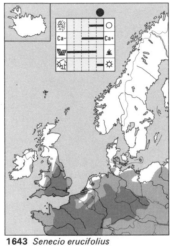

1643 *Senecio erucifolius*
Hoary Ragwort

1644 *Senecio jacobaea*
Ragwort

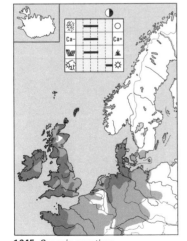

1645 *Senecio aquaticus*
Marsh Ragwort

1646 *Senecio crispatus*

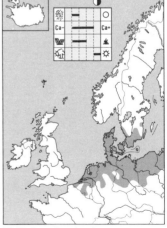

1647 *Senecio palustris*
Marsh Fleawort

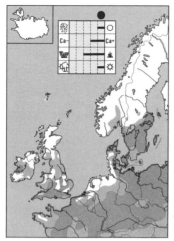

1648 *Carlina vulgaris*
Carline Thistle

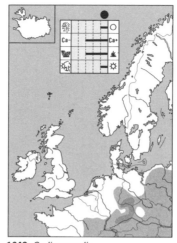

1649 *Carlina acaulis*
Stemless Carline Thistle

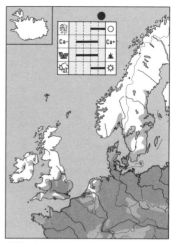

1650 *Arctium lappa*
Greater Burdock

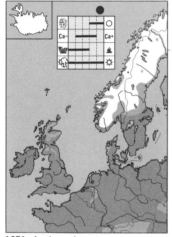

1651 *Arctium minus* N
Lesser Burdock

1652 *Saussurea alpina*
Alpine Saw-wort

1653 *Jurinea cyanoides*

1654 *Carduus tenuiflorus*
Slender Thistle

1655 *Carduus nutans*
Musk Thistle

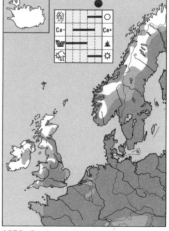

1656 *Carduus crispus agg.* N
Welted Thistle

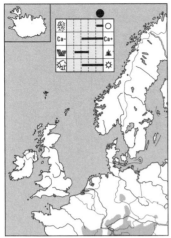

1657 *Carduus defloratus*

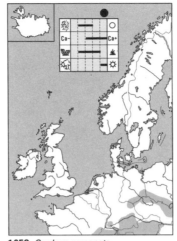

1658 *Carduus personata*
Great Marsh Thistle

1659 *Carduus pycnocephalus*

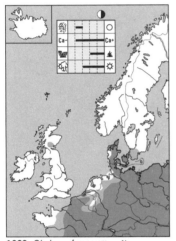

1660 *Cirsium oleraceum* N
Cabbage Thistle

1661 *Cirsium eriophorum*
Woolly Thistle

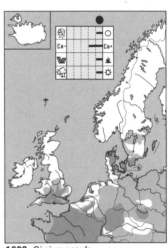

1662 *Cirsium acaule*
Dwarf Thistle

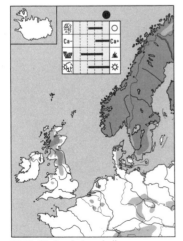

1663 *Cirsium heterophyllum*
Melancholy Thistle

1664 *Cirsium dissectum*
Meadow Thistle

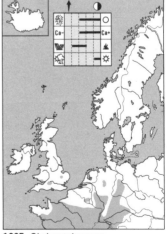

1665 *Cirsium tuberosum*
Tuberous Thistle

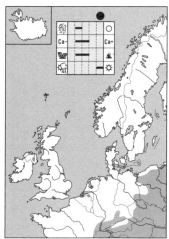

1666 *Cirsium rivulare*

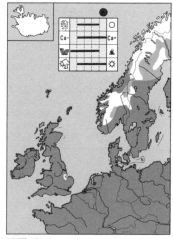

1667 *Cirsium palustre*
Marsh Thistle

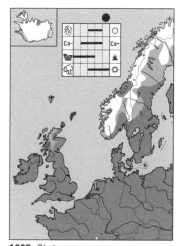

1668 *Cirsium arvense*
Creeping Thistle

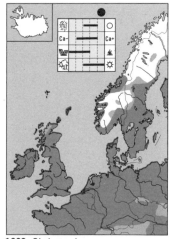

1669 *Cirsium vulgare*
Spear Thistle

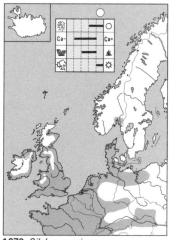

1670 *Silybum marianum*
Milk Thistle

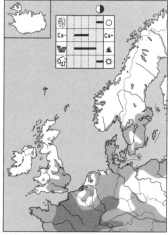

1671 *Onopordum acanthium* N
Cotton Thistle

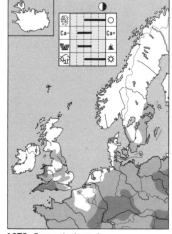

1672 *Serratula tinctoria*
Saw-wort

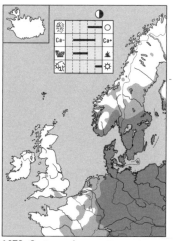

1673 *Centaurea jacea* N
Brown Knapweed

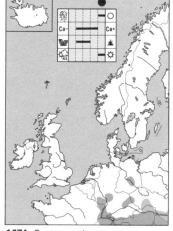

1674 *Centaurea nigrescens* N

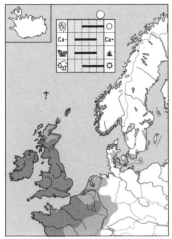

1675 *Centaurea nigra* N
Black Knapweed

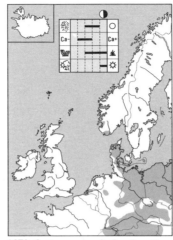

1676 *Centaurea pseudophrygia* N

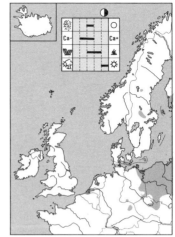

1677 *Centaurea phrygia* N

1678 *Centaurea stoebe* N

1679 *Centaurea maculosa* N

1680 *Centaurea scabiosa* N
Greater Knapweed

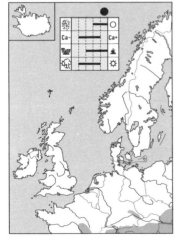

1681 *Centaurea triumfetti* N

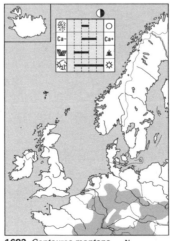

1682 *Centaurea montana* N
Perennial Cornflower

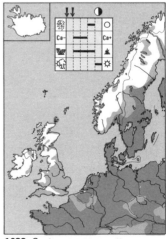

1683 *Centaurea cyanus* N
Cornflower

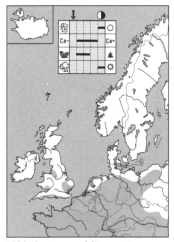

1684 *Centaurea calcitrapa* N
Red Star-thistle

1685 *Centaurea aspera* N
Rough Star-thistle

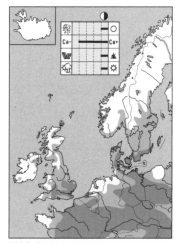

1686 *Cichorium intybus*
Chicory

1687 *Lapsana communis*
Nipplewort

1688 *Aposeris foetida*

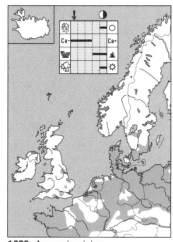

1689 *Arnoseris minima*
Lamb's Succory

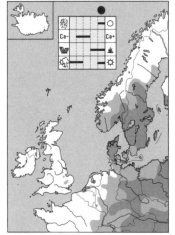

1690 *Hypochaeris maculata*
Spotted Catsear

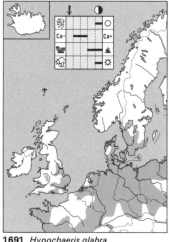

1691 *Hypochaeris glabra*
Smooth Catsear

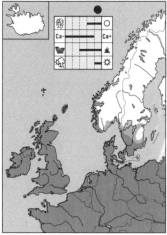

1692 *Hypochaeris radicata*
Common Catsear

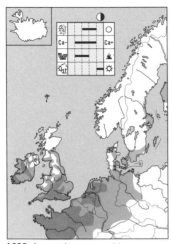

1693 *Leontodon taraxacoides*
Lesser Hawkbit

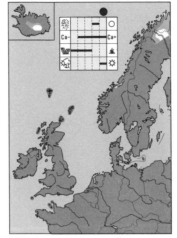

1694 *Leontodon autumnalis*
Autumn Hawkbit

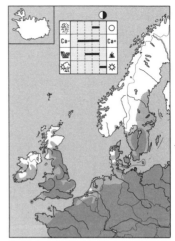

1695 *Leontodon hispidus*   N
Rough Hawkbit

1696 *Leontodon helveticus*

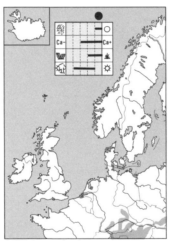

1697 *Leontodon incanus*

1698 *Picris hieracioides*
Hawkweed Oxtongue

1699 *Picris echioides*
Bristly Oxtongue

1700 *Tragopogon dubium*

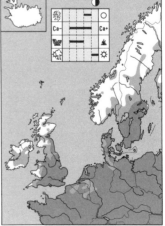

1701 *Tragopogon pratensis*
Goatsbeard

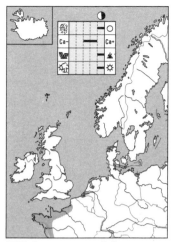

1702 *Tragopogon crocifolius*

1703 *Scorzonera humilis*
Viper's Grass

1704 *Scorzonera purpurea*
Purple Viper's Grass

1705 *Scorzonera hispanica*

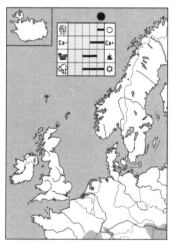

1706 *Scorzonera austriaca*

1707 *Podospermum laciniatum*

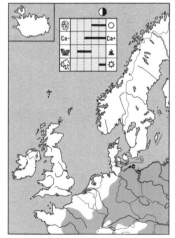

1708 *Chondrilla juncea*
Chondrilla

1709 *Willemetia stipitata*

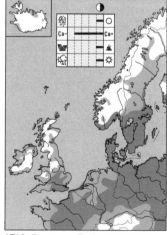

1710 *Taraxacum Erythrosperma*
Lesser Dandelion

1711 *Taraxacum Palustria*
Marsh Dandelion

1712 *Taraxacum Arctica*
Arctic Dandelion

1713 *Taraxacum Ceratophora*

1714 *Taraxacum Spectabilia*
Red-veined Dandelion

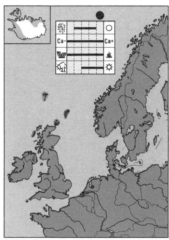

1715 *Taraxacum Vulgaria*
Dandelion

1716 *Cicerbita alpina*
Alpine Sow-thistle

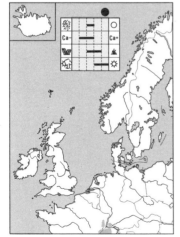

1717 *Cicerbita plumieri*

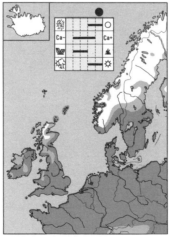

1718 *Sonchus oleraceus*
Smooth Sow-thistle

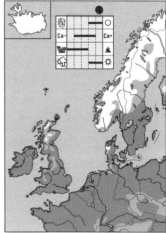

1719 *Sonchus asper*
Prickly Sow-thistle

213

Daisy Family · Compositae

1720 *Sonchus arvensis*
Perennial Sow-thistle

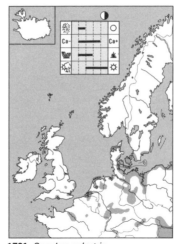
1721 *Sonchus palustris*
Marsh Sow-thistle

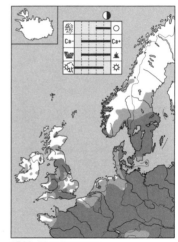
1722 *Mycelis muralis*
Wall Lettuce

1723 *Lactuca perennis*
Blue Lettuce

1724 *Lactuca saligna*
Least Lettuce

1725 *Lactuca virosa*
Great Lettuce

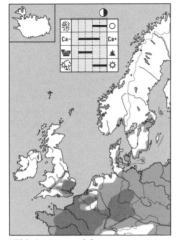
1726 *Lactuca serriola*
Prickly Lettuce

1727 *Lactuca quercina*

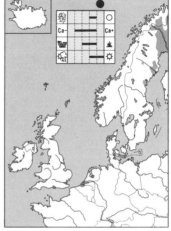
1728 *Lactuca sibiricum*

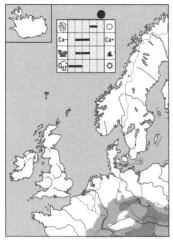

1729 *Prenanthes purpurea*
Purple Lettuce

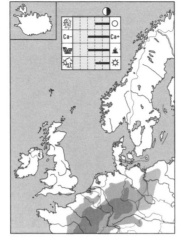

1730 *Crepis foetida*
Stinking Hawksbeard

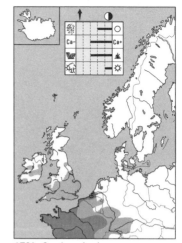

1731 *Crepis vesicaria*
Beaked Hawksbeard

1732 *Crepis praemorsa*

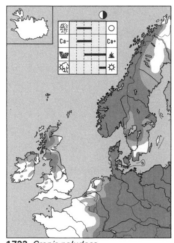

1733 *Crepis paludosa*
Marsh Hawksbeard

1734 *Crepis pulchra*

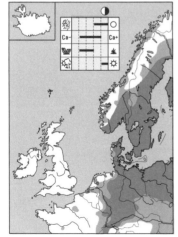

1735 *Crepis tectorum*

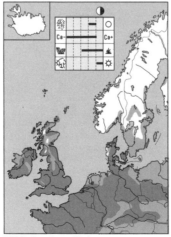

1736 *Crepis capillaris*
Smooth Hawksbeard

1737 *Crepis mollis*
Northern Hawksbeard

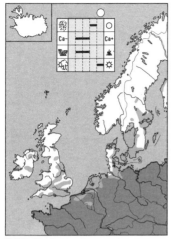

1738 *Crepis biennis*
Rough Hawksbeard

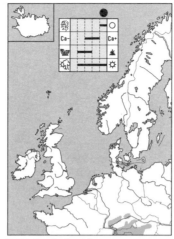

1739 *Crepis alpestris*

1740 *Hieracium Amplexicaulia*

1741 *Hieracium Alpina*
Alpine Hawkweed

1742 *Hieracium Carinthoidea*

1743 *Hieracium Oreadea*

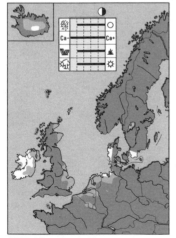

1744 *Hieracium Vulgata*
Common Hawkweed

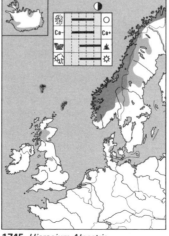

1745 *Hieracium Alpestria*

1746 *Hieracium Prenanthoidea*

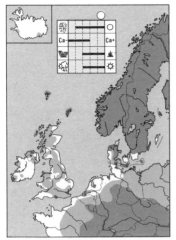

1747 *Hieracium Tridentata*

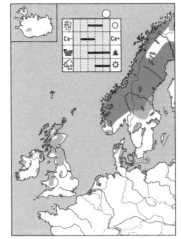

1748 *Hieracium Foliosa*

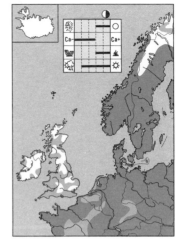

1749 *Hieracium Umbellata*
Leafy Hawkweed

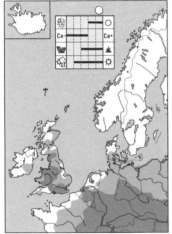

1750 *Hieracium Sabauda*

1751 *Hieracium Italica*

1752 *Hieracium Intybacea*

1753 *Hieracium Heterodonta*

1754 *Hieracium Nigrescentia*

1755 *Hieracium Depilata*

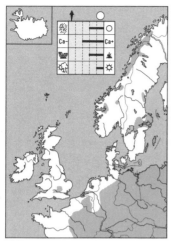

1756 *Pilosella Praealtina*

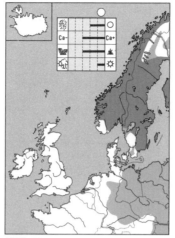

1757 *Pilosella Stiptolepidea*

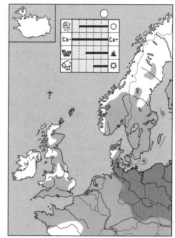

1758 *Pilosella Pratensina*

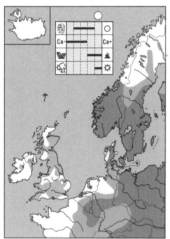

1759 *Pilosella Auriculina*
Orange Hawkweed

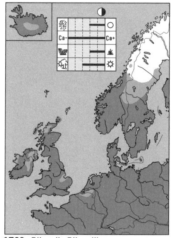

1760 *Pilosella Pilosellina*
Mouse-ear Hawkweed

1761 *Typha angustifolia*
Lesser Bulrush

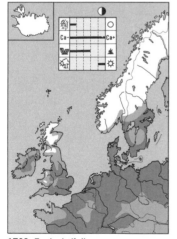

1762 *Typha latifolia*
Bulrush

1763 *Typha shuttleworthii*

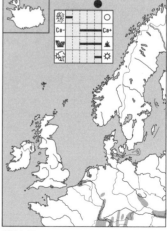

1764 *Typha minima*

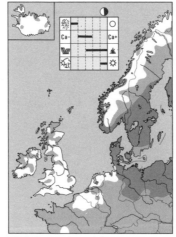

1765 *Sparganium angustifolium*
Floating Bur-reed

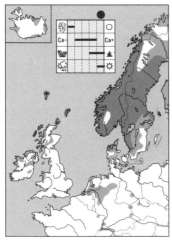

1766 *Sparganium minimum*
Least Bur-reed

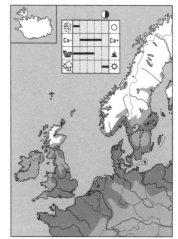

1767 *Sparganium erectum*
Branched Bur-reed

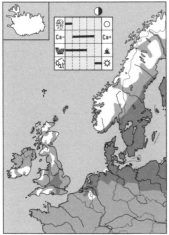

1768 *Sparganium simplex*
Unbranched Bur-reed

1769 *Sparganium glomeratum*

1770 *Sparganium hyperboreum*

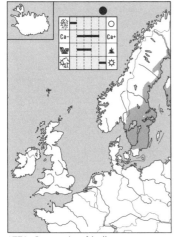

1771 *Sparganium friesii*

1772 *Zostera marina* N
Eel-grass

1773 *Zostera nana*
Dwarf Eel-grass

Pondweed Family · Potamogetonaceae

1774 *Potamogeton natans*
Broad-leaved Pondweed

1775 *Potamogeton polygonifolius*
Bog Pondweed

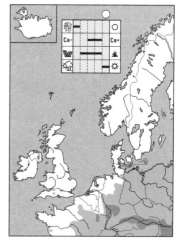

1776 *Potamogeton nodosus*
Loddon Pondweed

1777 *Potamogeton coloratus*
Fen Pondweed

1778 *Potamogeton alpinus*
Reddish Pondweed

1779 *Potamogeton gramineus*
Various-leaved Pondweed

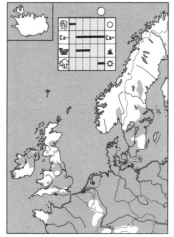

1780 *Potamogeton lucens*
Shining Pondweed

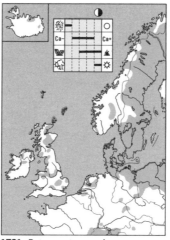

1781 *Potamogeton praelongus*
Long-stalked Pondweed

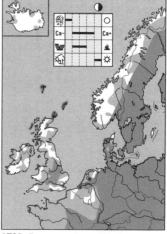

1782 *Potamogeton perfoliatus*
Perfoliate Pondweed

1783 *Potamogeton epihydrus*
American Pondweed

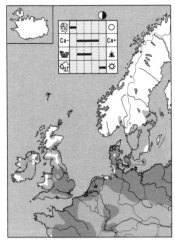

1784 *Potamogeton crispus*
Curled Pondweed

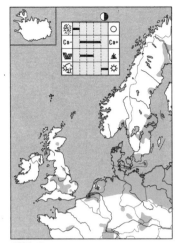

1785 *Potamogeton compressus*
Grasswrack Pondweed

1786 *Potamogeton acutifolius*
Sharp-leaved Pondweed

1787 *Potamogeton obtusifolius*
Blunt-leaved Pondweed

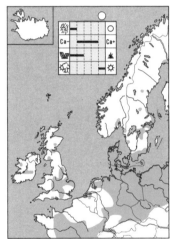

1788 *Potamogeton friesii*
Flat-stalked Pondweed

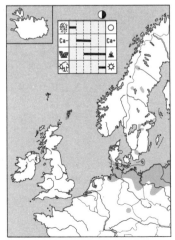

1789 *Potamogeton rutilus*
Shetland Pondweed

1790 *Potamogeton pusillus* N
Lesser Pondweed

1791 *Potamogeton trichoides*
Hair-like Pondweed

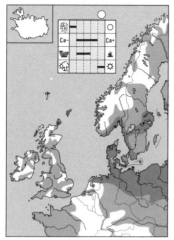

1792 *Potamogeton berchtoldii*
Small Pondweed

1793 *Potamogeton pectinatus*
Fennel Pondweed

1794 *Potamogeton vaginatus*

1795 *Potamogeton filiformis*
Slender-leaved Pondweed

1796 *Potamogeton helveticus*

1797 *Groenlandia densa*
Opposite-leaved Pondweed

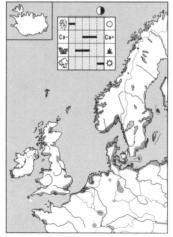

1798 *Ruppia maritima*
Beaked Tasselweed

1799 *Ruppia spiralis*
Spiral Tasselweed

1800 *Zannichellia palustris*
Horned Pondweed

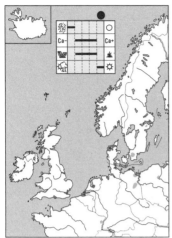

1801 *Najas flexilis*
Slender Naiad

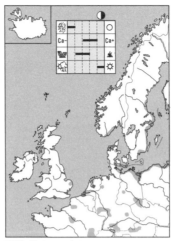

1802 *Najas marina*
Holly-leaved Naiad

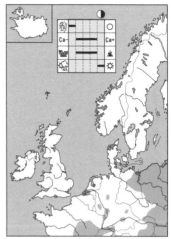

1803 *Najas minor*

1804 *Triglochin maritimum*
Sea Arrow-grass

1805 *Triglochin palustre*
Marsh Arrow-grass

1806 *Scheuchzeria palustris*
Rannoch Rush

1807 *Eriocaulon septangulare*
Pipewort

1808 *Alisma plantago-aquatica*
Common Water-plantain

1809 *Alisma lanceolatum*
Narrow-leaved Water-plantain

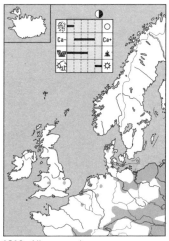

1810 *Alisma gramineum*
Ribbon-leaved Water-plantain

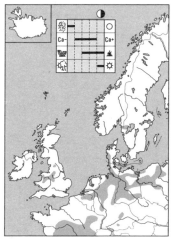

1811 *Luronium natans*
Floating Water-plantain

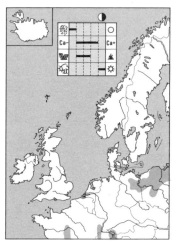

1812 *Caldesia parnassifolia*
Parnassus-leaved Water-plantain

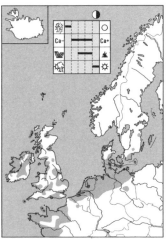

1813 *Baldellia ranunculoides*
Lesser Water-plantain

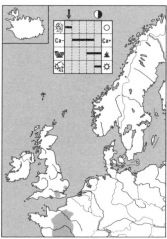

1814 *Damasonium alisma*
Star-fruit

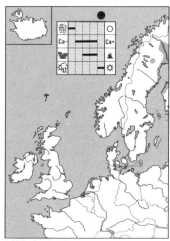

1815 *Sagittaria natans*

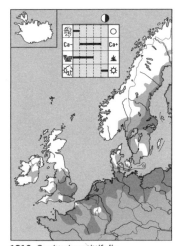

1816 *Sagittaria sagittifolia*
Arrowhead

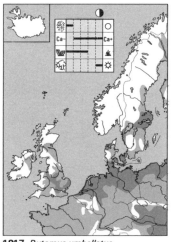

1817 *Butomus umbellatus*
Flowering Rush

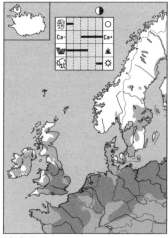

1818 *Elodea canadensis*
Canadian Waterweed

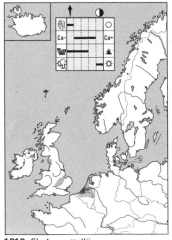

1819 *Elodea nuttallii*
Nuttall's Waterweed N

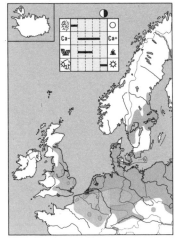

1820 *Stratiotes aloides*
Water Soldier

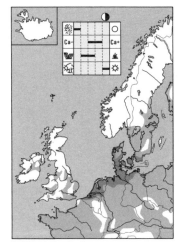

1821 *Hydrocharis morsus-ranae*
Frogbit

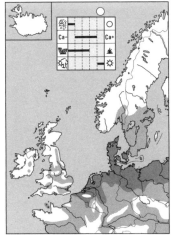

1822 *Acorus calamus* N
Sweet Flag

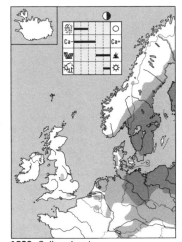

1823 *Calla palustris*
Bog Arum

1824 *Arum maculatum*
Lords and Ladies

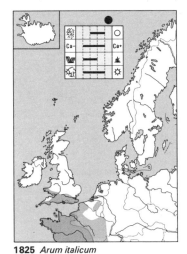

1825 *Arum italicum*
Large Cuckoo Pint

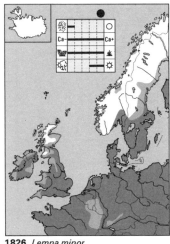

1826 *Lemna minor*
Common Duckweed

1827 *Lemna trisulca*
Ivy-leaved Duckweed

225

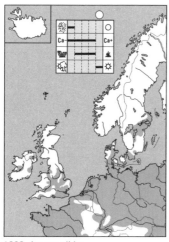

1828 *Lemna gibba*
Fat Duckweed

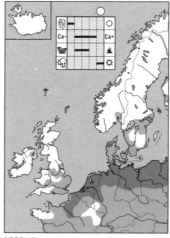

1829 *Spirodela polyrrhiza*
Greater Duckweed

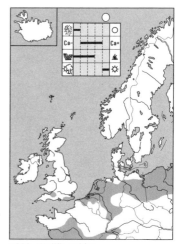

1830 *Wolffia arrhiza*
Rootless Duckweed

1831 *Tofieldia calyculata*
German asphodel

1832 *Tofieldia pusilla*
Scottish Asphodel

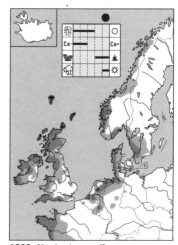

1833 *Narthecium ossifragum*
Bog Asphodel

1834 *Veratrum album*
False Helleborine

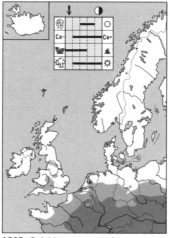

1835 *Colchicum autumnale*
Meadow Saffron

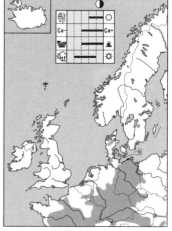

1836 *Anthericum liliago*
St Bernard's Lily

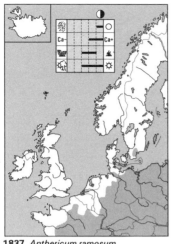

1837 *Anthericum ramosum*

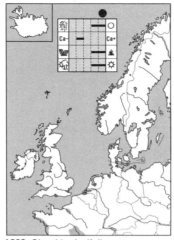

1838 *Simethis planifolia*
Kerry Lily

1839 *Ornithogalum pyrenaicum*
Spiked Star of Bethlehem

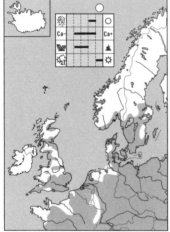

1840 *Ornithogalum umbellatum*
Common Star of Bethlehem

1841 *Ornithogalum gussonei*

1842 *Allium victorialis*

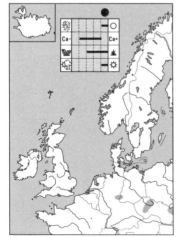

1843 *Allium strictum*

1844 *Allium angulosum*

1845 *Allium senescens*
German Garlic

227

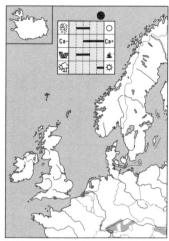

1846 *Allium suaveolens*

1847 *Allium ursinum*
Ramsons

1848 *Allium carinatum*
Keeled Garlic

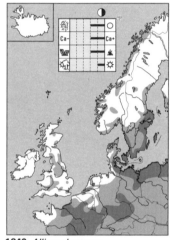

1849 *Allium oleraceum*
Field Garlic

1850 *Allium schoenoprasum*
Chives

1851 *Allium rotundum*

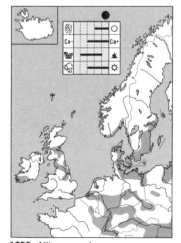

1852 *Allium scorodoprasum*
Sand Leek

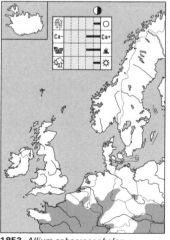

1853 *Allium sphaerocephalon*
Round-headed Leek

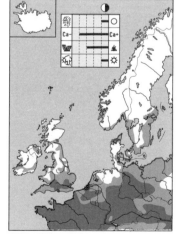

1854 *Allium vineale*
Crow Garlic

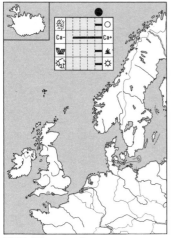

1855 *Allium ampeloprasum*
Wild Leek

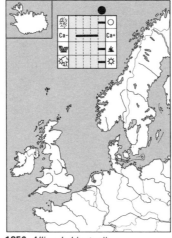

1856 *Allium babingtonii*
Babington's Leek

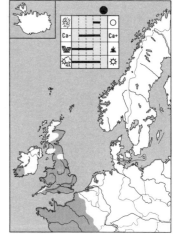

1857 *Ruscus aculeatus*
Butcher's Broom

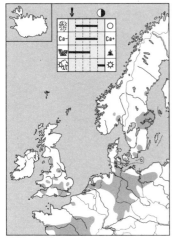

1858 *Fritillaria meleagris*
Fritillary

1859 *Gagea arvensis*

1860 *Gagea bohemica*

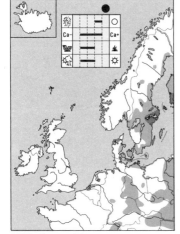

1861 *Gagea minima*
Least Gagea

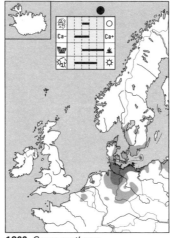

1862 *Gagea spathacea*
Belgian Gagea

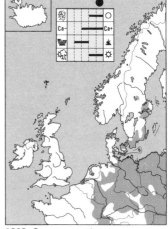

1863 *Gagea pratensis*
Meadow Gagea

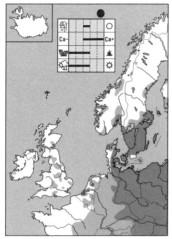

1864 *Gagea lutea*
Yellow Star of Bethlehem

1865 *Scilla verna*
Spring Squill

1866 *Scilla bifolia*
Alpine Squill

1867 *Scilla autumnalis*
Autumn Squill

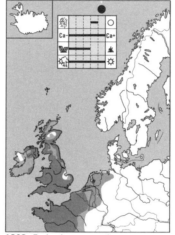

1868 *Endymion non-scriptus*
Bluebell

1869 *Asparagus officinalis*
Wild Asparagus

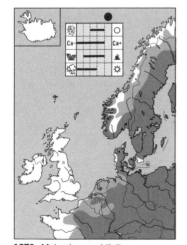

1870 *Maianthemum bifolium*
May Lily

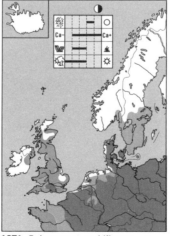

1871 *Polygonatum multiflorum* N
Common Solomon's Seal

1872 *Polygonatum odoratum*
Angular Solomon's Seal

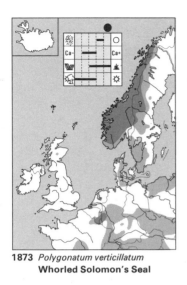

1873 *Polygonatum verticillatum*
Whorled Solomon's Seal

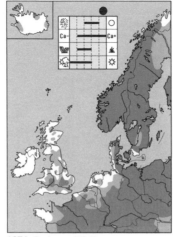

1874 *Paris quadrifolia*
Herb Paris

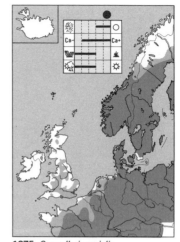

1875 *Convallaria majalis*
Lily of the Valley

1876 *Streptopus amplexifolius*

1877 *Tulipa sylvestris* N
Wild Tulip

1878 *Lloydia serotina*
Snowdon Lily

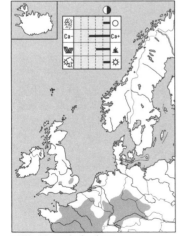

1879 *Muscari atlanticum*
Grape Hyacinth

1880 *Muscari neglectum*

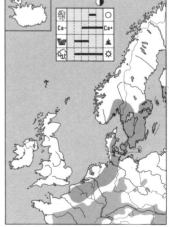

1881 *Muscari botryoides*
Small Grape Hyacinth

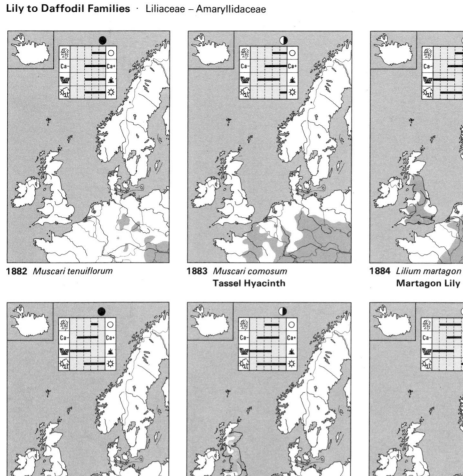

1882 *Muscari tenuiflorum*

1883 *Muscari comosum*
Tassel Hyacinth

1884 *Lilium martagon*
Martagon Lily

1885 *Lilium bulbiferum*

1886 *Galanthus nivalis*
Snowdrop

1887 *Leucojum vernum*
Spring Snowflake

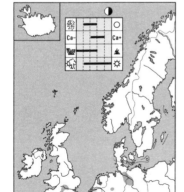

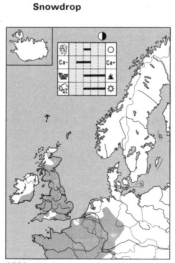

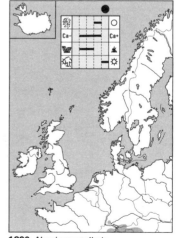

1888 *Leucojum aestivum*
Summer Snowflake

1889 *Narcissus pseudonarcissus*
Wild Daffodil

1890 *Narcissus stellaris*

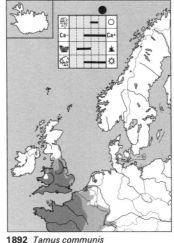

1891 *Narcissus obvallaris*
Tenby Daffodil

1892 *Tamus communis*
Black Bryony

1893 *Crocus albiflorus*
Spring Crocus

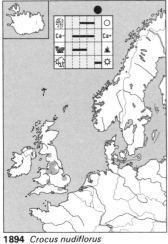

1894 *Crocus nudiflorus*
Autumn Crocus

1895 *Romulea columnae*
Sand Crocus

1896 *Sisyrinchium bermudianum*
Blue-eyed Grass

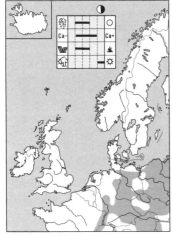

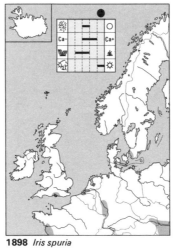

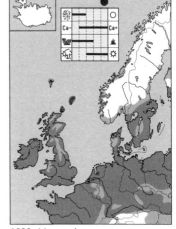

1897 *Iris sibirica*
Siberian iris

1898 *Iris spuria*
Butterfly Iris

1899 *Iris pseudacorus*
Yellow Iris

233

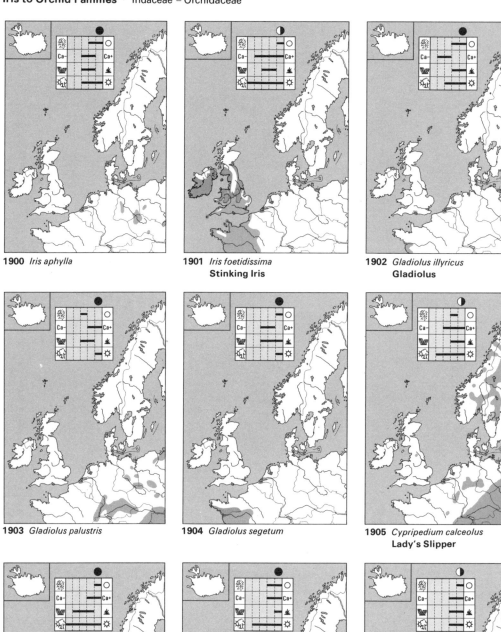

1900 *Iris aphylla*

1901 *Iris foetidissima*
Stinking Iris

1902 *Gladiolus illyricus*
Gladiolus

1903 *Gladiolus palustris*

1904 *Gladiolus segetum*

1905 *Cypripedium calceolus*
Lady's Slipper

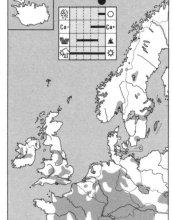

1906 *Ophrys insectifera*
Fly Orchid

1907 *Ophrys apifera*
Bee Orchid

1908 *Ophrys sphegodes*
Early Spider Orchid

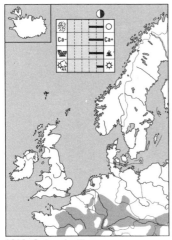

1909 *Ophrys fuciflora*
Late Spider Orchid

1910 *Anacamptis pyramidalis*
Pyramidal Orchid

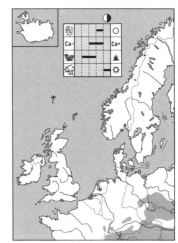

1911 *Traunsteinera globosa*

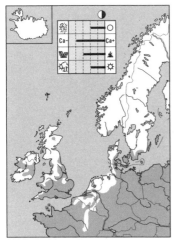

1912 *Orchis morio*
Green-winged Orchid

1913 *Orchis coriophora*
Bug Orchid

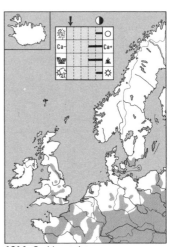

1914 *Orchis ustulata*
Burnt Orchid

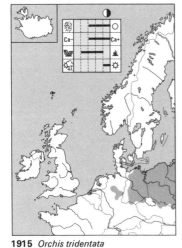

1915 *Orchis tridentata*
Toothed Orchid

1916 *Orchis simia*
Monkey Orchid

1917 *Orchis militaris*
Military Orchid

Orchid Family · Orchidaceae

1918 *Orchis purpurea*
Lady Orchid

1919 *Orchis mascula*
Early Purple Orchid

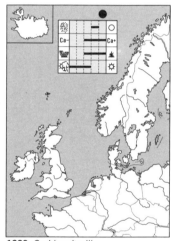

1920 *Orchis pallens*
Pale-flowered Orchid

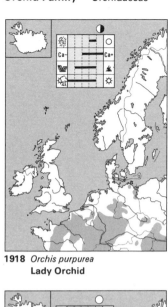

1921 *Orchis palustris*

1922 *Orchis laxiflora*
Loose-flowered Orchid

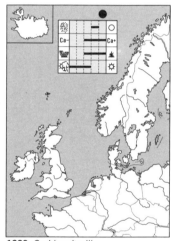

1923 *Orchis spitzelii*

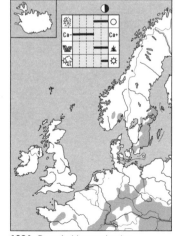

1924 *Dactylorhiza sambucina*
Elder-flowered Orchid

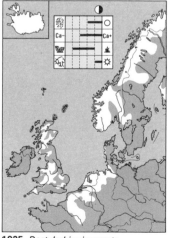

1925 *Dactylorhiza incarnata*
Early Marsh Orchid

1926 *Dactylorhiza cruenta*
Flecked Marsh Orchid

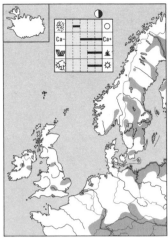

1927 *Dactylorhiza traunsteineri* N
Pugsley's Marsh Orchid

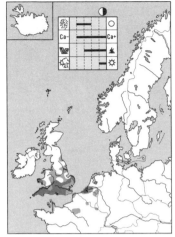

1928 *Dactylorhiza praetermissa*
Southern Marsh Orchid

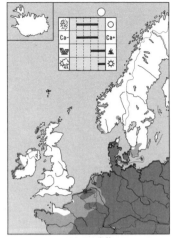

1929 *Dactylorhiza majalis*
Broad-leaved Marsh Orchid

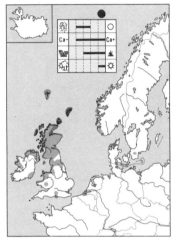

1930 *Dactylorhiza purpurella*
Northern Marsh Orchid

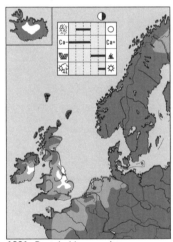

1931 *Dactylorhiza maculata*
Heath Spotted Orchid

1932 *Dactylorhiza fuchsii*
Common Spotted Orchid

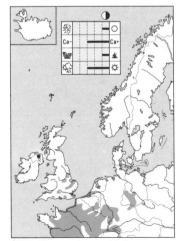

1933 *Himantoglossum hircinum*
Lizard Orchid

1934 *Neotinea intacta*
Dense-flowered Orchid

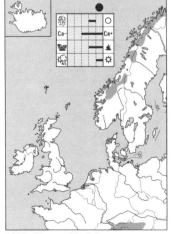

1935 *Chamorchis alpina*
False Musk Orchid

237

Orchid Family · Orchidaceae

1936 *Leucorchis albida*
Small White Orchid

1937 *Nigritella nigra*
Black Vanilla Orchid

1938 *Gymnadenia conopsea*
Fragrant Orchid

1939 *Gymnadenia odoratissima*

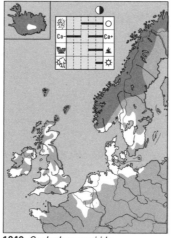

1940 *Coeloglossum viride*
Frog Orchid

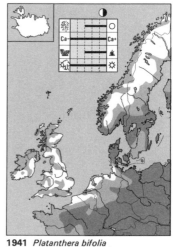

1941 *Platanthera bifolia*
Lesser Butterfly Orchid

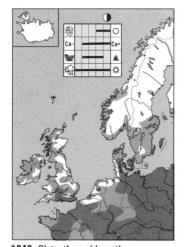

1942 *Platanthera chlorantha*
Greater Butterfly Orchid

1943 *Platanthera oligantha*

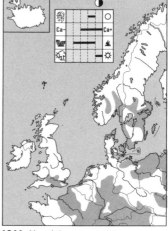

1944 *Herminium monorchis*
Musk Orchid

238

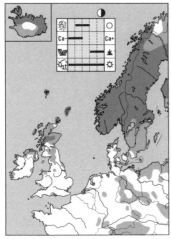

1945 *Listera cordata*
Lesser Twayblade

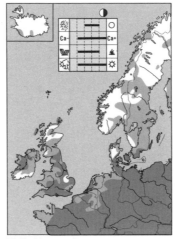

1946 *Listera ovata*
Common Twayblade

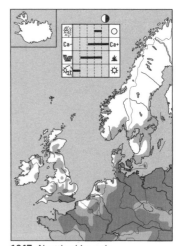

1947 *Neottia nidus-avis*
Birdsnest Orchid

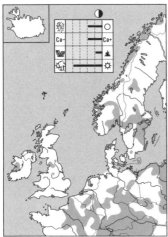

1948 *Epipactis atrorubens*
Dark Red Helleborine

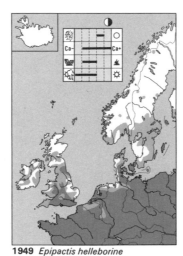

1949 *Epipactis helleborine*
Broad-leaved Helleborine

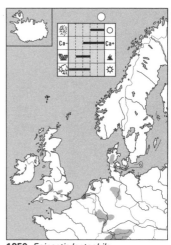

1950 *Epipactis leptochila*
Narrow-lipped Helleborine

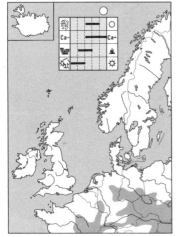

1951 *Epipactis microphylla*

1952 *Epipactis muelleri*

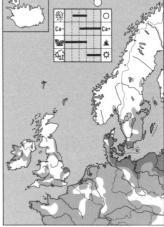

1953 *Epipactis palustris*
Marsh Helleborine

239

Orchid Family · Orchidaceae

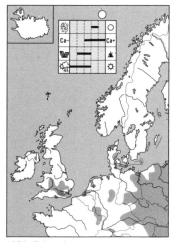

1954 *Epipactis purpurata*
Violet Helleborine

1955 *Epipactis phyllanthes*
Green-flowered Helleborine

1956 *Epipactis dunensis*
Dune Helleborine

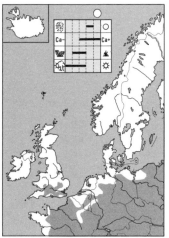

1957 *Cephalanthera damasonium*
White Helleborine

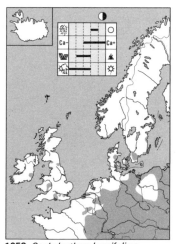

1958 *Cephalanthera longifolium*
Narrow-leaved Helleborine

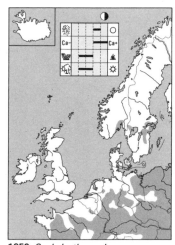

1959 *Cephalanthera rubra*
Red Helleborine

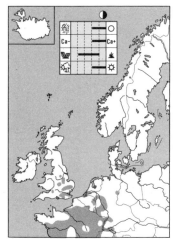

1960 *Aceras anthropomorphum*
Man Orchid

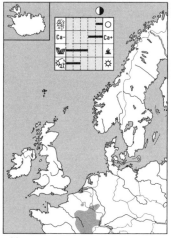

1961 *Limodorum abortivum*
Violet Birdsnest Orchid

1962 *Epipogium aphyllum*
Ghost Orchid

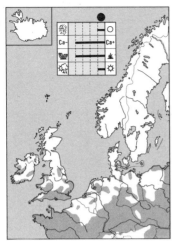

1963 *Spiranthes spiralis*
Autumn Lady's Tresses

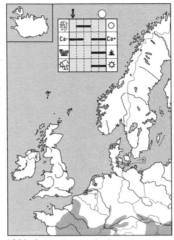

1964 *Spiranthes aestivalis*
Summer Lady's Tresses

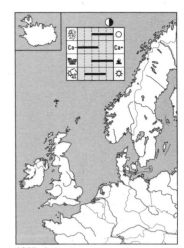

1965 *Spiranthes romanzoffiana*
Irish Lady's Tresses

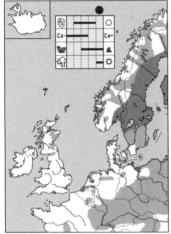

1966 *Goodyera repens*
Creeping Lady's Tresses

1967 *Malaxis monophyllos*
One-leaved Bog Orchid

1968 *Malaxis paludosa*
Bog Orchid

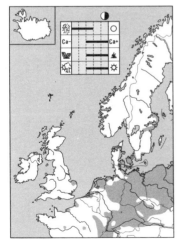

1969 *Liparis loeselii*
Fen Orchid

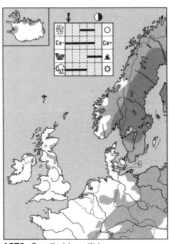

1970 *Corallorhiza trifida*
Coralroot Orchid

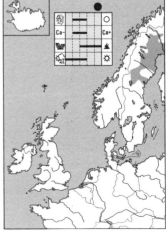

1971 *Calypso bulbosa*
Calypso

Orchid Family · Orchidaceae

1972 *Habenaria hyperborea*

Notes on the maps

1 *Abies alba*: native distribution; widely planted
2 *Picea abies*: very commonly planted
3 *Pinus sylvestris*: widely planted and naturalised
4 *P. mugo*: occasionally planted and naturalised, especially in Scandinavia
6 *Taxus baccata*: often planted, particularly in churchyards
9 *Salix alba*: much planted
10 *S. fragilis*: much planted
11 *S. triandra*: much planted
16 *S. glauca*: including *S. stipulifera*
22 *S. nigricans*: including *S. borealis*
24 *S. cinerea*: including *S. atrocinerea*
27 *S. coaetana*: probably under-recorded
31 *S. repens*: including *S. rosmarinifolia*
35 *S. viminalis*: very widely planted
37 *S. purpurea*: sometimes planted
38 *S. daphnoides*: casual elsewhere
39 *Populus alba*: very commonly planted
P. nigra and *P. canescens* are probably not native in the area
48 *Alnùs incana*: widely planted
51 *Carpinus betulus*: planted over much of N and W of range shown
53 *Fagus sylvatica*: much planted
54 *Quercus ilex*: much planted and sometimes naturalised
56 *Q. robur*: frequently planted
59 *Ulmus procera*: often planted; continental distribution unclear
62 *Humulus lupulus*: in much of range naturalised
78 *Aristolochia clematitis*: a medicinal plant, often naturalised in old herb gardens
79 *Asarum europaeum*: occasionally casual
83 *Polygonum aviculare*: including *P. boreale, P. rurivagum,* and *P. arenastrum*
104 *Rumex longifolius*: sometimes naturalised elsewhere
110 *R. pulcher*: sometimes casual
116 *Beta vulgaris*: ssp *vulgaris* commonly cultivated as sugar-beet, beetroot, etc.
117 *Chenopodium bonus-henricus*: native and naturalised distributions not separable
117–128 Most *Chenopodium* spp are frequently casual
127 *C. album*: including *C. striatum*
138 *Atriplex longipes*: probably throughout but distribution unknown
140 *Halimione pedunculata*: extinct as native in Britain, but occasionally casual
142 *Kochia laniflora*: casual elsewhere
146 *Salicornia procumbens*: including *S. dolichostachya* and *S. stricta*
149 *Salsola kali*: occasionally casual in S. of area
154 *Montia sibirica*: distribution on continent unknown
159 *Arenaria serpyllifolia*: including *A. leptoclados*

176   *Stellaria media*: including *S. neglecta* and *S. pallida*
204   *Sagina saginoides*: including *S. normaniana*
228   *Agrostemma githago*: as a weed throughout
241   *Silene noctiflora*: casual elsewhere
254   *Petrorhagia prolifera*: including *P. nanteuilli*
255   *Dianthus gratianopolitanus*: occasionally established elsewhere
333   *Ranunculus peltatus*: including *R. penicillatus,* treated as subspecies for
         want of information
350   *Papaver lecoqii*: distribution very uncertain
353   *P. radicatum*: including *P. lapponicum, P. dahlianum,* and *P. laestahdianum*
354   *Meconopsis cambrica*: frequent garden escape
358, 361   *Corydalis bulbosa* and *C. solida*: occasional garden escapes
369   *Fumaria densiflora*: distribution uncertain; casual elsewhere
382   *Descurainia sophia*: range mostly as casual
388   *Bunias orientalis*: range mostly as casual
395   *Cheiranthus cheiri*: naturalised and native ranges mixed
399   *Barbarea stricta*: status unclear
404   *Rorippa sylvestris*: including *R. prostrata*
407   *Armoracia rusticana*: casual over much of range
408   *Nasturtium officinale*: including N. *microphyllum*
415   *Cardamine pratensis*: including *C. nymanii, C. matthiolii* and *C. palustre*
427   *Arabis hirsuta*: including *A. planisiliqua, A. sagittata,* and *A. brownii*
436   *Berteroa incana*: widespread as a casual
450   *Cochlearia officinalis*: including *C. pyrenaica*
456   *Camelina sativa*: including *C. alyssum* and *C. macrocarpa*
467   *Iberis amara*: garden escape elsewhere
481   *Brassica oleracea*: very common as casual in places
525   *Saxifragis nivalis*: including *S. tenuis*
533   *S. osloensis*: hybrid of *S. tridactylites* and *S. adscendens*
547   *Chrysosplenium alternifolium*: including *C. tetrandrum*
572   *Rosa vosegiaca*: including *R. glauca*
577   *R. canina*: including 10 micro-species
578   *R. tomentosa*: including *R. scabriuscula, R. sherardii, R. villosa* and *R. mollis*
579   *R. rubiginosa*: including *R. elliptica, R. agrestis,* and *R. micrantha*
595   *Potentilla chamissonis*: including *P. hookeriana*
607   *P. tabernaemontani*: including *P. pusilla*
654   *Malus sylvestris*: often planted
655   *Sorbus aucuparia*: often planted
659   *S. aria*: including *S. graeca, S. rupicola,* etc; often planted
633   *S. intermedia*: widely planted and often naturalised elsewhere
664   *Amelanchier ovalis*: widely planted
707   *Vicia tenuifolia*: occasional casual elsewhere; native range uncertain
711   *V. villosa*: native range uncertain; casual elsewhere
730   *Lathyrus latifolius*: including *L. heterophyllus*: frequent garden escape
747   *Medicago sativa*: native range is ssp *falcata*
753–778   Many *Trifolium* spp are cultivated for fodder and may establish
780   *Lotus tenuis*: distribution uncertain
794   *Coronilla varia*: casual elsewhere
797   *Onobrychis viciifolia*: common fodder crop
842   *Euphorbia exigua*: native range uncertain
849   *E. cyparissias*: native range uncertain

858 *Acer platanoides*: commonly planted

860 *A. pseudoplatanus*: not native in area

861 *A. monspessulanus*: occasionally planted and naturalised

862 *Impatiens noli-tangere*: native distribution unclear

866 *Ilex aquifolium*: much planted

870 *Buxus sempervirens*: widely planted and naturalised

889 *Hippophae rhamnoides*: widely planted

947 *Circaea intermedia*: hybrid of *C. lutetiana* and *C. alpina*

948 *Oenothera biennis*: including *O. rubricaulis, O. suaveolens* and
    O. erythrosepala

950 *O. muricata*: including *O. parviflora, O. silesiaca, O. ammophila,* and
    O. rubricuspis; information very uncertain

961 *Epilobium tetragonum*: including *E. adnatum* and *E. lamyi*

980 *Cornus mas*: planted and occasionally naturalised elsewhere

985 *Astrantia major*: occasional garden escape

996 *Myrrhis odorata*: probably only native in Alps

1002 *Aegopodium podagraria*: native range unclear

1087 *Ledum palustre*: including *L. groenlandicum*

1115 *Anagallis arvensis*: including *A. foemina*

1141 *Armeria maritima*: including various inland races sometimes separated as
    species

1147 *Limonium binervosum*: including *L. dodartii*

1151 *Fraxinus excelsior*: often planted

1152 *Ligustrum vulgare*: British distribution is of both native and introduced
    range; continental distribution is native range only

1154 *Nymphoides peltata*: distribution very poorly known

1157 *Blackstonia perfoliata*: including *B. serotina*

1175 *Gentianella campestris*: including *G. baltica*

1178 *G. amarella*: including *G. uliginosa*

1185 *Calystegia sepium*: including *C. sylvaticum*

1193 *Polemonium caeruleum*: widespread as a garden escape

1206 *Galium pumilum*: including *G. sterneri* and *G. suecicum*

1212 *G. spurium*: including *G. vaillantii*

1229 *Myosotis decumbens*: distribution in Britain unknown

1232 *M. laxa*: including *M. caespitosa*

1233 *M. stolonifera*: probably under-recorded

1245 *Asperugo procumbens*: casual elsewhere

1251 *Pulmonaria longifolia*: including *P. maculosa* and *P. obscura*

1253 *P. mollis*: including *P. mollissima*

1255 *Anchusa officinalis*: casual elsewhere

1263 *C. stagnalis*: including *C. platycarpa, C. verna,* and *C. palustris*

1265 *C. hermaphroditica*: including *C. truncata*

1281 *Galeopsis tetrahit*: including *G. bifida*

1288 *Lamium maculatum*: common garden escape

1316 *Thymus praecox*: including *T. humifusus* and *T. drucei*

1318 *T. pulegioides*: including *T. froelichianus*

1325 *Mentha longifolia*: distribution in W. Europe very uncertain as most records
    refer to *M. spicata*

1326 *Salvia verticillata*: native range uncertain

1337 *Datura stramonium*: casual in most of range

1345 *Verbascum phoeniceum*: casual elsewhere

1355 *Scrophularia umbrosa*: including *S. alata*
1358 *S. auriculata*: including *S. aquatica* and *S. balbisii*
1380 *Veronica austriaca*: including *V. teucrium*
1410–1436 *Euphrasia*: most species probably under-recorded
1477 *Utricularia vulgaris*: including *U. neglecta*
1478 *U. minor*: including *U. bremii*
1479 *U. intermedia*: including *U. ochroleuca*
1483 *Plantago indica*: often casual elsewhere
1488 *Centranthus ruber*: native distribution unclear; frequent garden escape
1550 *Erigeron acer*: including *E. politum*
1569 *Antennaria alpina*: including *A. porsildii*
1588 *Anthemis tinctoria*: native range unclear: frequent casual elsewhere
1593 *Achillea ptarmica*: including *A. cartilaginea*
1602 *Tripleurospermum maritimum*: including *T. inodorum*
1634 *Senecio fuchsii*: occasional casual
1642 *S. squalidus*: long-established introduction
1651 *Arctium minus*: including *A. nemorosum, A. pubens* and *A. tomentosum*
1656 *Carduus crispus*: including *C. acanthoides*
1660 *Cirsium oleraceum*: occasionally established elsewhere
1671 *Onopordum acanthium*: native distribution unclear, casual over much of
         range
1673–1685 *Centaurea*: the taxonomy of this genus is so confused that it is often
         difficult to know to which species older records refer
1675 *C. nigra*: including *C. nemoralis* and *C. pratensis*
1682 *C. montana*: often casual elsewhere
1695 *Leontodon hispidus*: including *L. hyoseroides*
1772 *Zostera marina*: including *Z. hornemanniana* and *Z. angustifolia*
1790 *Potamogeton pusillus*: synonymous with *P. panormitanus; P. berchtoldii*
         (1792) is sometimes referred to as *P. pusillus*
1819 The distribution in N. England and Ireland is of Esthwaite Waterweed,
         referred to in many floras as *Elodea nuttallii*, but which is in fact *Hydrilla
         verticillata*
1822 *Acorus calamus*: introduced throughout range in 16–17th centuries
1871 *Polygonatum multiflorum*: many of the introduced records probably refer to
         P. × hybridum
1877 *Tulipa sylvestris*: native range uncertain
1927 *Dactylorhiza traunsteineri*: including *D. russowii*

Main sources of information

The books and articles listed here are those from which most of the information for the maps was taken. In addition, I have used many maps and records published in scattered journals and books, too numerous to detail.

Great Britain and Ireland

Perring, F. and Walters, S. M. Atlas of the British Flora. London, 1962.
Clapham, A. R., Tutin, T. G., and Warburg, E. F. Flora of the British Isles. Cambridge, 1962.
Miscellaneous records published in *Watsonia* and elsewhere.

France

Coste, H. Flore de France. Paris, 1900–6.
Bonnier, G. Flore de France. Paris.
Miscellaneous records published in the *Bulletin du Société Botanique de France.*

Belgium, Netherlands, and Luxembourg

van Rompaey, E. and Delvosalle, L. Atlas de la Flore Belge et Luxembourgeoise. Brussels, 1972.
de Langhe, J-E. *et al.* Nouvelle Flore de la Belgique, du Grand-Duché de Luxembourg, du Nord de la France et des Régions voisines. Brussels, 1973.
Sloff, J. G. Plant maps for the Netherlands. *Blumea* 2, 1935; *Nederl. Kruidk. Arch.* 46–51, 1936–1941.

Germany and Central Europe

Meusel, H. *et al.* Vergleichende Chorologie der zentraleuropäischen Flora. Jena, 1965.
Garcke, A. Illustrierte Flora von Deutschland. 22nd Edn, Hamburg, 1972.
Hegi, G. Flora von Mitteleuropa. Munich, 1959–1971.
Christiansen, W. Neue kritische Flora von Schleswig-Holstein. Rendsburg, 1953.
Meusel, H. and Schubert, R. Verbreitung der mitteldeutscher Leitpflanzen. *Hercynia* 1–3, 1937–1944; *Wiss. Z. Martin-Luther Universität, Halle-Wittenberg,* 1953–1969.
Miscellaneous maps published in *Berichte der Bayerische Botanische Gesellschaft.*

Scandinavia

Hultén, E. Atlas över Växternas utbrednings i Norden. Stockholm, 1971.

Main sources of information

Odum, S., Pedersen, A., Hansen, A., *et al.* The distribution of plants in Denmark. *Bot Tidsskr.* 59–64, 1963–1969.

Löve, A. and D. Cytotaxonomical conspectus of the Icelandic Flora. *Acta Horti Gotoburg.* 20.

Hansen, K. The distribution of vascular plants in the Faeroes. *Dansk. bot. Arkiv* 24, 1966.

Miscellaneous records in *Blyttia, Svensk botanisk Tidsskrift,* etc.

General

Hultén, E. The Amphi-atlantic plants and their phytogeographical connections. Stockholm, 1958.

Hultén, E. The Circumpolar plants. Stockholm, 1962, 1971.

Checklist of the plants in the book

134 patula
135 calotheca
136 hastata
137 glabriuscula
138 longipes
139 Halimione
       portulacoides
140 pedunculata
141 Bassia hirsuta
142 Kochia laniflora
143 Arthrocnemum
       perenne
144 Salicornia europaea
145 pusilla
146 procumbens
147 Suaeda maritima
148 vera
149 Salsola kali
150 Carpobrotus edulis
151 Portulaca oleracea
152 Montia fontana
153 perfoliata
154 sibirica
155 Arenaria humifusa
156 norvegica
157 ciliata
158 gothica
159 serpyllifolia
160 Moehringia trinervia
161 lateriflora
162 muscosa
163 Minuartia viscosa
164 hybrida
165 mediterranea
166 rubra
167 setacea
168 recurva
169 verna
170 rubella
171 stricta
172 biflora
173 sedoides
174 Honkenya peploides
175 Stellaria nemorum
176 media
177 holostea
178 alsine
179 palustris
180 graminea
181 crassipes
182 longifolia
183 calycantha
184 crassifolia
185 humifusa
186 Holosteum
       umbellatum

187 Cerastium cerastoides
188 dubium
189 arvense
190 alpinum
191 arcticum
192 fontanum
193 brachypetalum
194 glomeratum
195 pumilum
196 semidecandrum
197 diffusum
198 Moenchia erecta
199 Myosoton aquaticum
200 Sagina nodosa
201 intermedia
202 caespitosa
203 subulata
204 saginoides
205 procumbens
206 apetala
207 maritima
208 Scleranthus perennis
209 annuus
210 Corrigiola litoralis
211 Herniaria glabra
212 ciliolata
213 hirsuta
214 Illecebrum
       verticillatum
215 Spergula arvensis
216 morisonii
217 pentandra
218 Spergularia rupicola
219 media
220 marina
221 segetalis
222 bocconii
223 echinosperma
224 rubra
225 Lychnis flos-cuculi
226 viscaria
227 alpina
228 Agrostemma githago
229 Silene italica
230 nutans
231 chlorantha
232 viscosa
233 tatarica
234 wahlbergella
235 furcata
236 otites
237 vulgaris
238 acaulis
239 rupestris
240 armeria
241 noctiflora

242 alba
243 dioica
244 linicola
245 gallica
246 conica
247 Cucubalus baccifer
248 Gypsophila fastigiata
249 repens
250 muralis
251 Saponaria officinalis
252 Vaccaria pyramidata
253 Petrohagia saxifraga
254 prolifera
255 Dianthus
       gratianopolitanus
256 seguieri
257 superbus
258 arenarius
259 deltoides
260 armeria
261 carthusianorum
262 gallicus
263 Nymphaea alba
264 candida
265 Nuphar lutea
266 pumilum
267 Ceratophyllum
       demersum
268 submersum
269 Helleborus foetidus
270 viridis
271 Nigella arvensis
272 Myosurus minimus
273 Trollius europaeus
274 Actaea spicata
275 erythrocarpa
276 Caltha palustris
277 Aconitum
       septentrionale
278 vulparia
279 variegatum
280 napellus
281 Consolida regalis
282 Anemone nemorosa
283 ranunculoides
284 narcissiflora
285 sylvestris
286 Hepatica nobilis
287 Pusatilla vernalis
288 vulgaris
289 alba
290 pratensis
291 patens
292 Clematis recta
293 vitalba
294 alpina

295 Adonis vernalis	349 dubium	404 sylvestris
296 flammea	350 lecoqii	405 islandica
297 aestivalis	351 argemone	406 pyrenaica
298 annua	352 hybridum	407 Armoracia rusticana
299 Ranunculus polyanthemos	353 radicatum	408 Nasturtium officinale
	354 Meconopsis cambrica	409 Cardamine bulbifera
300 nemorosus	355 Glaucium flavum	410 heptaphylla
301 repens	356 Chelidonium majus	411 pentaphyllos
302 lanuginosus	357 Corydalis claviculata	412 enneaphyllos
303 acris	358 bulbosa	413 trifolia
304 montanus	359 intermedia	414 amara
305 oreophilus	360 pumila	415 pratensis
306 sardous	361 solida	416 resedifolia
307 bulbosus	362 Fumaria occidentalis	417 bellidifolia
308 arvensis	363 capreolata	418 parviflora
309 parviflorus	364 purpurea	419 impatiens
310 illyricus	365 bastardii	420 flexuosa
311 paludosus	366 martinii	421 hirsuta
312 pygmaeus	367 muralis	422 Cardaminopsis arenosa
313 auricomus	368 densiflora	423 petraea
314 nivalis	369 officinalis	424 halleri
315 sulphureus	370 caroliniana	425 Arabis glabra
316 hyperboreus	371 schleicheri	426 pauciflora
317 sceleratus	372 vaillantii	427 hirsuta
318 lapponicus	373 parviflora	428 turrita
319 cymbalaria	374 Sisymbrium supinum	429 recta
320 ficaria	375 strictissimum	430 stricta
321 aconitifolius	376 loeselii	431 alpina
322 platanifolius	377 austriacum	432 Lunaria rediviva
323 glacialis	378 altissimum	433 Alyssum saxatile
324 flammula	379 orientale	434 alyssoides
325 reptans	380 officinale	435 montanum
326 lingua	381 Alliaria petiolata	436 Berteroa incana
327 ophioglossifolius	382 Descurainia sophia	437 Draba aizoides
328 hederaceus	383 Arabidopsis thaliana	438 alpina
329 omiophyllus	384 seucica	439 nivalis
330 tripartitus	385 Braya purpurascens	440 norvegica
331 ololeucos	386 linearis	441 cacuminum
332 baudotii	387 Isatis tinctoria	442 fladnizensis
333 peltatus	388 Bunias orientalis	443 daurica
334 aquatilis	389 Erysimum crepidifolium	444 cinerea
335 trichophyllus		445 incana
336 circinatus	390 odoratum	446 muralis
337 fluitans	391 hieracifolium	447 nemorosa
338 Aquilegia atrata	392 repandum	448 crassifolia
339 vulgaris	393 cheiranthoides	449 Erophila verna s.l.
340 Thalictrum aquilegifolium	394 Hesperis matronalis	450 Cochlearia officinalis
	395 Cheiranthus cheiri	451 danica
341 alpinum	396 Matthiola incana	452 aestuaria
342 minus	397 sinuata	453 anglica
343 simplex	398 Barbarea vulgaris	454 scotica
344 lucidum	399 stricta	455 Kernera saxatilis
345 morisonii	400 verna	456 Camelina sativa
346 flavum	401 intermedia	457 microcarpa
347 Berberis vulgaris	402 Rorippa austriaca	458 Neslia paniculata
348 Papaver rhoeas	403 amphibia	

251

459 Capsella bursa-
    pastoris
460 Hymenolobus
    procumbens
461 Hornungia petraea
462 Teesdalia nudicaulis
463 Thlaspi arvense
464   perfoliatum
465   alpestre
466   montanum
467 Iberis amara
468 Biscutella laevigata
469 Lepidium campestre
470   heterophyllum
471   ruderale
472   latifolium
473 Cardaria draba
474 Coronopus
    squamatus
475   didymus
476 Subularia aquatica
477 Conringia orientalis
478 Diplotaxis tenuifolia
479   muralis
480   viminea
481 Brassica oleracea
482   nigra
483   rapa
484 Sinapis arvensis
485   alba
486 Erucastrum
    nasturtiifolium
487   gallicum
488 Rhynchosinapis
    cheiranthos
489   wrightii
490   monensis
491 Cakile maritima
492   edentula
493 Rapistrum rugosum
494 Crambe maritima
495 Calepina irregularis
496 Raphanus
    raphanistrum
497 Reseda luteola
498   lutea
499 Sarracenia purpurea
500 Drosera rotundifolia
501   intermedia
502   anglica
503 Crassula tillaea
504   aquatica
505   vaillantii
506 Umbilicus rupestris
507 Jovibarba sobolifera
508 Sedum telephium

509   reflexum
510   forsteranum
511   acre
512   sexangulare
513   alpestre
514   album
515   anglicum
516   dasyphyllum
517   hirsutum
518   villosum
519   annuum
520   rubens
521   andegavense
522   hispanicum
523 Rhodiola rosea
524 Saxifraga hieracifolia
525   nivalis
526   stellaris
527   foliolosa
528   spathularis
529   hirsuta
530   rotundifolia
531   hirculus
532   tridactylites
533   osloensis
534   adscendens
535   aizoides
536   caespitosa
537   hartii
538   rosacea
539   hypnoides
540   granulata
541   cernua
542   rivularis
543   oppositifolia
544   cotyledon
545   paniculata
546 Chrysosplenium
    oppositifolium
547   alternifolium
548 Parnassia palustris
549 Ribes rubrum
550   spicatum
551   nigrum
552   petraeum
553   uva-crispa
554   alpinum
555 Aruncus dioicus
556 Filipendula vulgaris
557   ulmaria
558 Rubus chamaemorus
559   acticus
560   saxatilis
561   idaeus
562   sect. Rubus
    subsect:-
    caesii (caesius)

563   suberecti
564   silvatici
565   discolores
566   appendiculati
567 Rosa sempervirens
568   arvensis
569   pimpinellifolia
570   acicularis
571   majalis
572   vosegiaca
573   pendulina
574   gallica
575   stylosa
576   jundzilii
577   canina agg.
578   tomentosa agg.
579   rubiginosa agg.
580 Agrimonia eupatoria
581   procera
582 Aremonia
    agrimonoides
583 Sanguisorba
    officinalis
584   minor
585 Dryas octopetala
586 Geum rivale
587   urbanum
588   hispidum
589 Potentilla fruticosa
590   palustris
591   anserina
592   rupestris
593   multifida
594   nivea
595   chamissonis
596   argentea
597   collina agg.
598   inclinata
599   supina
600   norvegica
601   recta
602   thuringiaca
603   hyparctica
604   crantzii
605   aurea
606   heptaphylla
607   tabernaemontani
608   cinerea
609   erecta
610   anglica
611   reptans
612   alba
613   sterilis
614   montana
615   micrantha
616 Sibbaldia
    procumbens

617 Fragaria vesca
618   moschata
619   viridis
620 Alchemilla alpina
621   pallens
622   hoppeana
623   conjuncta
624   faeroensis
625   glaucescens
626   plicata
627   propinqua
628   monticola
629   crinita
630   strigulosa
631   subglobosa
632   sarmatica
633   subcrenata
634   cymatophylla
635   heptagona
636   acutiloba
637   gracilis
638   xanthochlora
639   filicaulis
640   minima
641   glomerulans
642   nebulosa
643   wichurae
644   murbeckiana
645   lineata
646   obtusa
647   glabra
648   coriacea
649   incisa
650 Aphanes arvensis
651   microcarpa
652 Pyrus pyraster
653   cordata
654 Malus sylvestris
655 Sorbus aucuparia
656   torminalis
657   chamaemespilus
658   domestica
659   aria
660   mougeotii
661   hybrida
662   meinichii
663   intermedia
664 Amelanchier ovalis
665 Cotoneaster
     integerrimus
666   nebrodensis
667   niger
668 Crataegus laevigata
669   calycina
670   monogyna
671 Prunus spinosa

672   fruticosa
673   avium
674   mahaleb
675   padus
676 Lembotropis
     nigricans
677 Cytisus scoparius
678 Chamaecytisus
     ratisbonensis
679   supinus
680 Genista tinctoria
681   pilosa
682   anglica
683   germanica
684 Ulex europaeus
685   minor
686   gallii
687 Chamaespartium
     saggitale
688 Colutea arborescens
689 Astragalus cicer
690   danicus
691   frigidus
692   penduliflorus
693   alpinus
694   norvegicus
695   glycyphyllos
696   exscapus
697   arenarius
698   baioniensis
699 Oxytropis lapponica
700   deflexa
701   campestris
702   halleri
703   pilosa
704 Vicia orobus
705   pisiformis
706   cracca
707   tenuifolia
708   cassubica
709   sylvatica
710   dumetorum
711   villosa
712   hirsuta
713   tenuissima
714   tetrasperma
715   sepium
716   sativa
717   lathyroides
718   lutea
719   bithynica
720   narbonensis
721 Lathyrus vernus
722   niger
723   japonicus
724   pannonicus

725   montanus
726   pratensis
727   palustris
728   tuberosus
729   sylvestris
730   latifolius
731   sphaericus
732 Lathyrus hirsutus
733   nissolia
734   aphaca
735 Ononis natrix
736   reclinata
737   pusilla
738   spinosa
739   repens
740   arvensis
741 Melilotus dentata
742   altissima
743   alba
744   officinalis
745 Trigonella
     monspeliaca
746 Medicago lupulina
747   sativa
748   marina
749   orbicularis
750   arabica
751   polymorpha
752   minima
753 Trifolium
     ornithopodioides
754   strictum
755   montanum
756   repens
757   hybridum
758   michelianum
759   retusum
760   glomeratum
761   suffocatum
762   fragiferum
763   spadiceum
764   aureum
765   campestre
766   dubium
767   micranthum
768   striatum
769   arvense
770   bocconii
771   scabrum
772   pratense
773   medium
774   alpestre
775   rubens
776   ochroleucum
777   squamosum
778   subterraneum

779 Dorycnium
    pentaphyllum
780 Lotus tenuis
781   corniculatus
782   uliginosus
783   subbiflorus
784   angustissimus
785 Tetragonolobus
    maritimus
786 Anthyllis vulneraria
787 Ornithopus
    perpusillus
788   pinnatus
789   compressus
790 Coronilla emerus
791   vaginalis
792   minima
793   coronata
794   varia
795 Hippocrepis comosa
796 Onobrychis arenaria
797   viciifolia
798 Oxalis corniculata
799   europaea
800   acetosella
801 Geranium
    sanguineum
802   pratense
803   sylvaticum
804   phaeum
805   palustre
806   bohemicum
807   lanuginosum
808   pyrenaicum
809   rotundifolium
810   molle
811   pusillum
812   columbinum
813   dissectum
814   lucidum
815   robertianum
816   purpureum
817 Erodium maritimum
818   cicutarium
819 Tribulus terrestris
820 Linum perenne
821   austriacum
822   leonii
823   flavum
824   bienne
825   viscosum
826   trigynum
827   tenuifolium
828   suffruticosum
829   catharticum
830 Radiola linoides

831 Mercurialis perenne
832   annua
833   ovata
834 Euphorbia peplis
835   palustris
836   hyberna
837   dulcis
838   brittingeri
839   platyphyllos
840   serrulata
841   helioscopia
842   exigua
843   peplus
844   portlandica
845   seguierana
846   paralias
847   lucida
848   esula
849   cyparissias
850   amygdaloides
851 Dictamnus albus
852 Polygala
    chamaebuxus
853   comosa
854   vulgaris
855   serpyllifolia
856   calcarea
857   amarella
858 Acer platanoides
859   campestre
860   pseudoplatanus
861   monspessulanum
862 Impatiens noli-
    tangere
863   capensis
864   parviflora
865   glandulifera
866 Ilex aquifolium
867 Euonymus europaeus
868   latifolius
869 Staphylea pinnata
870 Buxus sempervirens
871 Rhamnus saxatilis
872   catharticus
873 Frangula alnus
874 Tilia platyphyllos
875   cordata
876 Malva alcea
877   moschata
878   sylvestris
879   pusilla
880   neglecta
881 Lavatera cretica
882   arborea
883   thuringiaca
884 Althaea hirsuta

885   officinalis
886 Thymelaea passerina
887 Daphne mezereon
888   laureola
889 Hippophae
    rhamnoides
890 Hypericum
    androsaemum
891   hirsutum
892   pulchrum
893   montanum
894   elodes
895   linariifolium
896   humifusum
897   tetrapterum
898   undulatum
899   maculatum
900   perforatum
901   elegans
902   canadense
903 Viola odorata
904   alba
905   hirta
906   collina
907   mirabilis
908   rupestris
909   reichenbachiana
910   riviniana
911   canina
912   lactea
913   persicifolia
914   pumila
915   elatior
916   uliginosa
917   palustris
918   epipsila
919   selkirkii
920   biflora
921   lutea
922   hispida
923   tricolor
924   arvensis
925   kitaibeliana
926 Tuberaria guttata
927 Helianthemum
    nummularium
928   appeninum
929   oelandicum
930   canum
931 Fumana procumbens
932 Tamarix gallica
933 Myricaria germanica
934 Frankenia laevis
935 Elatine alsinastrum
936   hydropiper
937   triandra

938   hexandra
939 Bryonia alba
940   cretica
941 Lythrum salicaria
942   hyssopifolia
943   borysthenicum
944   portula
945 Trapa natans
946 Circaea lutetiana
947   × intermedia
948   alpina
949 Oenothera biennis
950   muricata agg.
951 Ludwigia palustris
952 Epilobium
       angustifolium
953   latifolium
954   dodonaei
955   hirsutum
956   parviflorum
957   duriaei
958   montanum
959   collinum
960   lanceolatum
961   tetragonum
962   obscurum
963   roseum
964   palustre
965   davuricum
966   nutans
967   anagallidifolium
968   hornemanii
969   lactiflorum
970   alsinifolium
971   glandulosum
972   adenocaulon
973   brunnescens
974 Myriophyllum
       verticillatum
975   spicatum
976   alterniflorum
977 Hippuris vulgaris
978   tetraphylla
979 Cornus sanguinea
980   mas
981   suecica
982 Hedera helix
983 Hydrocotyle vulgaris
984 Sanicula europaea
985 Astrantia major
986 Eryngium maritimum
987   campestre
988 Chaerophyllum
       hirsutum
989   bulbosum
990   aureum

991   temulentum
992 Anthriscus sylvestris
993   nitida
994   caucalis
995 Scandix pecten-
       veneris
996 Myrrhis odorata
997 Smyrnium olusatrum
998 Bunium
       bulbocastaneum
999 Conopodium majus
1000 Pimpinella major
1001   saxifraga
1002 Aegopodium
       podagraria
1003 Sium latifolium
1004 Berula erecta
1005 Crithmum maritimum
1006 Seseli libanotis
1007   montanum
1008   annuum
1009   hippomarathrum
1010 Oenanthe fistulosa
1011   pimpinelloides
1012   silaifolia
1013   peucedanifolia
1014   lachenalii
1015   crocata
1016   fluviatilis
1017   aquatica
1018 Aethusa cynapium
1019 Athamanta cretensis
1020 Foeniculum vulgare
1021 Silaum silaus
1022 Meum athamanticum
1023 Physospermum
       cornubiense
1024 Conium maculatum
1025 Pleurospermum
       austriacum
1026 Bupleurum
       rotundifolium
1027   longifolium
1028   baldense
1029   gerardi
1030   tenuissimum
1031   falcatum
1032 Trinia glauca
1033 Apium graveolens
1034   nodiflorum
1035   repens
1036   inundatum
1037 Petroselinum
       segetum
1038 Sison amomum
1039 Cicuta virosa

1040 Ptychotis saxifraga
1041 Falcaria vulgaris
1042 Carum carvi
1043   verticillatum
1044 Cnidium dubium
1045 Selinum carvifolia
1046   pyrenaum
1047 Ligusticum scoticum
1048   mutellina
1049 Conioselinum
       tataricum
1050 Angelica palustris
1051   sylvestris
1052   archangelica
1053 Peucedanum
       officinale
1054   gallicum
1055   carvifolia
1056   alsaticum
1057   oreoselinum
1058   palustre
1059   lancifolium
1060   cervaria
1061   ostruthium
1062 Pastinaca sativa
1063 Heracleum
       sphondylium
1064 Tordylium maximum
1065 Laser trilobum
1066 Laserpitium latifolium
1067   prutenicum
1068   siler
1069 Torilis nodosa
1070   arvensis
1071   japonica
1072 Caucalis platycarpos
1073 Turgenia latifolia
1074 Orlaya grandiflora
1075 Daucus carota
1076 Chimaphila umbellata
1077 Moneses uniflora
1078 Monotropa hypopitys
       s.l.
1079 Orthilia secunda
1080 Pyrola minor
1081   media
1082   rotundifolia
1083   norvegica
1084   grandiflora
1085   chlorantha
1086 Diapensia lapponica
1087 Ledum palustre
1088 Loiseleuria
       procumbens
1089 Rhododendron
       lapponicum

1090	Andromeda polifolia	1143	Limonium vulgare	1194		acutiflorum
1091	Chamaedaphne calyculata	1144	humile	1195	Asperula tinctoria
		1145	bellidifolium	1196		arvensis
1092	Arctostaphylos uva-ursi	1146	auriculae-ursifolium	1197		odorata
				1198		cynanchica
1093	Arctous alpina	1147	binervosum	1199	Cruciata laevipes
1094	Calluna vulgaris	1148	recurvum	1200	Galium boreale
1095	Erica herbacea	1149	transwallianum	1201		verum
1096	tetralix	1150	paradoxum	1202		sylvaticum
1097	cinerea	1151	Fraxinus excelsior	1203		palustre
1098	erigena	1152	Ligustrum vulgare	1204		mollugo
1099	mackaiana	1153	Menyanthes trifoliata	1205		saxatile
1100	ciliaris	1154	Nymphoides peltata	1206		pumilum
1101	vagans	1155	Vinca minor	1207		debile
1102	Daboecia cantabrica	1156	Cynanchum vincetoxicum	1208		uliginosum
1103	Vaccinium vitis-idaea			1209		tricornutum
1104	uliginosum	1157	Blackstonia perfoliata	1210		parisiense
1105	myrtillus	1158	Centaurium tenuiflorum	1211		aparine
1106	oxycoccus			1212		spurium
1107	microcarpus	1159	scilloides	1213		rotundifolium
1108	Phyllodoce caerulea	1160	littorale	1214		glaucum
1109	Cassiope hypnoides	1161	pulchellum	1215		trifidum
1110	tetragona	1162	erythraea	1216		triflorum
1111	Arbutus unedo	1163	Lomatogonium rotatum	1217	Rubia peregrina
1112	Empetrum nigrum			1218	Sherardia arvensis
1113	hermaphroditum	1164	Cicendia filiformis	1219	Heliotropium europaeum
1114	Anagallis tenella	1165	Exaculum pusillum		
1115	arvensis	1166	Gentiana nivalis	1220	Cerinthe glabra
1116	minima	1167	utriculosa	1221		minor
1117	Androsace maxima	1168	cruciata	1222	Onosma arenaria
1118	lactea	1169	verna	1223	Echium plantagineum
1119	septentrionalis	1170	pneumonanthe	1224		vulgare
1120	elongata	1171	detonsa	1225	Buglossoides arvense
1121	Cyclamen purpurascens	1172	purpurea	1226		purpuro-caeruleum
		1173	lutea	1227	Lithospermum officinale
1122	Glaux maritima	1174	asclepiadea		
1123	Hottonia palustris	1175	Gentianella campestris agg.	1228	Myosotis sylvatica
1124	Lysimachia nemorum			1229		decumbens
1125	nummularia	1176	austriaca	1230		palustris
1126	thyrsiflora	1177	germanica	1231		caespititia
1127	vulgaris	1178	amarella	1232		laxa
1128	Primula vulgaris	1179	anglica	1233		brevifolia
1129	veris	1180	aspera	1234		secunda
1130	elatior	1181	ciliata	1235		sicula
1131	farinosa	1182	tenella	1236		sparsiflora
1132	scotica	1183	aurea	1237		alpestris
1133	scandinavica	1184	Swertia perennis	1238		arvensis
1134	stricta	1185	Calystegia sepium	1239		ramosissima
1135	auricula	1186	soldanella	1240		discolor
1136	nutans	1187	Convolvulus arvensis	1241		stricta
1137	Samolus valerandi	1188	Cuscuta epilinum	1242	Mertensia maritima
1138	Soldanella montana	1189	epithymum	1243	Lappula squarrosa
1139	alpina	1190	europaea	1244		deflexa
1140	Trientalis europaea	1191	gronovii	1245	Asperugo procumbens
1141	Armeria maritima s.l.	1192	lupuliformis		
1142	alliacea	1193	Polemonium caeruleum	1246	Omphalodes scorpioides

1247 Cynoglossum
    germanicum
1248 officinale
1249 Pulmonaria officinalis
1250 angustifolia
1251 longifolia
1252 montana
1253 mollis
1254 Nonea pulla
1255 Anchusa officinalis
1256 arvensis
1257 Symphytum officinale
1258 tuberosum
1259 Pentaglottis
    sempervirens
1260 Verbena officinalis
1261 Callitriche
    obtusangula
1262 cophocarpa
1263 stagnalis
1264 hamulata
1265 hermaphrodita
1266 Ajuga genevensis
1267 chamaepitys
1268 reptans
1269 pyramidalis
1270 Teucrium botrys
1271 scorodonium
1272 montanum
1273 chamaedrys
1274 scordium
1275 Scutellaria minor
1276 hastifolia
1277 galericulata
1278 Marrubium vulgare
1279 Melittis
    melissophyllum
1280 Galeopsis speciosa
1281 tetrahit
1282 pubescens
1283 segetum
1284 ladanum
1285 angustifolium
1286 Lamium album
1287 molucellifolium
1288 maculatum
1289 amplexicaule
1290 hybridum
1291 purpureum
1292 Galeobdolon luteum
1293 Leonurus
    marrubiastrum
1294 cardiaca
1295 Ballota nigra
1296 Betonica officinalis
1297 Stachys recta

1298 annua
1299 arvensis
1300 alpina
1301 sylvatica
1302 palustris
1303 germanica
1304 Nepeta cataria
1305 pannonica
1306 Glechoma hederacea
1307 Dracocephalum
    ruyschiana
1308 Prunella grandiflora
1309 laciniata
1310 vulgaris
1311 Acinos arvensis
1312 Calamintha sylvatica
1313 nepeta
1314 Clinopodium vulgaris
1315 Origanum vulgare
1316 Thymus praecox
1317 serpyllum
1318 pulegioides
1319 Lycopus europaeus
1320 exaltatus
1321 Mentha pulegium
1322 arvensis
1323 aquatica
1324 suaveolens
1325 longifolia
1326 Salvia verticillata
1327 nemorosa
1328 glutinosa
1329 pratensis
1330 verbenaca
1331 Atropa bella-donna
1332 Hyoscyamus niger
1333 Physalis alkekengi
1334 Solanum dulcamara
1335 nigrum
1336 luteum
1337 Datura stramonium
1338 Gratiola officinalis
1339 Lindernia
    procumbens
1340 Limosella australis
1341 aquatica
1342 Mimulus guttatus
1343 luteus
1344 Verbascum blattaria
1345 phoeniceum
1346 virgatum
1347 lychnitis
1348 nigrum
1349 pulverulentum
1350 thapsus
1351 densiflorum

1352 phlomoides
1353 Scrophularia nodosa
1354 vernalis
1355 umbrosa
1356 scorodonia
1357 canina
1358 auriculata
1359 Misopates orontium
1360 Anarrhinum
    bellidifolium
1361 Chaenorrhinum
    minus
1362 Linaria vulgaris
1363 repens
1364 supina
1365 arvensis
1366 arenaria
1367 pelisseriana
1368 alpina
1369 Kickxia elatine
1370 spuria
1371 Digitalis purpurea
1372 lutea
1373 grandiflora
1374 Erinus alpinus
1375 Veronica alpina
1376 serpyllifolia
1377 fruticans
1378 urticifolia
1379 prostrata
1380 austriaca
1381 officinalis
1382 chamaedrys
1383 montana
1384 scutellata
1385 beccabunga
1386 anagalloides
1387 anagallis-aquatica
1388 catenata
1389 acinifolia
1390 praecox
1391 triphyllos
1392 arvensis
1393 verna
1394 dillenii
1395 peregrina
1396 agrestis
1397 polita
1398 opaca
1399 persica
1400 filiformis
1401 hederifolia
1402 longifolia
1403 spicata
1404 Sibthorpia europaea
1405 Melampyrum
    cristatum

1406	arvense	1460	reticulata	1513	Succisa pratensis
1407	nemorosum	1461	amethystea	1514	Campanula glomerata
1408	pratense	1462	picridis	1515	cervicaria
1409	sylvaticum	1463	minor	1516	rotundifolia
1410	Euphrasia rostkoviana	1464	hederae	1517	rhomboidalis
1411	rivularis	1465	caryophyllacea	1518	cochlearifolia
1412	anglica	1466	teucrii	1519	scheuchzeri
1413	vigursii	1467	elatior	1520	baumgartenii
1414	hirtella	1468	alsatica	1521	persicifolia
1415	arctica	1469	rapum-genistae	1522	rapunculus
1416	picta	1470	gracilis	1523	patula
1417	tetraquetra	1471	Globularia elongata	1524	rapunculoides
1418	nemorosa	1472	Pinguicula	1525	trachelium
1419	pseudo-kerneri		grandiflora	1526	latifolia
1420	confusa	1473	vulgaris	1527	barbata
1421	stricta	1474	alpina	1528	uniflora
1422	hyperborea	1475	lusitanica	1529	Wahlenbergia
1423	minima	1476	villosa		hederacea
1424	frigida	1477	Utricularia vulgaris	1530	Legousia
1425	foulaensis	1478	minor		speculum-veneris
1426	cambrica	1479	intermedia	1531	hybrida
1427	ostenfeldii	1480	Littorella uniflora	1532	Phyteuma spicatum
1428	marshallii	1481	Plantago coronopus	1533	nigrum
1429	rotundifolia	1482	maritima	1534	tenerum
1430	dunensis	1483	indica	1535	orbiculare
1431	campbelliae	1484	lanceolata	1536	Jasione perennis
1432	micrantha	1485	media	1537	montana
1433	scottica	1486	major	1538	Lobelia dortmanna
1434	atropurpurea	1487	Adoxa moschatellina	1539	urens
1435	bottnica	1488	Centranthus ruber	1540	Eupatorium
1436	salisburgensis	1489	Valeriana dioica		cannabinum
1437	Odontites verna	1490	officinalis	1541	Solidago virgaurea
1438	lutea	1491	sambucifolia	1542	Bellis perennis
1439	jaubertiana	1492	tripteris	1543	Bellidiastrum michelii
1440	Bartsia alpina	1493	Valerianella locusta	1544	Aster tripolium
1441	Parentucellia viscosa		agg.	1545	amellus
1442	Pedicularis sceptrum-	1494	Lonicera	1546	alpinus
	carolinum		periclymenum	1547	sibiricus
1443	foliosa	1495	xylosteum	1548	Crinitaria linosyris
1444	hirsuta	1496	nigra	1549	Erigeron borealis
1445	oederi	1497	alpigena	1550	acer
1446	flammea	1498	caerulea	1551	uniflorus
1447	palustris	1499	Linnaea borealis	1552	unalaschense
1448	sylvatica	1500	Sambucus nigra	1553	Conyza canadensis
1449	lapponica	1501	ebulus	1554	Filago lutescens
1450	Rhinanthus	1502	racemosa	1555	pyramidata
	groenlandicus	1503	Viburnum opulus	1556	vulgaris
1451	minor	1504	lantana	1557	gallica
1452	angustifolius	1505	Dipsacus fullonum	1558	minima
1453	alectorolophus	1506	pilosus	1559	arvensis
1454	Lathraea squamaria	1507	laciniatus	1560	Micropus erectus
1455	clandestina	1508	Knautia arvensis	1561	Gnaphalium
1456	Orobanche arenaria	1509	sylvatica		sylvaticum
1457	purpurea	1510	Scabiosa columbaria	1562	uliginosum
1458	caerulescens	1511	canescens	1563	luteo-album
1459	alba	1512	ochroleuca	1564	norvegicum

1565 supinum	1614 rupestris	1668 arvense
1566 undulatum	1615 borealis	1669 vulgare
1567 Antennaria dioica	1616 laciniata	1670 Silybum marianum
1568 carpatica	1617 norvegica	1671 Onopordum
1569 alpina	1618 Tussilago farfara	acanthium
1570 Helichrysum	1619 Petasites fragrans	1672 Serratula tinctoria
arenarium	1620 hybridus	1673 Centaurea jacea
1571 Inula hirta	1621 albus	1674 nigrescens
1572 conyza	1622 spurius	1675 nigra
1573 brittanica	1623 frigidus	1676 pseudophrygia
1574 salicina	1624 Homogyne alpina	1677 phrygia
1575 crithmoides	1625 Adenostyles alliariae	1678 stoebe
1576 helvetica	1626 Arnica montana	1679 maculosa
1577 germanica	1627 alpina	1680 scabiosa
1578 Pulicaria vulgaris	1628 Doronicum	1681 triumfetti
1579 dysenterica	pardalianches	1682 montana
1580 Buphthalmum	1629 plantagineum	1683 cyanus
salicifolium	1630 Senecio	1684 calcitrapa
1581 Bidens cernua	spathulifolius	1685 aspera
1582 connata	1631 integrifolius	1686 Cichorium intybus
1583 frondosa	1632 paludosus	1687 Lapsana communis
1584 radiata	1633 fluviatilis	1688 Aposeris foetida
1585 tripartita	1634 fuchsii	1689 Arnoseris minima
1586 Galinsoga parviflora	1635 nemorensis	1690 Hypochaeris
1587 ciliata	1636 vulgaris	maculata
1588 Anthemis tinctoria	1637 viscosus	1691 glabra
1589 austriaca	1638 sylvaticus	1692 radicata
1590 arvensis	1639 vernalis	1693 Leontodon
1591 cotula	1640 cineraria	taraxacoides
1592 Chamaemelum nobile	1641 erraticus	1694 autumnalis
1593 Achillea ptarmica	1642 squalidus	1695 hispidus
1594 millefolium	1643 erucifolius	1696 helveticus
1595 nobilis	1644 jacobaea	1697 incanus
1596 setacea	1645 aquaticus	1698 Picris hieracioides
1597 collina	1646 rivularis	1699 echioides
1598 pannonica	1647 palustris	1700 Tragopogon dubius
1599 Otanthus maritimus	1648 Carlina vulgaris	1701 pratensis
1600 Matricaria	1649 acaulis	1702 crocifolius
matricaroides	1650 Arctium lappa	1703 Scorzonera humilis
1601 recutita	1651 minus	1704 purpurea
1602 Tripleurospermum	1652 Saussurea alpina	1705 hispanica
maritimum	1653 Jurinea cyanoides	1706 austriaca
1603 Chrysanthemum	1654 Carduus tenuiflorus	1707 Podospermum
segetum	1655 nutans	laciniatum
1604 Leucanthemum	1656 crispus	1708 Chondrilla juncea
vulgare	1657 defloratus	1709 Willemetia stipitata
1605 Tanacetum	1658 personata	1710 Taraxacum
corymbosum	1659 pycnocephalus	Erythrosperma
1606 vulgare	1660 Cirsium oleraceum	1711 Palustria
1607 Cotula coronopifolia	1661 eriophorum	1712 Arctica
1608 Artemisia absinthium	1662 acaule	1713 Ceratophora
1609 vulgaris	1663 heterophyllum	1714 Spectabilia
1610 campestris	1664 dissectum	1715 Vulgaria
1611 maritima	1665 tuberosum	1716 Cicerbita alpina
1612 pontica	1666 rivulare	1717 plumieri
1613 austriaca	1667 palustre	1718 Sonchus oleraceus

259

1719 asper	1773 nana	1824 Arum maculatum
1720 arvensis	1774 Potamogeton natans	1825 italicum
1721 palustris	1775 polygonifolius	1826 Lemna minor
1722 Mycelis muralis	1776 nodosus	1827 trisulca
1723 Lactuca perennis	1777 coloratus	1828 gibba
1724 saligna	1778 alpinus	1829 Spirodela polyrrhiza
1725 virosa	1779 gramineus	1830 Wolffia arrhiza
1726 serriola	1780 lucens	1831 Tofieldia calyculata
1727 quercina	1781 praelongus	1832 pusilla
1728 sibiricum	1782 perfoliatus	1833 Narthecium
1729 Prenanthes purpurea	1783 epihydrus	ossifragum
1730 Crepis foetida	1784 crispus	1834 Veratrum album
1731 vesicaria	1785 compressus	1835 Colchicum autumnale
1732 praemorsa	1786 acutifolius	1836 Anthericum liliago
1733 paludosa	1787 obtusifolius	1837 ramosum
1734 pulchra	1788 friesii	1838 Simethis planifolia
1735 tectorum	1789 rutilus	1839 Ornithogalum
1736 capillaris	1790 pusillus	pyrenaicum
1737 mollis	1791 trichoides	1940 umbellatum
1738 biennis	1792 berchtoldii	1841 gussonei
1739 alpestris	1793 pectinatus	1842 Allium victorialis
1740 Hieracium	1794 vaginatus	1843 strictum
Amplexicaulia	1795 filiformis	1844 angulosum
1741 Alpina	1796 helveticus	1845 senescens
1742 Cerinthoidea	1797 Groenlandia densa	1846 suaveolens
1743 Oreadea	1798 Ruppia maritima	1847 ursinum
1744 Vulgata	1799 spiralis	1848 carinatum
1745 Alpestria	1800 Zannichellia palustris	1849 oleraceum
1746 Prenanthoidea	1801 Najas flexilis	1850 schoenoprasum
1747 Tridentata	1802 marina	1851 rotundum
1748 Foliosa	1803 minor	1852 scorodoprasum
1749 Umbellata	1804 Triglochin maritimum	1853 sphaerocephalon
1750 Sabauda	1805 palustre	1854 vineale
1751 Italica	1806 Scheuchzeria	1855 ampeloprasum
1752 Intybacea	palustris	1856 babingtonii
1753 Heterodonta	1807 Eriocaulon	1857 Ruscus aculeatus
1754 Nigrescentia	septangulare	1858 Fritillaria meleagris
1755 Depilata	1808 Alisma plantago-	1859 Gagea arvensis
1756 Pilosella Praealtina	aquatica	1860 bohemica
1757 Stiptolepidea	1809 lanceolatum	1861 minima
1758 Pratensina	1810 gramineum	1862 spathacea
1759 Auriculina	1811 Luronium natans	1863 pratensis
1760 Pilosellina	1812 Caldesia parnassifolia	1864 lutea
1761 Typha angustifolia	1813 Baldellia	1865 Scilla verna
1762 latifolia	ranunculoides	1866 bifolia
1763 shuttleworthii	1814 Damasonium alisma	1867 autumnalis
1764 minima	1815 Sagittaria natans	1868 Endymion non-
1765 Sparganium	1816 sagittifolia	scriptus
angustifolium	1817 Butomus umbellatus	1869 Asparagus officinalis
1766 minimum	1818 Elodea canadensis	1870 Maianthemum
1767 erectum	1819 densa	bifolium
1768 simplex	1820 Stratiotes aloides	1871 Polygonatum
1769 glomeratum	1821 Hydrocharis morsus-	multiflorum
1770 hyperboreum	ranae	1872 odoratum
1771 friesii	1822 Acorus calamus	1873 verticillatum
1772 Zostera marina	1823 Calla palustris	1874 Paris quadrifolia

1875	Convallaria majalis	1909	fuciflora	1942	chlorantha
1876	Streptopus	1910	Anacamptis	1943	oligantha
	amplexifolius		pyramidalis	1944	Herminium
1877	Tulipa sylvestris	1911	Traunsteinera		monorchis
1878	Lloydia serotina		globosa	1945	Listera cordata
1879	Muscari atlanticum	1912	Orchis morio	1946	ovata
1880	neglectum	1913	coriophora	1947	Neottia nidus-avis
1881	botryoides	1914	ustulata	1948	Epipactis atrorubens
1882	tenuiflorum	1915	tridentata	1949	helleborine
1883	comosum	1916	simia	1950	leptochila
1884	Lilium martagon	1917	militaris	1951	microphylla
1885	bulbiferum	1918	purpurea	1952	muelleri
1886	Galanthus nivalis	1919	mascula	1953	palustris
1887	Leucojum vernum	1920	pallens	1954	purpurata
1888	aestivum	1921	palustris	1955	phyllanthes
1889	Narcissus	1922	laxiflora	1956	dunensis
	pseudonarcissus	1923	spitzelii	1957	Cephalanthera
1890	stellaris	1924	Dactylorhiza		damasonium
1891	obvallaris		sambucina	1958	longifola
1892	Tamus communis	1925	incarnata	1959	rubra
1893	Crocus albiflorus	1926	cruenta	1960	Aceras
1894	nudiflorus	1927	traunsteineri		anthropomorphum
1895	Romulea columnae	1928	praetermissa	1961	Limodorum
1896	Sisyrinchium	1929	majalis		abortivum
	bermudianum	1930	purpurella	1962	Epipogium aphyllum
1897	Iris sibirica	1931	maculata	1963	Spiranthes spiralis
1898	spuria	1932	fuchsii	1964	aestivalis
1899	pseudacorus	1933	Himantoglossum	1965	romanzoffiana
1900	aphylla		hircinum	1966	Goodyera repens
1901	foetidissima	1934	Neotinea intacta	1967	Malaxis monophylla
1902	Gladiolus illyricus	1935	Chamorchis alpina	1968	Hammarbya paludosa
1903	palustris	1936	Leucorchis albida	1969	Liparis loeselii
1904	segetum	1937	Nigritella nigra	1970	Corallorhiza trifida
1905	Cypripedium	1938	Gymnadenia	1971	Calypso bulbosa
	calceolus		conopsea	1972	Habernaria
1906	Ophrys insectifera	1939	odoratissima		hyperborea
1907	apifera	1940	Coeloglossum viride		
1908	sphegodes	1941	Platanthera bifolia		

Index of English names

265

Index of scientific names

271

Index of scientific names